SAM WALTON

The Inside Story of America's Richest Man

VANCE H. TRIMBLE

A SIGNET BOOK

SIGNET
Published by the Penguin Group
Penguin Books USA Inc., 375 Hudson Street,
New York, New York 10014, U.S.A.
Penguin Books Ltd, 27 Wrights Lane,
London W8 5TZ, England
Penguin Books Australia Ltd, Ringwood,
Victoria, Australia
Penguin Books Canada Ltd, 10 Alcorn Avenue,
Toronto, Ontario, Canada M4V 3B2
Penguin Books (N.Z.) Ltd, 182–190 Wairau Road,
Auckland 10, New Zealand

Penguin Books Ltd, Registered Offices:
Harmondsworth, Middlesex, England

Published by Signet, an imprint of Dutton Signet,
a division of Penguin Books USA Inc.

First Signet Printing, November, 1991
10 9 8 7 6 5

 REGISTERED TRADEMARK—MARCA REGISTRADA

Printed in the United States of America

The author thanks the following for kind permission to quote extracts from pertinent
articles in their publications: The *Arkansas Times* magazine, the *Arkansas Gazette*,
U.S. News & World Report, the *Kansas City Star* magazine, the *Tulsa* (Okla.) *World*
and the *Tulsa Tribune*, *Financial World*, *Forbes*, *Fortune*, *Architectural Digest*, *Business Week*, *The Wall Street Journal*, the *Wal-Mart World*, *Discount Store News*, *The
New York Times Magazine* and Jon Bowermaster, and *An Outdoor Journal*, Jimmy
Carter (1988), Bantam Books, New York.

Photographs and illustrations for this work were obtained from the following sources,
to whom the author expresses his gratitude for permission to reproduce them:
    The (Little Rock) *Arkansas Gazette*, the *Tulsa* (Okla.) *World*, the *Tulsa* (Okla.)
Tribune, the *Pryor* (Okla.) *Daily Times*, the *Springdale* (Ark.) *News*, the *Cincinnati*
(Ohio) *Post*, the *San Diego* (Calif.) *Union*, Drury College, University of the Ozarks,
Sam M. Walton for annual reports of Wal-Mart Stores Inc., The National Transportation
Safety Board, private sources, and the author's collection.

To two sweethearts,
Elzene and Carol Ann

Contents

Contents

Acknowledgments

This book was undertaken without the cooperation of Sam Walton and his family. Sam was pleasant and polite and got on a first-name basis right from the start. He said he was "in sympathy" with my effort to write his biography, but was unable to help me for a very specific reason—competition. In April 1989 Sam was attempting to write his autobiography. He felt two books on his life would be one too many and suggested I drop my work. I told him I was already committed to a New York publisher and intended to go ahead.

Our initial contact occurred when I accosted him at the end of a University of Arkansas luncheon in Little Rock. We talked for two or three minutes, and I told him I wanted to come to Bentonville and interview him. Sam tentatively agreed to see me and asked me to confirm with his secretary. When I reached Bentonville, she told me Sam had misunderstood the purpose of my interview and couldn't see me. However, she arranged for me to spend an hour visiting with Wal-Mart president David Glass.

Sam Walton is honest and fair-minded, and he didn't like it when some of his employees began deliberately trying to thwart my research. Someone said Sam's publisher wanted him to "dry up all sources." When I complained about this in a letter to Sam, he telephoned me and said he would consider letting me come to Bentonville for a little talk. Next day he'd reconsidered and called to cancel, saying any meeting between us would be unfair to his publisher.

I had no reason to be angry with Sam. After all, he was going to bring out his own book on his astounding career, and perhaps mine would have somehow diminished his. I accepted that; if I had been writing the story of my own life, I wouldn't want somebody else competing with me.

So I continued my research. And despite Wal-Mart roadblocks, it was really rather easy to obtain authentic information about this amazing man and his spectacular career. Many official records are available and thousands of words about him have been printed in newspapers and magazines. I sought out past and present Wal-Mart employees, Walton neighbors and friends, certain officials of his company, and some of their wives and kinfolk, as well as executives among his retailing rivals, editors, publishers, government officials, and others. Amazingly, nearly everyone was willing to tell what they know about Sam and his family and Wal-Mart.

In some respects, the lack of ready access to the Waltons and the corporate archives makes this a better book because it necessitated much old-fashioned police reporter legwork and careful digging, developing and exploiting leads, and putting the Walton life story together by practically laying one brick atop another.

This absolutely is not an authorized biography, but I am certain Sam Walton and his family would find it accurate, reasonably complete, and above all fair to him. Many of my informants appear just as amazed at Sam's brilliant rise to megabillionaire as are the multitudes who have heard little of him. Undoubtedly, many more fascinating episodes might have been uncovered about his life and career, but the ones assembled here seem adequate to delineate an unorthodox and complicated character, even if they don't fully unravel the mysteries of his personality.

Sam surprised me later with a few phone calls. He had heard I was digging into the Ron Mayer episode, and thought I had the facts garbled. He called to make sure I got it right, and I used his version of the event in this book. I would have been pleased to talk to him about other events, but managed to pretty well get everything in perspective, mainly through secondhand sources who were in the know.

I was distressed by his announcement early this year that he has been stricken with an aggressive bone cancer, multiple myeloma, and wish him a full recovery of health. His friends in Bentonville say that because of this illness Sam has shelved his autobiography for a couple of years. In that circumstance, I trust this book will fill the void for interested readers until he can tell his own story.

Nobody writes a biography without help. As previously, my wife, Elzene Miller Trimble, lent her considerable talents as a co-researcher and as a gifted and sharp-eyed editorial critic, detecting not a small number of skipped beats as well as questioning any doubtful or unsatisfactory passages. I gratefully acknowledge her help and her tolerant understanding of my too frequent absence from the bridge table.

Instead of a bibliography and reference notes, I chose mainly to indicate in the manuscript sources of information being given, but also have listed specific permissions granted. For their kind assistance, in large and small ways, in my research, I wish to thank the following:

In Arkansas—at Bentonville: Judge William Enfield, Wesley Hunnicutt, Tom Harrison, Dr. Neil Compton, J. Dickson Black, Bob Bogle, Ferold Arend, Steve Trollinger, Charles Craig, Burton and Shirley Stacy, David and Ruth Glass, Becky Elliott, John D. Wright, Mary Jane Clemmer, Mary Jarnigan, James T. Henry,

Larry W. Dimmit, Sharon Simmons, Wilson Powell, Charles Gocio, Marilois Bach, Carrie McSpadden.

In Rogers: Tony Lundquist, Jo Soderquist, Melvin L. Rakestraw, Steve Wanasek, Clarence Leis, Gwen Batie. In Springdale: Harold Hardin, Jim Morris, Paul Neal, Bob Beson. In Fayetteville: Ernie and Lois Deane, Ellen Shipley, E. Fay Jones, Mary Ann Gunn, Ralph Treat.

In Little Rock: David Petty, "Mr. Witt" and Jack Stephens, Mike Smith, Vernon Giss, Steve Stephens, William Bowen, Jackie Carfango, John Brummett, Robert Dunn, Jim Hopkins, Mara Leveritt, Beverly Holcomb, J. William Becker, Melva Harmon, Ernie Dumas, John Ciasca Jr.

In Newport: Fred and Eran Pickens, Paul K. Holmes Jr., Newport Public Library staff, Mrs. Joe Williams, Michael Rail.

Elsewhere in Arkansas: Jack Moseley of Fort Smith; Floyd Bohannan of Siloam Springs; District Attorney Chris Raff, Sheriff Jerry Johnson, and Tommy Jackson, all of Searcy; Colonel David Fitton and his brother Garvin, Shirley Cox, Grace McCutcheon, and Bud Hendricks, all of Harrison.

In Missouri—at Columbia: Clay C. Cooper Jr., Frederick Tim Allen, Jan Summers, John C. Crighton, Charles Digges Sr., W. H. Bill Conboy, Major Michael Brewer. At Springfield: James E. Dodson, Dr. John E. Moore. At Shelbina: Ron Smoot, Walt Lucas, Isabel Bowen Hutcherson, Chris Ahern, Tim Dunaway. At Buffalo: Jim Hamilton, Mary Jane Beckner, Junior Turner. Also: Audrey Walton of Versailles; Don Spindel and Phillip Abbenhaus, of St. Louis; Wilma Fisher of Lexington; Carter Blanton of Paris.

In Oklahoma—at Tulsa: Alex Adwan, Michael Wallis, John Wooley, Henry Will, Robert L. McGowen. At Oklahoma City: Billy Jo Gourley, Frank Boggs. At Kingfisher: Mrs. Floyd Rasp, Gary Reid, Irwin Bollenbach, Gina Hyatt. At Norman: Louise Beard Moore, Paula Baker, Mary Lou Strickland, Dan Symcox, Mary Reid. At Enid: Dr. Gary Miller, Randy King. At

Claremore: John Harvey Burrows, Bob Chambers, Eliza Arnold, Philip Viles Jr., Deena Bassman. At Pryor: Terry Aylward, Austin Acuff, Jimmy Kitchens, Tony Jack Lyons. Also Nick Robson of Catoosa, and Ruth Wooley of Foyil.

In Texas—Bill Roberts, Leon Davis and Dr. Jorge Quesada of Houston; Roy Bode and Joan Gosnell of Dallas; George Carmack of San Antonio; Joe Taylor and Norman Anthony of Falfurrias; Dick Jones of Corpus Christi; Walter Schiel of Waller.

In California—John Walton of Chula Vista; James H. Jones of Burlingame; Charlie Barr of Long Beach; Peter Barnes of Los Angeles; Everett Orr Topping of Seal Beach.

In Kansas—Bob Solter and Dave Bergemier of Abilene; Fran Jabara of Wichita; Lee Finch of Dodge City; Sidney A. McKnight, Shawnee Mission.

In Indiana—Ronald D. Mayer, Harvey Jacobs, Chris Katterjohn, all of Indianapolis.

And elsewhere—Lionel Linder and Kitty Acuff, Memphis; Jack Kuhn, Nashville; Jay Ambrose, Denver; Jay Gourley, Frank Browning, Dan Thomasson, and Peter Copeland, Washington, D. C.; Paul Knue, Pat Carnes, and W. W. Oliver, Cincinnati; Laurance Eustis III, New Orleans; Coach Glenn C. Smith, Pittsfield, Illinois; Colleen Mueller, Vero Beach, Florida; Kenneth Hornbeck, Park Hills, Kentucky; Lois Houser, Wooster, Ohio; Dr. Kenneth Stone, Ames, Iowa; Richard Oppel, Charlotte; Sharon Reier, St. Augustine; Mayor Bob Bodin, New Iberia, Louisiana; Tony Lisanti, Stephen Taub and Doris Lantiotis, New York; Vance Packard, New Canaan, Connecticut.

And finally I thank Dick Marek for contracting this book for Dutton, and Arnold Dolin and Rosemary Ahern at NAL for creative editing.

— 1 —

Flirting with the Dark Angel

Potential disaster hovered over a small-town airport in the southwestern corner of Missouri one afternoon in May of 1969. Weather was not a problem; it was a pretty day. But three fliers unknowingly but inexorably were heading for a close brush with death. They were, as the locals would say, within spitting distance of eternity.

Out of the Kansas sky came a sleek and shiny twin-engine Beech Baron, eastbound. It passed over Joplin, and twelve miles further east started dropping down on Carthage, a town of about 11,000 that had a small airfield.

Typical of a little-used local airport, the Carthage field was served by no airline, had no control tower, although the woman holding down the office could communicate with traffic by radio. Nestled beside U.S. 71, it had a 3,000-foot strip used mainly by a few dozen training and pleasure aircraft, including three crop dusters, gawky-looking with tubes and nozzles and pumps anchored to their wings. They sat idle, parked near a cluster of four silvery hangars at the north end of the field.

Sam Walton was piloting the Beech Baron. Flying with him was Ronald G. Mayer.

While conversing with his passenger, Sam Walton

occasionally glanced down at the highway he had been
following, but mainly swiveled his gaze skyward to see
if any other planes were in the vicinity before he
committed his craft to a landing pattern. He also wanted
a good look at the sock to check wind direction so he
could land into it.

Sam Walton anticipated a totally routine touchdown.
He was an old hand at flying—twenty-seven years. He
had flown in and out of this Carthage field perhaps
thirty or forty times. The Baron was behaving beautifully; he and Mayer had already landed and taken off
this day from three other small airports in Oklahoma
and Kansas. They were scheduled for another Missouri stop after Carthage.

The wind was from the south. Sam Walton maneu-
vered until he had the plane's nose lined up with the
north end of the runway. He studied the airfield and
saw no activity except two men in mechanic's coveralls
trundling a small monoplane into the largest of the
hangars.

As he had done hundreds of times, in preparation
for landing, he adjusted the fuel mixture to *rich*, raised
the carburetor heat, trimmed the tabs to slightly ele-
vate the nose, and began descending.

In a relaxed crouch, with both hands on the yoke,
Sam Walton looked nonchalant and rumpled, a man
of no pretense. He was fifty-one, with close-cropped
thinning and graying hair, a long sober face, and rather
grim agate eyes. His loose posture in the airplane
disguised the fact that he retained the strength and
agility that had made him a star quarterback in high
school, and in adult life a crackerjack tennis competitor. His hand-eye coordination was excellent, honed
by a few thousand days afield with a 28-gauge shotgun
and bird dogs as a quail hunter.

He wore a nondescript tie, and his sports jacket and
shirt were ordinary and haphazard. His lone badge of
affluence was a gold wristwatch—and this $100,000
six-passenger airplane.

From the left seat, he extended his right arm, grasped

both throttle knobs, and eased them off to retard his two 260-horsepower engines. Beginning his descent, he was at ease and confident—and also proud; his Beech Baron was known as the Cadillac of small planes. It would do practically anything he asked of it.

Sam Walton was still talking to his passenger. He has a country, folksy voice, with a tendency to drawl some words while putting a brittle edge on others, mainly for emphasis. But his speech was clear and strong. Occasionally he would "uh" and hesitate. But there was no mistaking his earnestness; he had about him a sort of Billy Graham–like evangelistic fervor.

He was trying to hire Ron Mayer. It would take about as much selling as Sam Walton could muster. Ron Mayer already had an excellent job as financial vice-president of a well-established merchandising concern in Kansas. Sam wanted him to become the main money man for his own new Wal-Mart discount store chain.

Both knew it would be something of a gamble.

Ron Mayer—for good reason—could recall that whole episode twenty years later with indelible clarity: "Sam told me, 'I'll show you our stores. Then you make up your mind.' "

The Walton chain then consisted of twenty-four stores in Arkansas, Oklahoma, Kansas, and Missouri. The men were flying around to visit about half of them. Sam Walton kept vigorously asserting that he intended to spread out and open up many more stores. So far, Mayer had not been too impressed by the outlook for success of the stores. In his eyes they had quite a few shortcomings. He was, however, impressed by Sam Walton, the aggressive, outspoken entrepreneur from a rustic little town in Arkansas, a discounter who was beginning to startle the Eastern retail giants by the magical way his cash registers were making music.

The Carthage airport lay silent in the sun, looking almost deserted. The Baron dropped out of the clear sky, gliding swiftly toward the north end of the runway. It touched down gracefully at about seventy or eighty miles an hour. There was a mild thud, the quick screech of rubber as tires hit asphalt, spewing unseen puffs of smoke.

Sam Walton reached again for the throttle knobs and slid them all the way back, talking to Ron Mayer while the plane's speed gradually fell off, dropping to about fifty miles an hour. The Beech Baron whizzed past the little white airport shack, 100 yards off the landing strip. In another 1,000 feet the airplane would roll to a stop, and the pilot could make a U-turn and come back and park. No sweat.

All of a sudden Sam Walton's mouth fell open in midsentence, his face turned ashen. He gripped the yoke so fiercely his knuckles glowed white. Ron Mayer gave him a startled look, then turned and stared out the windshield. He jumped and let out a gasp of fright and felt his heart go wild.

Up ahead, perhaps no more than 200 yards away, a small plane, a Piper Cub trainer, was pulling onto the landing strip directly in the path of the incoming airplane.

The Beech Baron was still whizzing forward at fifty miles an hour. It could not stop, and it was too late to turn off the runway. In only a few seconds it appeared doomed to smash into the intruding Piper Cub!

Walton's automatic reflexes exploded into furious action. His right hand jammed forward both throttle knobs. The two engines instantly revved up to full power with a thundering jolt. His left hand jerked back the yoke, and he felt the airplane shudder.

He had only one chance to escape. He must get airborne immediately, leap high enough to hurdle the Piper Cub.

The instant the engines screamed, Sam Walton's free-flying hands were knocking down carburetor heat to prevent an explosion, resetting the elevator tabs, and yanking loose the fire extinguisher—so it would be ready if they didn't make it. Any crash would be fiery.

In the Piper Cub, the careless student pilot who was

playing the fool by pulling onto the runway without first checking, had to be frightened out of his wits. It was too late now for him; there was no way he could get out of the Baron's path.

Sam Walton, with the straining engines battering his ears, felt his plane tremble and rise just a little off the runway, struggling against drag to lift its nose skyward. The Baron again shuddered and wobbled slightly, but couldn't seem to start climbing. The undercarriage still skimmed along barely three or four feet above the runway. The Baron bore down furiously on the hapless trainer, with Sam Walton pressing the yoke back against his chest with both hands, and muttering a prayer.

At the last instant, the Baron lifted barely another foot or two, whizzed over the Piper Cub—and zoomed back up into the sky.

"Our wheels," Ron Mayer recalled, "didn't clear that student plane more than a foot. It was unbelievable!"

As a pilot, Sam Walton had been in tight squeezes before—too many times. Lady Luck had always smiled on him. He realized that in these last few awesome seconds she had practically gathered him into her arms and kissed him!

Years later he was still remembering it and describing it as his most hairy flying adventure. "It was the closest I ever came to getting killed in an airplane," he said grimly in an interview.

An hour later, their nerves no longer jangling over the close call, Sam Walton led Ron Mayer into the Carthage Wal-Mart store, up and down the aisles, explaining the advantages of his various techniques. In the cubbyhole office, he got out the books to show what kind of volume and profit margin his local manager was achieving.

Sam was enormously proud of what his new company had done so far.

In his own mind, Ron Mayer, thirty-five, was weighing the offer of a Wal-Mart job against the position he already held with the A.L. Duckwall Company back in Dwight Eisenhower's hometown, Abilene, Kansas. Duckwall, with more than 100 stores, was much bigger than Wal-Mart. The businesses were rivals and in general alike—discounters in small Midwestern and Southern towns. Ron Mayer weighed this contrasting element. How could he be better off to jump ship and go to a smaller outfit? It had been only seven years since Sam Walton had transformed what was a prosperous string of small variety stores into a growing discount chain.

Nationally, that field was dominated by the giant K mart Corporation, a modern and direct outgrowth of the S. S. Kresge variety store chain, which had its beginning back in 1899. Now, seventy years later, there were about 200 K marts, and trade experts predicted growth to 1,000, perhaps 2,000, stores. Already Kresge–K mart annual sales volume topped $1 billion! With K mart opting for America's metropolises while the Wal-Marts were being opened up in small towns (around 2,000 to 3,000 population), how could Sam Walton, skimping along and with only rosy dreams for resource capital, compete with the giant retailers? The Duckwall man couldn't come up with a satisfactory answer.

Despite his friendly feeling for the Arkansas man, Ron Mayer saw too many disadvantages and said: "No thanks." It was not Sam Walton's first rebuff, and says a good deal for his sangfroid. That single failure didn't terminate the courtship. For weeks he continued wooing Ron Mayer, upping the ante with a larger salary and more generous bonus. Sam really wanted the man. Finally, Ron Mayer weakened, and decided to come aboard on July 1, 1969 as Wal-Mart's financial vice-president.

Ron Mayer moved with vigor into Wal-Mart headquarters at Bentonville, Arkansas. He immediately impressed other key corporate men with his brilliance, aggressiveness, and effectiveness. Sam Walton, beaming with self-satisfaction, was certain he had a prize executive. Perhaps this was the man who could suc-

ceed him as chairman and chief executive officer. It
was something to think about—very carefully.

For more than a year, Sam Walton considered making Ron Mayer his heir to the chairmanship. He admired the man, and thought he could trust him with
Wal-Mart's destiny. But later the corporate headquarters scenario began to change drastically. Instead of
hero and man of the hour, Ron Mayer by early 1976
took on the dark hues of villain.

For Sam Walton this turned out to be the most
serious and disruptive period in his amazing retailing
saga. He found himself and his new protégé on a
collision course—with the risks high, somehow remi-
niscent of the frightening episode on the Carthage
runway.

Once again, Sam Walton took instinctive action for
survival.

The deadly near miss at Carthage and his debacle with
Ron Mayer are significant. They are but two of numerous critical and dramatic episodes in the life and
times of Samuel Moore Walton that are generally un
known to the American public. Even Wall Street in
siders have yet to hear a full account of the explosive
aftermath of the Ron Mayer contretemps.

For his first fifty or sixty years, Sam Walton was not
at all a national figure. He remained in the shadows,
off the beaten track—down in rustic Bentonville, a
town of only 2,900 when he took up residence there in
1950. He likes small towns. With high-octane imagination, plus down-home genius, ungodly long hours of
work and tons of luck, he began creating magic in the
retail trade. Even so, he and Wal-Mart Discount City
were slow to become known beyond the Sunbelt.

It was only in the early 1980s that a startled public
discovered that the richest man in America was not a
Rockefeller, a du Pont, a Trump, a Kennedy, a Getty,
or a Perot but an unglamorous Arkansawyer named

Sam Walton. And with—at that time—a family fortune of $6.3 billion!

Then, of course, the national media descended on
his little Dixieland hometown to find out all about this
country fellow with the big bucks. Their digging soon
enabled them to write in their notebooks that he grew
up in Missouri in the Depression, worked his way
through college, lived a clean Christian life, served
stateside in World War II, married an Oklahoma banker's daughter, opened up his first five-and-dime store
in backwater north central Arkansas, and raised four
healthy kids. Pretty darned ordinary.

But only on the surface. Sam Walton underneath
was no ordinary man.

He was a genius in business, with an iron mind—
some said pig-headed—unwilling to compromise any
of his carefully thought-out policies and principles.

He hated being America's wealthiest. "Aw, shucks—
it's just paper."

To him, making money was only a game, a test of
his imagination and expertise to see how far he could
drive a business concept. Wall Street had a hard time
getting the drift of that. Sam's idea, he readily admitted, was absurdly simple: Buy cheap. Sell low. Every
day. And while doing it smile!

In other words, open a discount store called Wal-
Mart; recruit cold-eyed buyers, as well as friendly,
hand-shaking managers and hard-working clerks; add
new stores just as fast as you can; expand across the
Sunbelt and the Midwest; and watch your sales volume shoot toward the moon!

What really sets him apart is his life-style. With all
that money he could loll around Palm Springs, whoop
it up in the most posh arenas that New York, London,
or Paris can offer, take the sun on a sleek yacht off
Monte Carlo, drive a Lamborghini roadster, drape
wife Helen in emeralds and sables, build his own Taj
Mahal on an Ozark mountaintop (as John D. Rockefeller's grandson did), quit work forever, take life
easy, and live like a king.

He did none of those things.

Instead he lived in a beautiful and modern but modest Frank Lloyd Wright–style three-bedroom house, a few blocks from one of his warehouses, with an old pickup truck in the driveway, a dusty Chevy sedan in the garage, a couple of muddy bird dogs romping in his yard. He was still attending potluck dinners at the Presbyterian church, where he once taught Sunday school. And rising before dawn, often breakfasting at the Holiday Inn (now Days Inn), and driving his battered pickup (minus two hubcaps) to his office, located in a single-story warehouse complex. His desk sits in an unpretentious cubicle about eight by twelve feet, fronting a secretaries' bullpen. He is messy. Papers are piled a foot high on his desk, which once had a fifty-nine-cent wire in-basket on its scratched top and an early Holiday Inn look.

Sam Walton out-Spartans the Spartans. It is just part of his real life.

He's a man of a thousand stories.

He's good, decent, honorable, likable—a Southern man of his word, and perhaps a rarity in modern billion-dollar-business, a man whose handshake you can rely on in any kind of deal.

Quail hunting, tennis, and flying are his passions. He's a crack shot and loves his bird dogs. Tennis is fading, on account of bad knees. He only took up flying because driving mountain curves was too slow. His friends shake their heads, and a few mutter that he's a careless pilot, and marvel that he hasn't splattered himself on an Ozark mountain peak.

The fact that *Forbes* magazine set him at the top of the list of America's Four Hundred Richest disturbed him greatly. So did all the journalistic prying into his Bentonville haunts. He granted very few interviews. He turned his back on most TV cameras. He shuddered each time another magazine piece appeared, even when it was favorable, and in such prestigious journals as *Fortune*, *Business Week*, *Financial World*.

In addition to having a lucky streak, Sam Walton is

flexible. If he adopts a business course that doesn't work out, he's neither too vain nor too blind to see his mistake, to say so, and change his heading 180 degrees. Of course, it usually requires major persuasion by trusted lieutenants or his own recognition of unusual circumstance, to let reason override his natural inflexibleness.

His life has not been all upbeat. His marriage was so good and true nothing could rupture it. He is enormously proud of his children, three sons and a daughter, but for a time couldn't convince them to follow him into retailing. It was a wrenching disappointment that none wanted to understudy for his Wal-Mart kingship. In fact, sons John and Jim both virtually told their father to take the business and shove it. When that was reported in the national press, Sam shook his head and said it wasn't that bad.

But all the children grew disenchanted after a teenage introduction to the five-and-dime business, which their father figured could be successful only with dawn-to-past-dusk hard work and iron-hand discipline. They chafed, too, at growing up as scions of a rich and influential man, and yearned to succeed on their own merit, and perhaps in other fields.

Daughter Alice went through reckless exploits before settling down to a sensible business career. First-born Rob and Jim have finally securely tied themselves to the discount corporation and allied interests and to hometown Bentonville. Alice trained herself to handle investments of the family billions, which she largely does while living nearby on a horse farm. However, John, building sailboats in San Diego, remains a free-spirited maverick, but with his full share of the family wealth.

In 1982 Sam came down with hairy cell leukemia, a form of cancer that can be fatal. Doctors gravely told him they might save his life by removing his spleen. He wouldn't hear of it. The only alternative was to become a guinea pig for experimental medicine. He didn't want to do that either. In his stubborn way, he rejected all treatment, and holed up in Bentonville to "meditate."

Would Lady Luck smile on him once again? He wondered about that, counted on it! She had always been such a huge factor in his life and his career.

Beating the odds has become the veritable trademark for this "richest man in America." Sam Walton's genius and uncanny good fortune have been part of an incomparable business odyssey that is also one of America's most spectacular personal success stories of this century.

And the multi-billion-dollar saga appears not yet to have reached its zenith.

It was back in the 1950s when Sam Walton began trying to devise ways to turn five-and-ten-cent stores into a great chain of discount retailing establishments. He was a pioneer in business. Perhaps, the hand of fate spurred him to strike out for new horizons. That should not be surprising, for a hearty appetite for challenge and adventure dominated Walton men from his great-grandfather's day. Nor is his choice of retailing so unusual; his grandfather ran a general store in horse-and-buggy days in Missouri.

The Waltons were courageous pioneers from Virginia who dared the frontiers of the American West, and it was because of the Indian Territory land rush of 1889 that Samuel Moore Walton began life out on the wild, bleak, and grassy prairie of northwestern Oklahoma.

—2—

Indians and Buffalo Grass

Morning dew was not yet dry on the prairie wildflowers when a keen-eyed adventurer named J. W. Walton, out of Missouri, broke camp beside a muddy creek, doused his coffee fire, collected his Winchester, his canteen, and bedroll, and saddled up his spirited horse to ride pell-mell into the most dramatic human stampede in the American West.

Two hours later at Buffalo Springs, on the northern border of Oklahoma's "unassigned" Indian lands, Walton encountered a mammoth and motley array of covered wagons, oxcarts, buggies, men on horseback and on foot—side by side in a line stretching as far as the eye could see. Facing them, guarding against impromptu invasion, were U.S. Cavalry troops.

Walton reined up and edged into the line, guiding his stallion between two grizzled men who looked as dangerous as cattle rustlers. This scene was almost identical to what was taking place on all four sides of the vast, raw Indian Territory, according to the cavalrymen. All told, they said, at least 50,000 people were lined up, including hundreds aboard two special Santa Fe trains, with steam up waiting on the north at Arkansas City and on the south at Purcell.

It was a rare day in history—Monday, April 22, 1889. Within an hour or so, at straight-up noon, sol-

diers would fire their carbines into the lazy blue sky.
This would be the official signal to start the "run"—
turning loose the land-hungry mob to rush in and
stake a claim on one of 10,000 quarter-section home-
steads or city lots the federal government was giving
away. It would prove larger than the Forty-niner Gold
Rush.

Walton had never seen this land on which he would
stake his new future. But he and the others had heard
it was a welcoming place with "the finest climate in
the world, an abundance of water, timber, and stone.
Springs gush from every hill. The grass is green the
year round." That was the description put out all
across America by the Katy, Frisco, and Santa Fe
railroads as well as by the illegal "Boomers"—aggressive
colonists who for years had sneaked in to start little
abortive frontier settlements before U.S. troops chased
them out.

Back in his home state, J. W. Walton had been a
lawman, first elected sheriff of Cooper County in central Missouri, and later in 1883, filling the same office
in Webster County, just east of Springfield. The Waltons were restless pushers. Emigrating from the Brit-
ish Isles to the Atlantic seaboard, they struggled west
with the pioneer surge out of Virginia, ambitious to
escape hardscrabble life, and adventuresome enough
to wrestle fate and the frontier for better days.

Now J. W. Walton was taking a new gamble on
what was being called President Benjamin Harrison's
horse race into this near mythical land of Indian and
buffalo, endless prairie grass, with deep rich red virgin
soil waiting to be broken by plow.

Everybody—men and women twenty-one and older
who did not own as much as 160 acres elsewhere—had
a chance. All it took to capture a homestead was
getting there first. J. W. Walton figured his big horse,
well rested, would cover ground fast.

His hope was to reach the area where government
surveyors had laid out a town to be called Kingfisher—

and to arrive before all the nearby choice land was staked.

The pioneers were making big talk about the unborn town of Kingfisher. It would straddle the stage route from Buffalo Springs south to Fort Reno, about midway. Statehood was surely coming for Oklahoma Territory (which it did in 1907), and everyone expected Kingfisher to be the capital. (It was a close call, but Oklahoma City would beat out both rivals, Guthrie and Kingfisher.)

Straight through these "unassigned lands" had come the old Chisholm Trail over which Texas ranchers drove 10 million cattle to the Abilene, Kansas, railhead after transportation was bottled up in the Civil War by Union blockade of Confederate ports.

At Buffalo Springs, J. W. Walton and his fretful companions watched the sun climb overhead, but kept their eyes on the soldiers whose watches had been synchronized with Greenwich time.

Then came the moment—noon. The *Daily Oklahoman* recalled in an anniversary edition:

> Then, at spot after spot along the borders, there was a soldier's gunshot, and a bugler's blare, and the crowd responded with a mighty yell that became a roar. The tense silence was shattered with the din of pounding hooves, rattling harness, grinding wheels. Men and beasts and vehicles pushed beyond their limits to be there first.
>
> They tumbled off the trains, throwing their bags before them, and then ran. Great clouds of dust stirred and swirled in as many directions as the settlers took. Household goods fell from wagons and littered the prairie. Nobody dared stop. The wildflowers were trampled . . .

The start of the race resembled a roar of low thunder, settlers observed later, and the ground seemed to tremble. J. W. Walton burst forward with the leaders. Suddenly, one "cattle rustler" racing alongside was thrown out of the saddle when his horse stepped into a gopher hole and broke a leg. Glancing back, J. W. Walton saw the downed man had the presence of mind to grab his stake and pound it into the ground with a hatchet to claim the homestead on which he fell.

Bringing up the rear of the headlong scramble were family-ladened, ramshackle wagons with slogans like "Oklahomy or Bust" painted on their shabby canvas.

By nightfall, a stake bearing the name J. W. WALTON had been driven into the grassy hillock of a beautiful quarter-section within easy riding distance of the Kingfisher townsite. There a mad scramble was going on. Ten thousand people came in overnight. They now mingled raucously, marking off streets and alleys; putting up tents; trying to start makeshift saloons, general stores, blacksmiths, boardinghouses; buying scarce drinking water at a quarter a gallon, arguing with unscrupulous "Sooners" they suspected of sneaking in under cover of darkness ahead of the "run" and grabbing off some of the best land.

After driving his stake, the ex-Missouri sheriff had to ride into the federal land office at either Guthrie or Kingfisher and pay a $14.75 filing fee. He must live on the land five years to get a patent (legal ownership).

Into the pitiful conglomeration of pioneers—virtually all desperately poor—J. W. Walton settled, after first returning to Missouri to bring his family, household wares, and livestock to the desolate center of Oklahoma.

Like their neighbors, the J. W. Waltons found homesteading wasn't easy or for the faint of heart. Oklahoma, with all her beauty and charm, could be—and was—a formidable adversary with her extreme heat and cold, tornadoes, hailstorms and dust storms, floods and droughts, not to mention the necessity of dealing with rattlesnakes, tarantulas, centipedes, and hordes of insects.

Neighbor pitched in to help neighbor. Wells were dug. Sod houses were built. Gardens were put in. Shelters for animals were constructed. Bois d'arc (bow wood) trees were planted as hedgerows to separate the farms. They would provide some windbreak, as well as keep herds separated (and provide a makeshift place to dry laundry).

Days were long. Work was hard, as were the times. It took four horses to pull a gang plow that cut a 2-foot wide swath on the Mathies Kuver farm, and a full month to break 80 acres. Fortunately wild game was plentiful, including squirrels, cottontails, prairie chickens, jackrabbits, wild turkeys, quail, ducks, geese, some bear, and hundreds of deer.

The J. W. Waltons fared perhaps no better nor any worse than anyone else during their five years of homesteading, but the head of the family was too ambitious, imaginative, and aggressive to settle down to the routine of farming. His bent was for business, and he saw an opportunity in real estate sales and farm loans. Scores of disgruntled settlers were willing to give up their claims for, say, a gun, a horse, fifty or a hundred dollars, and a train ticket back north. Anxious settlers could squat on their land just fourteen months and then buy it from Uncle Sam for $1.25 an acre. In all this land flurry, there was room for an agent. J. W. Walton opened an office in Kingfisher.

How well he succeeded, and why, is indicated in a business blurb published September 5, 1901, in the weekly *Kingfisher Times* labeling him one of the prominent citizens, adding:

This gentleman has always been identified with every movement for the advancement of the interests of either our city or county. He is a man of progressive ideas, a man who is always on the side of right, and one who has the highest regard for his name and reputation. He is a firm believer in the future of Kingfisher city and county, knowing, as he does, that no section in the United States can surpass this for agricultural and horticultural pursuits and for the raising of livestock . . .

Mr. Walton for the past nine years has conducted an exclusive loan agency. Confining his business to farm loans. . . . He makes his own examinations, closes up the deals himself, and can furnish the money wanted at any time. By dealing with him the borrower does not have any tedious delays, but can obtain his money as soon as the papers are made out.* Then too, Mr. Walton is a very safe man with whom to deal. He treats everybody fairly and honestly, and we are safe in saying his record is without blemish in a field which admits of much peculation.

The *Kingfisher Times* pointed out that Walton was serving his second term as city councilman, with a "good record," and was a member of the Ancient Order of United Workmen, the Woodmen of the World, and the Knights and Ladies Security orders.

Such prominence and success in the booming Indian Territory made J. W. Walton appear back in Webster County, Missouri, an attractive magnet to draw from the old home place several kinsmen who were looking for adventure or a chance for a better life.

First to come to Kingfisher—in about 1895—was his courageous and enterprising teenage niece, Mollie Walton. Her father, Samuel W. had come from Virginia with his parents, three sisters, and three brothers, settling in Cooper County, and on growing up he had established a general store in Lamine. Several years later he sold out and went to Webster County, opening a general store in the little town of Diggins,† also harvesting railroad ties and running a large fruit farm. Mollie was the only child of his first marriage. After his wife died, he married again and fathered three sons, Earl, Freeman, and Thomas, all born in Diggins. While Thomas, who was to become Sam Walton's father, was still a baby, Samuel W. and his second

---

*Though no mention is made of his source of ready cash, presumably Walton had arranged to act as an agent, as did other Missouri kinsmen for the Metropolitan Life Insurance Company, or for a prosperous big city bank.

†Sam and Bud Walton helped finance a park on this site, and went to Diggins in 1987 to attend its dedication.

wife died within a few months of each other. Lacking a home, his "second family" was split up and the three boys "farmed out" individually to Webster County uncles or aunts.

On arriving in Indian Territory, Mollie dedicated herself to hard work and education. Within a year or two she graduated from high school, passed her teacher exam, and became a $35-a-month schoolmarm in Kingfisher.

Then she sent for the three boys and set up a home for them in Kingfisher. The youngest was only about four or five—Thomas, born June 21, 1892. Earl and Freeman were several years older. Mollie proved a forthright and judicious "little mother," setting the three youngsters to an increasingly arduous regimen of chores and schoolbooks.

The first schoolhouse was built of logs. The books and furniture were used. The Walton boys went through the McGuffey readers and spellers, Ray's arithmetic, and Barnes's history. There was no running water; a large pail was hand carried from a nearby well, and equipped with a communal dipper. A potbellied wood stove provided heat. Behind the schoolhouse were boys' and girls' outhouses.

In 1904 Earl and Freeman graduated from high school. Earl went on to the University of Oklahoma and came out a pharmacist. Eventually he opened a Rexall Drug Store in Kingfisher, which he operated for nearly sixty years.

Uncle J. W. took little Tom under his wing and began training him in the farm appraisal and mortgage business. Energetic, spry, ambitious, and a confirmed straight-shooter, Tom Walton caught on in a hurry. He observed the doughty Kingfisher County farmers, and learned lifelong lessons in how they coped with a variety of everyday perils. They had to keep alert in the tall buffalo grass for the sound of rattlesnakes. Tarantulas were just as plentiful. But the work had to go on.

By the time Mollie married a Dr. Williams and

moved away, the three orphan boys from Missouri were on their own. Tom was now a full-fledged farm appraiser and mortgage agent for his uncle. He was conscious of no life except that on the Oklahoma plains. The young man had adapted well; doubtless his mentor-uncle's high principles had rubbed off on him. He got along well. Everybody liked him.

Slight of build, but articulate and bright-eyed, Tom Walton was now in his midtwenties. He found numerous occasions to visit the farm of Reuben and Ellen James Lawrence, who had escaped the rigors of Kansas by migrating to Kingfisher County, bringing along three sons and five daughters. It was one of the latter, a shy eighteen-year-old named Nancy Lee, who caught Tom's amorous eye. He wooed her the same way he handled farm mortgages—vigorously.

They were married in 1917 and began housekeeping on a farm Tom Walton had acquired a few miles outside of the town of Kingfisher.

On Friday, March 29, 1918, their first child, a boy, was born. Tom cradled the infant proudly in his arms. It struck him that he had only the vaguest memory of his own father, and none at all of his mother, except that her name was Clara Etta Layton. He decided to make his own son his father's namesake—Samuel Moore Walton.

Not even by the world's most powerful crystal ball could this young Kingfisher couple have foretold on that day—or even years afterward—to what heights their first-born would rise in the modern dog-eat-dog business world.

Sam Walton remembers little of his early years. He does not know the location of the farmhouse where he was born. He has been remarkably blasé about his roots. His father took pains to scribble some historical notes for his two sons.

The second boy, James L., known as Bud, was born in 1921. "He was born," Tom always told his in-laws, "on the shortest day of the year—December twenty-first. And you know I was born on the longest day—

June twenty-first." That was merely a good story. Bud's birth certificate shows he was born on the twentieth of December.

Tom Walton's Kingfisher string was beginning to play out. An agricultural depression had started and was blitzing across the once-proud western plains. Ready money just about disappeared through the floor and frustration and anger sent tempers through the roof.

It probably was time, Tom Walton told Nancy, to take the kids and try to find a new life, perhaps a new career somewhere else. He had no inkling of the terrible struggle he would soon endure to keep body and soul together and food on the table in the coming Great Depression of the 1930s, when he would be merely one of the millions scrambling for scarce and precious nickels and dimes.

When the Walton family packed up to depart Kingfisher, Sam was about five years old, and Bud around two.

—3—

A Sort of Tom Sawyer

Think of the adventures of Tom Sawyer and Huckle-berry Finn and Tom's sweetheart Becky Thatcher in Missouri in the long-ago 1880s. But change the cast of characters. Make the names Samuel Moore Walton and his buddy Everett Orr and Sam's teenage flapper heartthrob Isabel Bowen.

Also jump the date forward to 1932 or 1933 and play out this new drama of school-days innocence in the little Missouri farming town of Shelbina, popula-tion not quite 2,000.

It so happened that Sam, Everett, and Isabel were right smack dab in authentic Mark Twain country, forty miles due west of Hannibal, where the famous steamboat pilot–author laid the lively scenes of his classic fiction.

Sam Walton, fifteen years old, was shy and certainly no rambunctious Tom Sawyer. But he was smart and good-looking, a scholar and an athlete. Isabel, spirited brunette daughter of the town druggist—who was very strict, too strict to let her date at fifteen—was smitten with Sam. She bribed Everett, who was an orphan like Huck Finn, to come by her house and get her out. Her father trusted Everett, having known him as a fine lad since the second grade. The bribe usually was ten cents.

21

Everett Orr was outgoing, a bull of a fellow, a superb athlete who lettered in football, basketball, track, "and just about everything," but he had a sad, heart-tugging background. His parents divorced in Long Island, New York, when he was four and fought nastily over their five children. Everett remembered a welfare worker pinning a tag on his coat, then perching him on the tailgate of an express wagon that jolted him across New York City. He was herded aboard one of the celebrated "orphan trains" that took children out West to new homes.

At the Shelbina depot, he was taken in by George Orr and his wife, who were then the wealthiest farmers in northeastern Missouri. They gave him love and a good home.*

Once Everett and Isabel were out of sight of Mr. Bowen, Everett would hand the girl over to his best buddy, Sam Walton. Druggist Bowen never caught on. Thus Isabel went happily off on a forbidden date with Sam—to a movie, a school party, or elsewhere. Isabel paid Everett the dime.

"Sometimes I'd let Sam borrow my parents' car that I often drove, a thirty-one Model A coupe," said Everett Orr. "I guess they'd go park and smooch a little." He laughed. "That's about as far as it went."

Along with courting Isabel, Sam was going out for football and basketball, learning to play tennis, making As and more friends, grinding away on merit badges in hopes of becoming an Eagle Scout, regularly attending Sunday school, and scrambling after odd jobs such as grass mowing that might put two bits or a half dollar in his pocket.

No one in the Walton household worked harder,

---

*Adoption laws prohibited Everett from investigating his roots until he reached age twenty-one. When a St. Louis welfare worker in the 1940s took him to lunch and opened his file, he found his name was Everett Topping and he was the son of a Sag Harbor, New York, fisherman. In later years, all the Topping "orphans" met in a reunion.

except his father. "The secret is work, work, work," said Thomas Gibson Walton. "I taught the boys how to do it."

The father of Sam and Bud was drilling in this lesson largely by example—and mostly while on the run. Though he was headquartered in Shelbina, most townsfolk thought of him as a "traveling salesman." His job as a farm loan agent kept him mainly out of town, traveling dusty country roads by car, often having to drive a hundred miles a day. He was a bear for work, and wouldn't tolerate sons who were not likewise industrious, ambitious, and decent.

Tom had set out for Webster County for two specific reasons. Foremost was to take a reading on business possibilities there, in hopes of finding a new job that would lift his family a few notches above their current commonplace existence.

Second, he had a nagging curiosity about his roots. Having grown up in the remote Indian Territory, he knew hardly anything about his lineage and heritage. He despised being a stranger to his own past. So once back in Webster County he went around getting acquainted with kinsmen and talking about pioneer days.

He was very interested in the history of the adjacent villages of Seymour and Diggins, where he was born, and the county seat, Marshfield. The first white settlers, he learned, had come to this region of southeastern Missouri in 1830. Previously it had been the hunting grounds of the Osage, Delaware, and Kickapoo Indians and other tribes. Near what became Seymour the first burial grounds of the Shawnees west of the Mississippi River were found. Daniel Boone and his buckskin-clad long rifles had roamed these wooded uplands and rich valleys drained by many rivers, creeks, and springs. Webster County lies on the summit of the Ozark range, with Marshfield being 1,505 feet above tidewater at Mobile Bay, and 1,081 feet above St. Louis.

It was not until the 1850s that the Waltons arrived. They came near the tail end of the caravans of pio-

neers flowing westward from Virginia, Kentucky, and
Tennessee. Tom's forebears in the main were sturdy
and hard-working farmers. Tom found that a few kinsmen opted to become merchants, lawmen, preachers,
bankers—professional people.

Not much printers' ink was needed locally for Walton family exploits. For the entire year of 1891, the
weekly *Marshfield Chronicle* carried only three items
about Tom's ancestral clan, viz: "J. F. Walton from
nearby Springfield bought the Swaggers blacksmith
shop on the east side of town." "S. S. Walton went to
Wright County to buy stock." And, S. W. Walton
from Springfield "spent Sunday in this place, returning
home on the evening train."

Tom discovered that the Moore side of his family
was all over the newspaper, as well as being active in
the political and business scenes. When Marshfield
was incorporated in 1877, F. W. Moore was listed as a
trustee and also elected town president. His name was
in the merchants' list in 1888. Perhaps most prominent
of the Moores was Joseph T., who came from Giles
County, Tennessee, and served as second lieutenant in
the 8th Missouri Cavalry, fighting gallantly at Pea
Ridge and Prairie Grove. A lifelong Republican, he
cast his first vote for Abraham Lincoln in 1864. Twice
(in 1886 and 1888) he was elected representative from
Webster County to the Missouri Legislature. Tom Walton noted with interest that Joseph Moore had been
appointed a federal land commissioner for the Oklahoma homesteading.

The quest for a better life that had drawn Tom
Walton back to Missouri did not meet with dazzling
success. He ran head-on into the hard times he was
trying to escape. No one offered him a plush job. In
the end, the best he could do was go back to the same
old grind he knew so well. That was to jump squarely
into the middle of the nationwide wrestling match that
pitted bitter, hard-up farmers deep in debt against
distraught bankers desperate to get their hands on
overdue interest and principal.

Tom went to work for his eldest half-brother, J. B. Walton, who operated the successful Walton Mortgage Company from headquarters in Butler, Missouri, sixty miles south of Kansas City. His job was to refinance delinquent loans, and to buy and sell farms. Springfield was his first base, and the family lived there a few months, long enough for Sam to start first grade.

Next Tom was transferred to Marshall, about seventy-five miles due east of Kansas City, in the same capacity. "We lived there several years," Sam Walton recalls. "My father quit the mortgage company and went into business for himself—real estate and insurance. Then came the Depression. Dad's business went down the drain. He went back to work for Walton Mortgage Company, and his brother sent him to Shelbina, which was a very small town about one hundred twenty-five miles northwest of St. Louis. Dad's job was to represent the company in the whole northeast corner of Missouri. That sure meant a lot of traveling."

In this humdrum fashion about ten prime years of Tom's and Nan's lives skittered away, with no perceptible climb for the family up the social or economic ladders. They were still lower middle-class, not poor, but dangerously close to it. Out in Oklahoma they had been pinched and forced to struggle against what started out merely as an agricultural recession. Now they—along with millions of other Americans—were in the cruel clutches of the Great Depression.

And in the summer of 1933, Tom was again considering pulling up stakes—at age forty-one—and leaving Shelbina to take his wife and sons to a strange new town.

To keep from warping their boys' dreams for a brighter tomorrow, the parents soft-pedaled the usual supper-table talk of their dismal finances. Sam and Bud were expected to work hard, earn some spending money if they could, to keep clean and be thrifty, and not be wasteful of anything.

As the new kid in town in the fall of 1931, when he

started the eighth grade in Shelbina, Sam Walton was already revealing the character traits that would dominate his future life. He stood out as an individual—different, no doubt about it. Sam cast a certain magic spell. He was soft-spoken and quiet, almost embarrassingly so. Yet despite being shy, he was a natural leader. By easily becoming class president or captain of the football team, he demonstrated that talent over and over again in his youth.

Most boys coming from farm families wore overalls to school in Shelbina. "Sam didn't," said Isabel Bowen. "He wore corduroy pants and a shirt and sweater, things of that sort. That helped make him stand out. He didn't have any trouble getting acquainted. I'd call him a sort of reserved person, until you knew him." His haircut also helped mark him. "Combed it straight back with no part in the middle," Everett Orr said. "Cut short. Just enough to comb straight back. In those days we put goop on our hair to make it lay down. I put an old stocking on my head to hold my hair in place."

Almost from the moment they met at school, Sam and Everett were pals and confidants. They were together as football players, in the Boy Scouts, at the Methodist Church, working odd jobs, hiking and camping out, and visiting overnight in each other's homes.

"Sam wouldn't run around with anybody that said a cuss word," said Everett Orr. "He was pretty straitlaced in that way. Sam would just cringe when somebody would cuss—if they even said 'hell.' His favorite word was 'darn.' That's as far as he would go. When he said 'darn' that was just as mad as he was going to get. I was very careful and we got along good for that reason, I think. That's where it started." Everett liked Sam's mild manner. "He never got excited about anything."

As a freshman, Sam lettered in football, playing halfback. "I know later on he was the quarterback, but not at Shelbina," said his school buddy. "He couldn't be quarterback because we had some pretty tough players, really tough."

In those years little Shelbina High School was a football power in northeastern Missouri. The team Sam Walton played on defeated larger schools such as Hannibal and Kirksville, badly trounced Palmyra, and finished the 1932 season undefeated. Next year Shelbina and Palmyra both ended their seasons undefeated, having battled each other to a scoreless tie in the final game.

"Sam was heavier than I," Everett Orr said. "He weighed . . . Well, he had a big butt and I remember he kind of walked with a waddle. I guess he weighed a hundred forty-eight or fifty in his freshman year."

Everett Orr remembered his school pal as very personable. "He made friends easily, even though he was shy; people sort of flickered toward him even when he was young. How such a shy guy could become a leader, I just can't understand. I'd have to think awful hard to find an answer to that."

His mother's influence had a lot to do with Sam's reticence, according to Everett. "I'd say he caught the quiet reserved part from his ma. It wouldn't come from his father; he was a traveling salesman—in his business, he had to be aggressive. The family seemed pretty well adjusted. I never saw any fights or anything. Of course, I didn't live there, just stayed overnight with Sam once in a while."

Everett Orr didn't recall seeing Tom Walton except on weekends. "He was a hard worker, and wasn't home much. I don't remember him much, just Sam's mother. She was really a nice person, quiet and reserved. If she said something it was always in a low tone. I never heard her holler at anybody, or speak loud about anything. It was a quiet family."

Isabel Bowen met Mrs. Walton only a few times. "I don't remember her ever coming to the school," she said. "She was a social person. She enjoyed playing bridge with the women of the community. She had a nice little garden and grew flowers." Sam's mother had "a very pretty face," both Isabel and Everett remembered, but was somewhat stocky and dressed matronly.

The Waltons lived a couple of blocks off Shelbina's main drag in a "nice" rented two-story house. It had a long front porch. "When Dizzy Dean was playing with the Gas House Gang in St. Louis," said Everett Orr, "and had a strikeout record going, well, I was helping Sam paint his front porch. We listened to the radio and kept score with a paintbrush, just made a brush mark for the strikes. Oh, that porch—we must have done a fast, sloppy job!"

Sam never pulled any pranks or got into trouble at school. "The teachers liked him," said Everett Orr. "He was probably the only one they knew who didn't have any bad words. He wouldn't smoke or nip a drink or anything like that. He sure didn't around me. But the other boys . . . You can't imagine—there were some town kids who were terrible town toughs. Sam was more country than town, I think."

Sam Walton translated his work ethic into quite a small-town honor—becoming the first Eagle Scout in Shelbina's history. Both he and pal Everett were diligently trying to acquire the requisite twenty-one merit badges. In addition, a candidate for Eagle Scout was required to demonstrate to an adult examiner that he was capable of saving a life by rescue or first-aid.

That part, by lucky happenstance, proved a snap for Sam. He became a real-life hero.

"We were all out at the class picnic on the Salt River," said Everett Orr. "It's a big river when it's swollen, and it had been raining a lot. I remember being along the riverbank with my girlfriend, keeping my eye on a big bottle of soda I had soaking to cool down at the edge of the water. A big bottle was something in those days. I didn't want anybody to discover it, and steal it.

"Donald Peterson, one of our classmates, fell in the river. Sam dived right in and pulled him out!"

A few weeks later the Eagle Scout ceremony was held in the basement of the red brick public library, which was fronted by a pretty, white-painted wooden gazebo, from which the municipal band played traditional Saturday evening summer concerts.

Sam raised his right hand in the Boy Scout salute, and repeated the oath, as his fifteen or twenty fellow Scouts and parents looked on.

His scoutmaster stepped forward to drape diagonally across his chest a wide sash on which his mother had sewed the twenty-one merit badges. Then around the fifteen-year-old's neck he hung a red, white, and blue ribbon from which dangled, glinting silver and majestic under the lights, the eagle that is the Boy Scouts' highest honor.

It was a night for all Shelby County to feel proud, and for Sam Walton clear and positive proof that he was being fed excellent advice by his father. If he wanted to achieve high and lofty goals, he must be willing to buckle down to work hard.

There was a close and even-tempered relationship between Sam and Buddy Walton, almost three years his junior, but the older brother was boss. "Sometimes Buddy would tag along, but mostly no," said Everett Orr. "I never heard them argue too much, except for Sam to say, 'You can't do it,' or 'You can't go,' something like that." Isabel Bowen agreed. "They got on just fine. Sam was interested in everything—academics, athletics, just everything. Bud was more carefree. Bud did all right, but he just never did let things bother him."

Tom Walton later said that he detected in their boyhood more promise in Bud than in Sam. However, he conceded to one of Sam's college pals: "Sam got his brains from his mother. She was the smart one in the family."

Even as a high school freshman, Sam showed business enterprise. He milked the family cow and bottled and delivered the excess milk. One customer was Isabel's father. He also did odd jobs that earned twenty-five or fifty cents, providing his own spending money.

Tom and Nan called in the boys one evening in late summer of 1933 and announced that September first the family would be moving again. This time they were going to a fairly large town—Columbia, located on Highway 40, just about the center of the state. It was an important college town, home of the University of Missouri and two well-known girls' schools, Stephens and Christian colleges. When all the students were in town, Columbia had a population of about 30,000.

Nan already was urging Sam to become a lawyer, and believed the move to a college town would make it easier for the sons to get a good education. Tom was all for it, even though shifting his base to Columbia would mean a longer drive to cover the same northeastern Missouri territory.

News of Sam's impending departure hit Isabel Bowen like a thunderbolt. It was no secret in Shelbina High School that Sam and Isabel were sweethearts. Their puppy love might have developed into a serious romance, given time. But that was not to be—aborted by the "move-on" syndrome that haunted Tom Walton's career. "We were just kids, you know," said Isabel. "We had never talked about getting married, or anything. We were both pretty unhappy about him leaving, but of course I don't know just how unhappy he was. I think he was disappointed, and I know for certain I was disappointed."

The sweethearts corresponded for a short time, then their romance faded, and they eventually lost track of each other.

Forty years later, when she was married to Dennis Hutcherson, living in nearby Clarence, and the mother of four children, she was invited to attend a surprise party for billionaire Sam Walton, and he greeted her with a kiss. Said Isabel Bowen Hutcherson: "We were not the least embarrassed."

—4—

"$2 and a Clean Shirt"

Hickman High School in Columbia, with its 650 students—many either genuinely sophisticated or smugly acting as if they were—could have proved too tough a hurdle for the sophomore from a little upstate country town. It wasn't. Sam Walton, even more so than at Shelbina, was a friendly fireball who practically set the place ablaze by the time he got his diploma in 1936.

Bad luck marred his entry into Hickman High. He hobbled in on crutches, having fractured his left leg sliding into home plate in a summer baseball game. But he went out for football and basketball in 1935 and 1936, and was quarterback of the undefeated Kewpie eleven and also lettered in basketball. He was elected vice-president of his junior class and president of the student body in his senior year. He had his full-page photo in the 1936 school annual, *The Cresset*, as "The Most Versatile Boy," and there could be no doubt about the validity of that title. Sam was in just about every club and organization on campus that amounted to anything—and he was active.

"Sam was a hard worker. He was optimistic all the time. He had a great smile on his face and felt like everybody was his friend and the world was something he could conquer," said Clay Cooper, who was Hickman

High's stellar halfback and leading scorer when "Sammy" —as he was now called—was the Kewpie quarterback.

"He really wasn't obnoxiously aggressive at all. He was just a good-boy type that everybody liked. He was smart and intelligent and did a good job."

Tom and Nan Walton took a two-story brick residence at 1309 Rosemary Lane, close to the University of Missouri campus. It had four upstairs bedrooms, three of which were rented to university students. Mrs. Walton did not regard that as a burden, Sam recalls. "She was just a great person," he says. "She took care of the house and kept those rooms clean. She was very ambitious, always read a lot, and grew flowers. Later she was president of the garden club in Columbia."

In those hard times the students' rent money helped out. Still Tom Walton began to see a glimmer of better days ahead as the city fathers of Columbia aggressively fought the rising tide of joblessness and poverty—with an arsenal of home-grown anti-Depression tactics.

To try to turn things around, Columbia dug into its $150,000 water and light fund surplus and built a new city hall and police station—to create jobs. Soon federal dollars began coming in from the New Deal in Washington. By December 1933, 450 women and 460 men were doing U.S. government paid work in Columbia and Boone County. Congressional public works funds also rolled into the city to help build a student center, library, new journalism building and labs and additions at the university, as well as airport runways, more streets and sewers, a water and light park, and a national guard armory.

Someone who came to Columbia in August 1938 was quoted in the *Tribune* as saying: "I have traveled over most of the United States in the last twelve months and this is the only city I have seen which apparently has not felt the depression."

Driving around the countryside, in daily contact with gaunt farmers and their ragged children, Tom Walton was seeing the grim realities of an economic crunch to which that visitor had been somehow blind. It was easy for Tom Walton to fix the origin of this trouble—World War I. U.S. farmers had been urged to expand cultivation. After the Armistice, farms in Europe that had been shut down began producing again. American farmers were left with a giant surplus of wheat, corn, meat, and cotton. Then came the Herbert Hoover years, which pinched the farmers even more than "Coolidge prosperity." Farmers all across the nation were caught in a squeeze between falling prices for agricultural commodities and the rising costs of industrial products.

Although not personally feeling the worst effects of the Depression, "Sammy" Walton was living up to his dad's "work, work, work" ethic at Hickman High School. In addition to his man-killing regimen in academics and athletics, he found time for odd jobs and was more and more becoming self-supporting. Rolling out of bed at dawn, he delivered a route for the M. U. journalism students' *Columbia Missourian*. Significantly, he also became a part-time helper in a Columbia five-and-ten-cent store.

Unless he was in a football or basketball uniform, Sam Walton never had his picture taken without a suit and tie, or wearing a good-looking sweater. He continued to comb back his hair, short, with no part. *The Cresset*'s photographs show his steady, clear-eyed gaze, and a hint of smile.

Hickman classmates felt that everything clicked into place for Sam. "He was an organizer," said Frederick Tim Allen, who played tackle on the Kewpie championship eleven, was Sam's confidant and many years later took a post-retirement job in a Wal-Mart store in Columbia. "He was student president, but didn't have to campaign. Sam really wasn't a politician, he just didn't waste time, always busy doing something."

"One difference about Sam," Allen said, "is he was always easy to get along with. I've never seen him lose his temper unless it was justified. No way. No extem-

poraneous temper—something pretty serious, somebody that's broke their word, or something like that. I
don't think there's anything abnormal about that. I get
mad, too, if somebody breaks their word."

The extent to which Tom Walton helped his sons
develop their drive and character is incalculable, in the
opinion of other Hickman High classmates of Sam's
who remained in Columbia and rose high in community business circles.

"Those were hard times, and Mr. Tom never really
. . . Well, he was just a small businessman," said
W. H. (Bill) Conboy of Shelter Insurance Company.
"He knew land and he knew people. Mr. Tom incul-
cated in both the boys a unique ability, in my opinion,
to know people. And I think both of the boys inher-
ited that rare quality of being able to put the calipers
on a person and decide whether they are the right type
of person for this particular endeavor."

Frederick Tim Allen said Sam was very close to his
father. "I think people underestimated him [Tom]. He
was a smart man. The reason I got to know him pretty
good was when we were playing football we didn't
have buses and stuff. Different people volunteered
cars and drove us players to out-of-town games.

"As a driver he was super. In those days if somebody drove a hundred miles a day, that was a lot of
miles. And I'd say he'd average pretty close to that.
That's why it wasn't any chore for him to take us to
the games. I saw him a lot of years later—I'd say he
was still driving up to ten days before he died, at
ninety-two."

Allen never detected any strife between Sam and his
kid brother. "Bud is very capable, a different type.
He's quieter. Sam is the enthusiastic type—real enthusiastic. Bud is more a thinker, I think. More of a
plodder. His dad always thought that Bud was in some
ways smarter than Sam, but just wasn't the type to be
ambitious, and always held back a little bit. Tom had a
banker's type of mentality. They believe in you work-

ing hard. Some of them don't work very hard, but they believe in *you* working hard!

"I think Bud is more the real estate type . . . It takes a different type person, and I think Bud is more like his father. Tom and Bud are more alike than Sam. Still, when things got to popping, Mr. Walton told me that he just couldn't believe that anybody—anybody—could be as capable as Sam. He was just amazed at Sam . . . just in awe of his ability."

By the time Sam was a Hickman High senior, his old flame in Shelbina had faded from the picture and he started dating a girl who lived two houses down on Rosemary Lane: Maxine Lennon. Her father, general agent for General American Insurance Company, urged Sam to seek his career in that field, and almost convinced him.

When he began his freshman year at the University of Missouri in the fall of 1936, Sam already had helpful contacts and friendships on campus, developed through association with a series of his mother's student roomers.

"Sam did all right with the girls," said Clay Cooper. "He was good-looking and it was a pretty active campus. In those days you had to live and try to get by, and you didn't have too much time for social life. But those were the big band days. Everyone had a big band come in; we had 'em all—Kay Kayser, Benny Goodman, you name it. There were dances at the frat houses, but the big ones were usually at the Tiger Hotel or Rothwell Gym."

Sam had to work his way through college, which helped hone his entrepreneurial talents. Not only did he deliver a route of 160 subscribers for the daily *Columbia Missourian*, he also contacted fraternity and sorority houses for bulk sales—typically orders for fifteen or twenty copies. His entrepreneurial exercises began back in high school when he first became acquainted with many of the treasurers and frat officers. "Usually that gave me an extra five-hundred dollars in commissions," he remembers. "For four or five years,

I was the newspaper's number one salesman." In the summers, Sam was a lifeguard at the Columbia municipal pool, and became the star of a swim team he organized. He also waited tables at the university in exchange for meals.

"His mettle was tested like everybody else's by the Depression," said Clay Cooper. "The Depression was a big leveler of people . . . Sam chose to rise above it. I think that's the biggest thing that Sam did. He was determined to be a success and go out in the business world and do something.

"He was constantly earning money. He had a number of jobs. That's something, isn't it! That's when if you had two dollars and a clean shirt, you were in business!"

Sam was a fraternity man, Beta Theta Pi, in a chapter that had close to fifty members. As in high school, his interests lay in every direction. He was strongly religious, and received the high honor of the presidency of the Burrall Class, a Sunday school group attended regularly by 1,200 Mizzou students (the largest Sunday school class in the world).

Sam Walton also taught a Sunday school for a large class of girls from prestigious Stephens College.

The leadership talent of Tom Walton's first-born seemed limitless in his four years at the University of Missouri. Perhaps his ultimate triumph was being selected for membership in an honor society called Q.E.B.H., founded on campus in 1879 as an exclusive group of unselfish and principled men devoted to their alma mater. Its goal was to preserve and maintain the university's "honored traditions and deep moral functions."

Perhaps because he was elected president of Q.E.B.H., Sam was included in a Big Man On Campus layout in the 1940 *Savitar*. (It should take away nothing that he was also one of the five-man governing board of this yearbook.) His face looked out from at least a dozen pages of the yearbook. Shortly before graduation, Sam was elected president of the senior class.

The university activity that was soon going to change the direction of Sam Walton's life was the R.O.T.C., in which he was a cadet from 1936 through 1940. Choosing the artillery, he was assigned to the Tiger battery and was promoted to cadet captain in his senior year.

In the summer of 1939—for six weeks from June 11 to July 22—Cadet Walton, along with other Mizzou artillery officers, fought dust, bugs, and grueling heat out on the Kansas plains. For going through training exercises first at Fort Leavenworth and then at Fort Riley, they got seventy cents a day, all the chow they wanted, and a taste of what General Sherman was referring to when he said that "war is hell."

World War II was on the immediate horizon in the summer of 1940, when Sam graduated and was commissioned second lieutenant in the reserves. Two years earlier, Tom and Nan had again pulled up stakes and moved to Lexington, Missouri, for a new traveling job, taking Bud along. Lexington, forty miles east of Kansas City, was the noted site of a crucial battle in the War Between the States. Bud did not choose to follow older brother to M. U., but for two years was a "day dodger" (off-campus student) at the local Wentworth Military Academy. The summer of Sam's graduation with a degree in business administration, his family was severely jolted. The strain of the Depression years had taken a toll on his parents, and they decided to separate. Nan moved to St. Louis and Tom went to Fulton, thirty miles east of Columbia.

"It had to bother Sam, of course," said his Hickman classmate Frederick Allen. "But he never mentioned it, and neither did I. It was one of those things we didn't talk about." Mrs. Walton was just a little over forty. There was no divorce, but the separation lasted a few years, and a decade later cancer was to cut short Nancy Walton's life.

Throughout his university years, Sam had expected to follow the advice of his girlfriend's father. But Sam deemed it necessary to attend the best insurance school

in the country, Wharton School at the University of
Pennsylvania.

Recalling that period fifty years later, he said: "I
just didn't have the money. Besides, I was tired. I was
glad to get out of the university. I worked harder and
put in more hours at the university than I have any
time since. My mother was very ambitious and she was
very proud of my accomplishments. More than anything else, I just wanted to see if I could do it."

As a little breather from the college grind before
taking up the even more grueling routine of full-time
business, Sam decided to see some of the rest of the
country, so he hitchhiked to Oklahoma, taking along a
buddy.

Perhaps subconsciously he was checking out his roots
in the old Indian and buffalo grass country. Arriving
in Kingfisher in late afternoon, he went to the Rexall
Drugs owned by his uncle, Earl Walton. He and his
companion were greeted warmly. Earl turned the store
over to a helper and drove the two college graduates
out to his house at 901 South Eighth Street in Kingfisher's best residential section.

"They surprised me, all walking in the back door,"
said Mrs. Helen (Floyde) Rasp, Earl Walton's widow,
who remarried after his death. "We never used the
front door much—this is a small town. The boys were
good-looking fellows. Sam was awfully friendly, just
like he is now. He was a tall old country boy; I don't
remember a thing about his friend.

"It so happened that I'd made a 'Red Earth' cake
that morning. That was one of Aunt Susan's recipes.
She was food editor of the *Daily Oklahoman* back in
those days. And whatever recipe she had was tops.
That cake is made with red food coloring, looks sort of
like our soil out here. Two-layer with white icing. That
was my kids' favorite."

Sam's Aunt Helen hit on the idea of having a picnic
in the shady backyard. "Made some sandwiches, probably ham, pimento cheese. Lemonade probably. Those
fellows got a big kick out of that. That was sometime

in May or June. They had just graduated. They were just traveling over the country. They didn't spend the night with us. They just went on, I remember watching them walking down the street."

Aunt Helen did not see her nephew again until about thirty years later when the Wal-Mart billionaire came to Kingfisher to cut the ribbon for the opening of one of his hundreds of discount stores.

Back in Columbia from his trip, Sam Walton virtually tossed all his dreams for the future up in the air to see how they landed. "I really had no idea what I would be," he said. "At one point in time I thought I wanted to be president of the United States."

More realistically, the twenty-two-year-old economics major came to the conclusion that retailing might be a better career than insurance. He met up with both Sears and J. C. Penney scouts who were combing the campuses for trainees.

"I interviewed Penney. I liked what I heard," Sam said. "I went to St. Louis and visited with the general manager and other folks there. They encouraged me and thought I had the kind of talent that would be useful for them. They offered me a job at eighty-five dollars a month."

Sam Walton grabbed it. The salary was nothing to write home about; even so he knew men with families who had been lucky to draw fifteen dollars a week in these rough times. As a management trainee, Sam was sent directly to the J. C. Penney store in Des Moines, Iowa.

Sam Walton plunged into this new world of merchandising, so much more upscale than the little variety store he had fiddled around in as "extra boy" help in Columbia, with the keen and furious dedication of a quarterback who was one touchdown behind, with two minutes to go.

He had no idea that he had started on the path that would lead him to the top of the modern-day discount store merchandising business.

But Sam was so favorably impressed at the outset

that he telephoned brother Bud and suggested he apply also to become a Penney trainee. Bud promptly did, was accepted, and sent to the store in Cedar Rapids, Iowa.

Until he arrived in Des Moines, Sam Walton knew little of the scope of the J. C. Penney Company chain—and absolutely no details of the personality and meteoric rise of the old man himself. He would learn more soon—including one profitable lesson taught him personally by James Cash Penney, when the founder was age sixty-five, at the wrapping counter in the Des Moines store.

Sam reported to Duncan Major, the manager of the Des Moines store, a patient, kindly, and expert merchandiser the Missouri recruit would quickly come to respect and admire. Manager Major handed him a printed copy of The Penney Idea, and told him to commit the seven tenets to memory. Sam suppressed a chuckle, thinking of Mizzou rah-rah stadium cheerleaders. Later he saw it more seriously.

The Penney Idea, adopted in 1913, was brief:

1. To serve the public, as nearly as we can, to its complete satisfaction.

2. To expect for the service we render a fair remuneration and not all the profit the traffic will bear.

3. To do all in our power to pack the customer's dollar full of value, quality, and satisfaction.

4. To continue to train ourselves and our associates so that the service we give will be more and more intelligently performed.

5. To improve constantly the human factor in our business.

6. To reward men and women in our organization through participation in what the business produces.

7. To test our every policy, method, and act in this wise: "Does it square with what is right and just?"

There were no employees or clerks at J. C. Penney's. They were "associates." The old man himself thought up that term in the early days when he decided to expand by letting his managers save up and go in with him as partners and help provide capital needed for opening new J. C. Penney stores.

The term was one Sam Walton would remember— and use. In fact, he would steal—or *borrow* is perhaps a more precise word— John Cash Penney's whole concept of how to succeed by putting customer satisfaction ahead of profit.

In 1940 J. C. Penney had 1,586 stores, and sales were running at $300 million. "The company strength," said Joan Gosnell, historian at J. C. Penney corporate headquarters in Dallas, "was in the small towns and smaller cities. The company sold mostly soft goods. Leading sellers in 1940 were brand items like Gaymode hosiery, Nation-wide sheets, and Super Big Mac work clothes."

There was a corporate training program, but it was really up to the local store manager to make certain his new-hires learned policy and how to "cut the mustard." Having Duncan Major for a boss was a lucky break for Sam Walton.

"Duncan Major [now deceased] was known as a store manager who gave his trainees a strong background," said Joan Gosnell. "In fact, there are two men who became J. C. Penney vice-presidents who worked in that Des Moines store."

Not many weeks after he became a Penney associate, Sam Walton found himself running faster than he ever had in high school track meets. He was in a race every day against another ambitious trainee who was driving like a fiend to make himself appear the Penney Company's most promising new man.

Sam pictured himself in that role. He worked just as hard as his rival—and tried to work even harder. They remained friendly, but Sam vowed that no one would beat him out for top new man. Working on a sales bonus, Sam limited his lunch break to fifteen minutes.

In the midst of their competition—as Sam told the story years later—J. C. Penney himself arrived in town and spent a lot of time wandering around the store.

A customer came in and bought something from Sam, and while he wrapped it for her, his rival fidgeted around because J. C. Penney was observing the transaction closely from a reasonable distance.

"I finished wrapping and tying the package, and the lady left," said Sam Walton. "Then Mr. Penney came over. 'Boys,' he said, 'I want to show you something.'

"And he took a box about the same size and he went around it with paper and let it overlap about like that . . . maybe a quarter inch. Then he went around it with twine one time like this and one time like that, and he tied it.

"He said, 'Boys, you know we don't make a dime out of the merchandise we sell, we only make our profit out of the paper and string we save!' "

Sam Walton related the incident to a friend and neighbor in Bentonville, Tom Harrison.

"Tom, I wish I was able to get work out of people like J. C. Penney did," said Sam Walton. "He could always get a lot of work out of people."

Tom Harrison gave his friend a knowing smile. "Sam, I think you've learned how to do that."

While he surely earned his eighty-five bucks a month,* in 1940 none of the brass in the Penney Company must have dreamed that this particular "associate" would become a major force in their retailing trade.

At least they didn't keep any records of either his flubs or his achievements. Nothing at all exists in the Des Moines office or at Dallas corporate headquarters that mentions any former trainee named Walton.

In Sam's memory those days are still vivid. "The manager, Duncan Major, was a fantastic trainer," Walton told a recent visitor. "He used to invite us out to

---

*His commissions soon brought his income up to about $115 a month, Sam remembers.

his house nearly every Sunday to play Ping-pong, to eat and talk. Business, of course. You could learn a lot. How to do it—and better. We had the free time; all us trainees were single. He was one manager who had a 25 percent bonus contract. He got his check, $65,000! He waved that around one Sunday. That just made us run faster and work harder."

Sam Walton's training time in Des Moines doubtless put several hundred dollars into the company till. And what he learned, and practiced up in the Iowa store, would eventually put a few billion into his own cash registers.

But at that time talk of war was in the air, and after about eighteen months of management training, Sam Walton knew his days in Des Moines were rushing to an end.

In his closet hung his old uniform with the gold bar of second lieutenant, Artillery, United States Army reserve. It was only a matter of time, he knew, before he would be ordered to put it on and report for active duty.

Sam resigned his Penney job. His impending military call-up was not the real reason he decided to leave town. It was something else—largely an escape from romance that, in light of his own later business principles, began in a vividly ironic manner.

—5—

The Lieutenant Takes a Bride

Hunching over her typewriter, the society editor of the *Daily Progress* in Claremore, Oklahoma, excitedly banged out her biggest story of 1943. She sent the copy in takes to the back shop where the rattling linotype spit it out in hot metal slugs. Didn't matter if it ran a column long. The publisher demanded she tell all about the bridal gown, the flowers, and the guests at the wedding of the only daughter of Leland Stanford Robson, the leading banker in this little town of 5,000.

She worried that the society page of the oil capital's *Tulsa World* might scoop her. They'd carry a big picture, too, and complete coverage. This was maybe Claremore's biggest social event in ten years. Only the upper-crust elite were invited, but everybody expected the *Progress* to print all the juicy details.

A wedding on St. Valentine's Day! And the bridegroom already on duty in the Army. His new bride having to tag along to God knows what miserable military camp. Not knowing when she'd have to kiss him good-bye while he sailed away to dodge flying bullets.

While the editor fussed over her story, making sure neither the Robson family nor the advertisers would find fault with her copy, twenty miles away in Tulsa printers at the *World* laid in the forms for the morning edition a six-by-eleven-inch zinc engraving of a bride standing in a voluminous wedding gown, under which the lead read:

Announcement is made of the marriage of Miss Helen Alice Robson, daughter of Mr. and Mrs. Leland Stanford Robson, Claremore, and Lieut. Samuel Moore Walton, Hawthorne, Cal., son of Mrs. Nan L. Walton, St. Louis, and Thomas G. Walton, Fulton, Mo.

Not the smallest detail was overlooked by either the *Tulsa World* or Claremore's *Daily Progress*. It was a beautiful candlelit ceremony held at 5:00 P.M. in the First Presbyterian Church, with the Rev. Clarence A. Campbell reading the service "in the presence of the families and a large group of friends."

Of course, the father gave away the bride. The organist played the traditional wedding marches. The soloist sang "Because" and "O Promise Me." The bride's gown was "designed with charming simplicity," said the *World* reporter.

Nothing was said about Sam's getup—regulation army dress uniform, khaki shirt and tie, with the artillery emblem on his lapels, the silver bar of a first lieutenant on his epaulets, the heavy Sam Browne belt and leather shoulder strap. The wedding photos showed him with full, wavy hair. His slender face appeared long, and his nose a trifle sharp and prominent. It was all very romantic because Sam had come in on a three-day pass and the young couple would be flying out of Tulsa back to Los Angeles with no time out for a honeymoon. There was a war on.

The papers printed paragraph after paragraph, too, about the reception "immediately afterward" at the Will Rogers Hotel, the three-tiered cake topped by figurines of a soldier couple, the tall baskets of Calla lilies and peach gladioli on either side of the receiving line. It was truly an elaborate and expensive wedding

thrown by perhaps the richest people in that northeastern corner of Oklahoma.

Sam's mother, Nan, came from St. Louis and stood
with Helen's mother. Bud got leave from Navy pilot
training in St. Paul long enough to stand in as best
man. Helen's brothers, Nick and Frank, were usher
and candlelighter.

Pretty brunette Helen Robson came from a truly
remarkable family. Her father was approximately a
contemporary of Sam's dad. Both men started out
with zero resources; but in creating his great wealth,
Leland Stanford Robson managed to beat Thomas G.
Walton hands down.

L.S. could hardly have had a more bleak start. Born
in Sandersville, Georgia, January 21, 1884—just eight
years before Tom Walton—he came to Oklahoma in
1909 to sell Bibles, pots and pans, and picture frames
to earn money to finish law school.

He collected enough to go back and graduate from
University of Georgia Law School in June 1910. He
again felt the lure of Oklahoma's new-state frontier;
he tried Tulsa but fled such a boom town and returned
to Claremore. He wanted to hang out his shingle as a
brand-new lawyer, but he had a problem. He was
broke.

Somebody loaned him fifty dollars. But for a twenty-
six-year-old greenhorn barrister clients were hard to
come by. Folks liked to see what a stranger was made
of first. Robson, in need, hatched a clever scheme to
make a little eating money. Fortunately, he had a
typewriter.

"Business was slow, and he typed for others at ten
cents a page," said his youngest son, Frank Carr
Robson.

The situation had improved enough by 1916 for
L. S. Robson to marry Hazel Corrine Carr of Claremore.
They had three sons, Leland Junior, Nick, and Frank,
and Helen, born December 3, 1919, thus making her
twenty months younger than her new husband. A second Robson daughter, Emma Louise, died at age two.

About the time Tom Walton was heading out of Oklahoma back to Missouri to seek his fortune, L. S. Robson was developing a successful law practice and looking around for other business opportunities. He, too, was interested in land—huge parcels of land. He plunged into ranching in 1929, buying some 18,500 acres of pasture in the corners of Rogers, Wagoner, and Tulsa counties from Russell Bilby, son of the famous cattle baron John S. Bilby.

He was adept at politics, holding office for twelve years as Claremore's city attorney. In 1941–1942 he was a member of the Oklahoma Highway Commission. His largest bonanza in business came from helping organize the Rogers County Bank at Claremore in 1936, where he held sway for thirty years as director, president, and chairman, retiring in 1966 at eighty-two. He died at age eighty-nine.

The Robsons lived in an ordinary house in the 400 block of East Sixth Street. "Mr. Robson was as tight as the bark on a tree," said Bob Chambers, a Claremore historian. Mrs. Robson was quiet and reserved. "Just a lovely, beautiful woman who was just a housewife," said Eliza Arnold, one of Helen's high school classmates. "She was interested in flowers and church. That's where Helen got her 'churchy' trait. She went to Sunday school at the Presbyterian Church all the time. She was very good."

Ruth Wooley of Chelsea, Oklahoma, remembers being Helen's classmate in Claremore: "She was so quiet you didn't even know she was in school." In high school Ruth Wooley dated Helen's brother, Leland Junior, whom she called Stan. Mrs. Wooley remembers how during the Depression Mrs. Robson brought to school enormous pots of vegetable soup "so none of the kids went hungry. It was pretty bad in those hard times. The Robsons, of course, had meat because they had the ranch."

In the eighth grade, Helen studied music and played the bassoon in the high school orchestra, and as a member of the band she made road trips with the

football team. She told a friend: "I loved playing in
the orchestra. I won the state high school bassoon
contest one year—I knew the piece and the others
didn't. I wasn't that much better. My piano playing
was kind of sad, though I took twelve years."

Maturing into an attractive, tall girl with long black
hair, Helen had a slight Indian facial cast, not uncom-
mon in Oklahoma. She has no direct Indian blood, but
her comment when the subject comes up runs like
this: "When you grow up in Oklahoma, you learn to
admire Indians, and a lot of your good friends are
Indians. The little girl who lived next door in Claremore
was Osage and Cherokee. So you just have a different
feeling about Indians than other people have. I have
second and third cousins who have Indian blood."

Claremore's gossip mongers speculated for years on
two assumptions: one, that the family was related to
cowboy-humorist Will Rogers, who was born in nearby
Oogolah; and two, whether the Robsons were multi-
millionaires.

"We are not related to Will Rogers," Helen once
told a friend. "My daddy represented him once in a
lawsuit, I think connected with the 1929 Paducah flood.
So he knew him and when Will came to Claremore to
talk at the high school, my daddy stopped him on the
street and introduced me. Will Rogers shook my hand.
For any youngster, that was a thrill!"

Even today Claremore old-timers will tell you L. S.
Robson handed each of his children one million dollars. Others say it was only $50,000, in a lump sum on
graduation from high school. The truth is that banker
Robson wanted all his children to fully comprehend
the value of money. To teach them, he gave each an
unlimited checking account with authority to draw on
it anytime for what they considered necessities.

Helen got her checking account at age thirteen. "It
was a sort of contest," she explains. "Dad kept track
of who had spent the most by the time we got out of
college. He took that as a benchmark and figured out
what each of the other three had coming as a bonus—

the difference between what we had spent and that highest figure."

How banker Robson and his wife actually shared the family wealth was to give all four children equal stakes in their 18,500-acre cattle ranch. Son Nick, a graduate of the University of Oklahoma, manages the ranch, which he jointly owns with brother Frank and Helen. He maintains a home and office at Catoosa, just outside Tulsa.

For two years, beginning in 1937, Helen was a student at Christian College (now Columbia College) in Columbia. Then she transferred to the University of Oklahoma at Norman, where she graduated in 1941 with a degree in economics.

Because both she and Sam Walton were in collegiate circles, living in the same city for two full school years, many of their friends took for granted that they met and fell in love there.

They did not meet in Columbia. Nor did they begin their romance during her two years at O.U., a period when Sam was still at J. C. Penney Company in Des Moines.

"Helen was popular, but she didn't act like a rich girl," says Billy Jo Gourley of Oklahoma City, who was her classmate both at Christian College and at Norman, and also a sorority sister in Kappa Kappa Gamma. Helen studied business administration and her other activities were similar at both schools: piano and bassoon, swimming, field hockey, fencing, and Y.W.C.A. She was athletic, strong, known as an "outdoors" girl. At O.U., where male students outnumbered girls four to one, pretty Helen Robson dated several men.

After graduating in the late spring of 1941, Helen returned to her parents' home in Claremore. She worked in her father's law office and also kept the ranch books. Sam was then selling shirts in the Des Moines J. C. Penney store. But fate was already scheming to bring these two strangers together.

About the time the Allies were preparing to invade

North Africa, Sam was given an Army physical in Des
Moines. The physicians gave him a surprise and a
shock. They discovered he had a "partial bundle branch
block," a malformation of nerves in the spine or heart.
He was rejected for overseas service but classified for
"limited duty."

Waiting to be called up, Sam kept working in the
Penney store, but his situation there was becoming
uncomfortable. Sam had started courting a cashier in
the store's office, a pretty Swedish brunette named
Beth Hamquist, about his age.

"She wanted to get married," Sam recalled recently.
"But I didn't."

On top of that, the J. C. Penney rules forbade any
employee dating another employee. Sam was romancing Beth on the sly. "I just didn't feel right about
that," he remembers. He knew, too, that eventually
Uncle Sam would call him up for stateside military
service. So in early January 1942 he just quit his job,
kissed Beth good-bye, and left town. (The irony is that
Sam Walton has that same prohibition against intraoffice
romance in effect for his 250,000 Wal-Mart employees.)

Sam hitchhiked south, feeling drawn to Oklahoma
for reasons he can't articulate. He went to Tulsa with
a vague notion of working for an oil company. He
applied at Carter and Humble and other refining companies. None would hire him because he would have
to soon leave and go into the Army.

At Pryor, seventeen miles east of Claremore, a giant
military gunpowder plant was being operated by E. I.
du Pont Corporation. Sam applied there and was hired
as a field investigator to check such things as the
references of job applicants. Sam telephoned brother
Bud, still working for J. C. Penney but trying to get
into Navy flying, and suggested he quit his store and
work at the du Pont plant while waiting. Bud came
down and took a job as rodman in a survey crew
laying out new gunpowder buildings.

Thousands of defense workers crowded in on Pryor
and Claremore, and housing in the two small towns

was scarce. The Claremore Chamber of Commerce appealed to residents to make their spare rooms available to the incoming defense workers. Homer McSpadden, head of Claremore's First National Bank, had a ten-room house. His wife, Carrie, agreed to rent two spare rooms, one to Sam.

A couple of months after hitting Claremore, Sam caught sight of Helen in a bowling alley one April evening. His line was pretty amateurish but proved effective. He walked over and smiled at her. "Don't I know you?" he said.

Helen's even gaze carefully appraised the handsome stranger, and it flashed through her mind that Claremore was suffering a dearth of eligible men because of the war's youth drain. She had been dating a couple of fellows and really liked one, but couldn't imagine spending her life as his wife.

"You do now," Helen merrily responded, and matched Sam's big grin.

Under wartime urgency, everything moved fast after that moment. Helen remembers they at once started dating "nearly every night."

Sam thought he was in love; she knew she was.

But Beth Hamquist came to town.

The cashier from Des Moines thought she still had a chance to marry Sam. En route south to take part in a friend's wedding, Beth decided to work in a visit with her old boyfriend.

"She was a pretty girl," recalls Carrie McSpadden, ninety-four and living now in a retirement home in Bella Vista, Arkansas. There was no room at the hotel. "I told Sam she was welcome to stay in my daughter's room, which was vacant, on the first floor."

Mrs. McSpadden recalls that Beth Hamquist stayed in Claremore about two weeks; Sam calculates it was two or three days. Both agree that the visit ended in a blow-up.

"Sam broke his engagement," Carrie McSpadden told me. "Oh, the girl was terribly upset. It was kind of a big row. The girl left on the next train."

Even now, say close friends, Helen seems to feel
Sam strung Beth along a little too far. But she's glad
she got him. The May 1989 *Ladies' Home Journal*
spotlighted the romances of wives of seven billionaires
and reported: "After forty-six years of marriage, it's
clear that Helen was right when she chose Walton
over another suitor. 'I thought life with him would be
so interesting,' she explains. Is it? 'Oh, lordy,' she
laughs. 'It seems to be.' "

Within weeks of meeting they were engaged. Then
Sam was off to war, inducted into service July 16,
1942. From his West Coast training base, Sam urged
Helen to set a wedding date. Finally she did, selecting
February 14 because it was romantic.

Despite no time for a honeymoon trip, Helen Walton found life as a wartime army officer's wife not too
grueling. His assignment sent them to Salt Lake City
as a captain with Company A, 777th Military Police
Battalion.

In 1944, Mrs. Walton was pregnant and happy about
it. However, she did not especially like living in Salt
Lake City. "I've heard Helen talk about how unfriendly they are if you are not a Mormon," said a
long-time friend, Mrs. Fred (Eran) Pickens of Newport,
Arkansas. "Being as friendly as she is, and a bride,
and away from home and expecting a baby, I imagine
it really hurt."

Helen came home so their first child, a boy, could
be born in Tulsa—October 28, 1944. Sam and Helen
decided on a combination of family names, Samuel
Robson Walton, and called the baby Rob.

Meanwhile, younger brother Bud Walton had completed pilot training stateside and shipped out for the
Pacific theater as a navy torpedo bomber pilot board
the *Manila Bay*, which saw furious action in the Sulu
Sea in the assault to recapture Okinawa.

With the war over in Europe, Captain Samuel Moore
Walton was given leave in June 1945, and left Salt
Lake City with his wife and son for a visit with Helen's

folks in Claremore. He was officially discharged from the military on August 16, 1945.

Bud, too, was quickly discharged by the navy and returned stateside, where he had a wife, Audrey, whom he had married in Chicago while undergoing flight training.

What, wondered both brothers, did the peacetime future hold for them?

— 6 —

First Five-and-Dime Days

When Sam Walton drove into the remote farming town of Newport, Arkansas, with Helen and eleven-month-old Rob, he thought Lady Luck was giving him a nifty break. He didn't know just how fickle she can be. He had been out of the army just a few weeks. And now he had stumbled into a chance to buy the franchise of a Ben Franklin five-and-dime store. Unless Helen vetoed the deal, he could return to civilian life at only twenty-seven as a small-town businessman.

Newport looked good to Sam. The population was barely 4,000, and it was off in the middle of nowhere, ninety miles northeast of Little Rock. Part of Jackson County, Newport dates from 1835, and for a half century served as headquarters for steamboats plying the White River, connecting metropolitan St. Louis to the Texas trade via the winding Arkansas River. Later the Iron Mountain Railroad, which went as far south as Mexico City, would come through and strangle virtually all river commerce. Jackson County in the 1940s mainly produced cotton, corn, and rice, although Newport had a shoe factory, a metal mill, and some other industry.

Sam and Helen were certain they would find in Newport the kind of self-reliant country folk they admired and could do business with. Also of great im-

54

portance to both was the opportunity to enjoy the outdoors life: boating and fishing on the two rivers that elbowed around the town—the White and the Black. There were also the fields, forests, and mountains for hiking and camping out. Another advantage was that Sam could indulge his new passion for quail hunting as birds were plentiful around Newport and in Jackson County.

Ben Franklin variety stores had sprung up in hundreds of towns too small to support S. H. Kress or Woolworth operations. The Newport store was No. 2480. To serve the host of Ben Franklins across the South, an office and warehouse had been established in St. Louis. All Ben Franklin stores operated under individual franchises controlled by the Butler Brothers Company of Chicago and St. Louis.

By chance, Sam Walton got word that the Newport franchise-holder, George Scharlott, wanted to sell out and return to St. Louis. In Claremore, Sam and Helen discussed this opportunity with L. S. Robson. To the lawyer-rancher-banker, it looked like a good business venture. He was willing to lend his son-in-law the $25,000 needed to swing the deal.

Scharlott would sell Sam his stock and fixtures, and Butler Brothers would assign both their franchise and their current lease on the Ben Franklin store, which at Front and Hazel streets, was located on perhaps the busiest corner in town.

Sam had no trepidation about plunging as a novice into the five-and-ten-cent-store business. At J. C. Penney in Des Moines he had diligently applied his sharp mind to getting a firm grasp on the techniques of retailing and studying the customer-satisfaction principles of old James Cash himself.

Besides, Butler Brothers had a "book" that told how to operate a Ben Franklin store. The manual explained what merchandise to buy, how to price it, and even contained numerous illustrations showing precisely how to display the hundreds of articles and items for sale along orderly aisles.

"Let's do it," Sam told Helen. "Newport, here come the Waltons!"

The Thursday, September 6, 1945, issue of the *Jackson County Democrat* carried at the top of page one a four-paragraph item with a single-column headline: "Sam M. Walton Buys Ben Franklin Store Stock." The piece ran just above a news story about the county Selective Service Board calling up forty-nine inductees, and next to a column headed "With the Boys," recounting the comings and goings of local soldiers and sailors and their families. The war was over, but U.S. armed forces were still very much in business.

As a matter of fact, Paul K. Holmes Sr., who was leasing the Ben Franklin location to Butler Brothers, had two sons, Paul K. Junior and Douglas, still serving in the military. This fact took on real significance later when Lady Luck decided to begin playing nasty games with the Walton family.

But for now their odyssey from Claremore to Newport advanced smoothly under sunny skies. On September 15, 1945, Sam Walton moved into his Newport quarters, a small house on Newport Avenue leased from Mrs. Elizabeth Maris.

The five-and-dime store did well from the start. It was large, 50 by 120 feet, and included a large rear storeroom. Sam was well satisfied with the lease, which set his rent at $200 a month, or 5 percent of gross profits. He put in long hours learning the ropes.

Always the leader, Sam quickly became involved in civic affairs, moving up fast in the chamber of commerce. He and Helen became part of the young social set and belonged to two bridge clubs, a potluck supper club, and the country club, which took over the defunct army airfield seven miles outside town. They also made it a point to find a family physician, Dr. Jabez Jackson, who practiced obstetrics. Mrs. Samuel Walton was expecting another child.

The wartime priorities that had gobbled up building materials all across America virtually stopped home building in Newport. The Waltons were eager to buy a more substantial house, but there was a shortage, with few for sale. Finally they got lucky. L. P. Mann, with a six-room white bungalow on Park Place, quit as school superintendent July 1, 1946, and left town. Sam and Helen snapped up his house for $12,500.

It was just in time for a growing family. Their second child, another boy, named John Thomas to honor his paternal grandfather, was born October 8, 1946. The family grew again June 7, 1948 with the arrival of James C. (for Carr, Helen's mother's side). Their last child, a daughter, was born October 7, 1949. On her, Helen bestowed her own middle name, Alice.

Newport knew the Waltons to be a lively, sociable, church-going family. Two of Sam and Helen's closest friends were Fred M. Pickens Jr., a lawyer and banker, and his Texas-born wife Eran. The couples socialized, and Fred Pickens represented Sam as an attorney and banker. "We had a lot of country people trade in this area in those days," said Fred Pickens. "They came to town on Saturday and they stayed all day. The way they felt about Sam was that he was just a common person, and the country people loved him."

"There's an expression in Arkansas," said Eran Pickens, "that I had never heard before: 'Common as anybody.' That's what they all said about Sam. And that's the greatest compliment the country folks can pay you."

Sam got to know most of his customers and called them by name when they stopped in his store. "I think his great memory was partly a gift and partly sincerity," said Fred Pickens. "For one thing he had a young brain—under thirty when he came to Newport. It was a regular Ben Franklin store people were used to. They liked the arrangement, the layout. You could find things. He was always there. He always greeted people."

Was the energetic and ambitious proprietor already looking ahead at this point, dreaming and scheming for great things to come? His neighbors in Newport saw no evidence of this. "He never did discuss any grand idea with any of us," said Fred Pickens. "His consuming idea when he was here was to be able to take care of his growing family."

The population of Newport had sagged during the war as hundreds of residents departed for Detroit, California, or elsewhere to work on war-plant production lines. Sam and the other members of the chamber of commerce puzzled over ways to attract new industry to bring at least some of these people back home.

As Sam and his fellow merchants explored possibilities for developing new business opportunities in Newport, President Harry Truman was proposing a hefty postwar tax increase to Congress. The new Ben Franklin proprietor had to consider what effect this would have on his volume of sales. He followed all the business news and kept up with new products on the commercial market such as aerosol "bug bombs," frozen orange juice, and one novelty item originally launched at $12.50 per unit, which Sam felt was bound to get much cheaper in mass production and would eventually sweep the country, ballpoint pens.

As president of the chamber of commerce, Sam worked on strategy to attract more industrial plants to Newport. In town already were an aluminum rolling mill of Revere Copper and Brass Company and Brown-Jordan Company, which manufactured expensive wrought-iron furniture, as well as the Airfoot Shoe Company, which shipped thousands and thousands of tennis shoes.

Recalling his Newport days in an interview forty-odd years later, Sam said: "The biggest thing I did was to go after a company in New Jersey that made metal tubes for Colgate toothpaste. Victor Muscat was its president. I got him down to Newport and talked to him. I invited Victor out to my house and he spent the night. We got along fine. He put a plant in a hangar out at the air base. It was Victor Metal Company, and ended up with about 650 employees."

One of Sam Walton's first acts as head of the chamber of commerce was to undertake to liquidate the

Jackson County Fair Board's $455 deficit. Contributions to public subscriptions for worthy civic causes frequently were listed on page one of the Newport newspapers, and the Ben Franklin store was always down for from $1.00 to $100. When the Business and Professional Women's Club raised money to build a downtown ladies lounge and rest room in the back of Dr. Ralph Appleton's clinic, Sam Walton forked over $10, the newspapers revealed.

For the Waltons, public life was attractive and invigorating. Sam became a member of the county levee board, and was on the public affairs board of the Newport city council, which passed on bids and contracts. He had learned much about buying and selling and was making himself a keen student of how to obtain merchandise at the absolute best bargain—so it could be handed on to the consumer at the lowest price. He was getting ideas.

Helen Walton was not a stay-at-home retiring Newport housewife. "Helen is one of the most gregarious people I have ever known," said Eran Pickens. "It's a mistake—and it has been done so often—to write up Sam as a great man and not give credit to Helen. It is not one of those silly things like behind every great man is a woman, or something like that. She just simply is."

It was accepted around town that Helen had given her husband monumental help by growing up to be a rich banker's daughter. "But one thing everybody would know about Sam," said Fred Pickens. "He paid back to Mr. Robson every penny of that loan. And you can bet your cotton crop that every payment was right on time!"

In a number of ways Helen was an ideal helpmate for Sam Walton's ultimate destiny. First, she shouldered her part of the load, whatever. Second, she had been taught to be thrifty—actually, frugal.

"My family had grown up in the Depression," said Helen. "People had to make choices. My dad used to say, maybe you won't get any new shoes or clothes or

other things but you will always have good healthy
food on the table. I guess that stuck with me. Health is
the most important part of my job. At that time we
just about all were in the same boat. We used to go
out to get fresh milk from a dairy cow, we bought eggs
from a chicken farm. People had to seek those things
out."

Even in Newport, Sam Walton "worked all hours,"
and his wife learned to accept his absence. "It was
difficult because he worked so much at night. Although I don't remember him getting up as early in
the morning as he does now. But always a lot of
hours," said Helen Walton. "I became accustomed to
putting the babies to bed at night alone. I always read
to the children, and we read a lot of good books that
way. They never went to bed without a story."

Eran Pickens said: "I wouldn't say they didn't have
a daddy when they lived here, but on the days like
Saturday Sam might have to be gone all day, and he
wasn't the kind of daddy that probably came home
and diapered the baby or hung out the diapers or
anything like that. . . . Of course, even people who
were struggling along had help, and Helen had full-
time good help, a black woman named Hazel."

Social life in this little Arkansas town was vigorous,
and perhaps at times hectic. The Waltons were invited
to many parties. Helen loved bridge, but her husband
only tolerated the game. With the Pickenses, the
Holmeses, and others, they belonged to the Thursday
Evening Bridge Club, a three-table group. Helen was
also a player in two ladies' afternoon foursomes.

"Sam definitely was not fascinated by bridge," said
Eran Pickens. "He just went along with Helen. He did
learn how to play. We had to drop some people from
our club because the husband didn't even learn how to
bid. Sam? Well, at the bridge table his mind was
always somewhere else."

The outdoors was infinitely more appealing to Sam,
and Helen too, than a card table. The beautiful Ozark
Mountains, which stretch across the entire northwest

corner of Arkansas, brought primitive wooded uplands within forty or fifty miles of Newport. The White River, wide and swift, lapped at the town's front door, and the smaller Black River was thirty minutes by auto. Frequently, the Walton clan would venture out for overnight camping, hiking, fishing, or just drinking in the fresh air and spectacular scenery.

In Newport Sam's bird dog—Peggy—was kept in a backyard pen. Given his passion for quail hunting, the assumption is he has done it since boyhood, under tutelage of his father. But he didn't take up the sport until reaching his late twenties, learning to hunt with L. S. Robson.

"My father-in-law was a great quail hunter and a tremendous trainer of dogs," Sam told a friend. "He loved to hunt. When I got out of the Army he took me bird hunting. I was hooked, just hooked! He was shooting a .28-gauge. That's a little lighter than a four-ten but not as heavy as a twenty. I thought if that's good enough for L. S., it ought to do for me. I used a .28 until switching to a twenty gauge four or five years ago."

With good forage and cover in the fields all over the Jackson County area, quail were plentiful twenty or thirty minutes beyond the city limits of Newport. And, with a shooting eye honed on the R.O.T.C. pistol club championship team, Sam was usually able to bag most any bird that rose within thirty yards of his .28-gauge muzzle.

"I'll tell you this," said Paul K. Holmes Jr., "bird hunting was something that fascinated him very much. He didn't neglect that any. I've had lots of cups of coffee and visited with him in the store, but I've never been hunting with him.

"Really, what he'd do a lot is just leave the store with his manager at some slack period and be gone two or three hours and come back and close up at quitting time or work some more in the store.

"I can't remember seeing him come back without his limit, or mighty close to it."

Strong ties were maintained between the parental Robsons and Waltons, and there was close three-way intercourse among the family bases in Newport and Oklahoma and Missouri. Helen's parents were frequent visitors. On occasion L. S. would drive over from Claremore to go fishing in the rivers or one of the numerous lakes in the Jackson County area. With the children, Sam and Helen would make the eight-hour motor trip up across the Ozark "summit" at Eureka Springs to Claremore for short weekend stays. A frequent visitor from Claremore was Helen's brother, L. S. Jr. He had an avid curiosity about the mystique of running a variety store, and finally opened one in Florida after moving there on account of asthma.

Tom Walton came occasionally for a visit, and on Easter Sunday, April 17, 1949, he went with the family to the First Presbyterian Church for the baptism of his grandson, Jim. What made the event doubly meaningful for Sam was that his mother Nan came with Tom, an indication that his parents had achieved some sort of reconciliation.

One family member who came to Newport as a permanent resident was brother Bud, who brought along his pretty war bride Audrey, known as "Audie." Being a torpedo plane pilot in some of the heaviest action in the Pacific had not changed Bud. He was still quiet and reserved, not given to idle conversation.

Utilizing and augmenting his kid brother's J. C. Penney training, Sam put him on the Ben Franklin store payroll as assistant manager and began schooling him in all the intricacies of five-and-dime retailing. Although generally receptive, Bud came to hate some of Sam's less conventional retail ploys.

Always looking for new ways to increase business, Sam jumped at the chance to buy a portable ice cream machine at the height of a sudden ice cream craze. The price was $1,250. Sam borrowed the money from Fred Pickens's newly opened Merchants and Planters Bank.

On Saturdays when the ice cream machine sat on

the sidewalk in front of the Ben Franklin, farmers and their families literally mobbed it with their nickels and dimes in hand. "Dollar for dollar," said Fred Pickens, "it might be the best single investment Sam Walton ever made."

But for Bud the machine held absolutely no charm. "He had to clean it," said Fred Pickens. "What a messy, repulsive chore!"

Sam Walton also discovered popcorn. "You can't imagine the crowds downtown on Saturday afternoons," said P. K. Holmes Jr. "On a fall day in Newport all these people would be on the street and Sam would have his popcorn machine fired up at the front of the store, and it was a going concern. It was the busiest part of the store. High profit, you understand, on popcorn."

Those were free and easy, Southern-style days of pleasant and uncomplicated living. The Waltons were young, in their thirties. They had a good living from the Ben Franklin store; in fact business was booming under Sam's friendly and inventive hand. Helen remained "churchy" and occupied with club activities, serving a term as president of P.E.O.'s Chapter R.* Sam kept up his civic leader role. The problems in Newport, however, did not require any big-time brain drain such as he would experience later on down the road.

The most important discovery Sam Walton made in Newport was that there was a charm and satisfaction in retailing that he had not fully expected. Sam Walton was crazy about selling and about satisfying customers. This was a darn good business, and it offered great opportunity. More members of the family circle ought to have five-and-dime stores. Helen's brother L. S. Jr., not greatly enamored of his law practice in

---

*P. E. O. is an international "philanthropic educational organization" founded in 1869 with headquarters at Des Moines, and 290,000 members in 49 states. P. E. O. funds an all-girls' school, Cottey College, in Nevada, Missouri, and awards other college scholarships.

Claremore, was interested. So was Bud Walton—at his older brother's vigorous urging.

With eyes and ears open, Sam monitored trade gossip for the news that suitable Ben Franklin franchises might be on the market. There'd have to be just the right kind of town to suit Bud—small, and near a fishing hole.

Just the right store turned up for sale in Versailles, a town of only about 2,000 in west-central Missouri, close by the Lake of the Ozarks. After checking out the store with Sam, Bud bought it. He would depend, as did Sam, on the Butler Brothers warehouse in St. Louis to wholesale him most of his merchandise, though he was free to buy from any source. However, unless he could purchase an item in carload lots and thus save 10 to 15 percent, the best price would be at Butler Brothers.

Sam was developing his keen eye for spotting experienced or promising retailers who could help his operations. When he took on H. W. Fisher as his assistant manager, a three-column by ten-inch Ben Franklin ad appeared in *Daily Independent* on July 27, 1948, proclaiming: "Mr. Fisher comes to us with the valued experience of 22 years in the variety store field. We feel that his qualifications will add greatly to the successful management of our store."

In the recesses of Sam Walton's mind there lurked volatile and not-to-be-denied impulses that drove him to challenge the status quo of many things and to conjure up risky new business experiments. One of his brainstorms erupted in Newport—The Eagle Department Store.

On Front Street his Ben Franklin was located next door to the J. C. Penney store. This was not a problem—they were quite different kinds of stores. Sam's chief local competitor was the Sterling variety store, operated by the aggressive Cash Wholesale Company of Little Rock. "They were a mighty good chain in that day and time," said P. K. Holmes Jr. "And they were on the corner, and so Sam's Ben Franklin and the Sterling store were right across the street from each other. We always said the Ben Franklin store sold the better merchandise, but I don't know that for sure."

The Sterling competition bothered Sam. He was on friendly terms with the manager, John Dunham, and talked shop with him over coffee occasionally. At the end of Sam's first year in Newport, the Sterling store's volume was $170,000; Sam's sales came to $80,000. If he were to win this race, he knew he'd have to become a better retailer.

John Dunham's store was already larger than the Ben Franklin, but the Sterling manager wanted even more space. He saw an opportunity to expand when a small store on his far side closed, leaving a twenty-five-by-one-hundred-foot location vacant. But Sam beat him to the punch. He rushed to Hot Springs, Arkansas, located the lady who owned the empty store, and leased the space.

"I really was just trying to block the expansion of Sterling," Walton said recently. "Their getting that extra space might have killed me."

Into the vacant store went Sam Walton's first brain child. Now he can chuckle about it; then it was a painful experiment, not a resounding success.

"It was just another variety store," said P. K. Holmes Jr. "It was smaller than his Ben Franklin. If it was a junior department store, it was mighty junior. A twenty-five-hundred-square-foot store just can't compete; a bigger store has more to offer. The Eagle store might have gone more into soft lines, like clothing, but there wasn't space for much."

The junior department store lasted just a couple of years, Sam Walton's first expansion—and first failure.

However, the Ben Franklin store was a definite and brilliant success. The sales volume grew astonishingly each year. For the year 1948, Sam racked up sales of $225,000, beating rival Sterling by $25,000. The Christmas trade was extraordinarily large and profitable. Sam Walton was pretty well established on Easy Street.

Then Lady Luck deserted him.

The fantastic way in which Sam built up and enlarged his sales volume beyond anything that had been done before by a Newport five-and-dime caught the eye of his landlord, P. K. Holmes Senior. The Holmes family had been Newport merchants since his patriarch father-in-law I. D. Price, opened an office supply and bookstore in 1882, which he operated until his death in 1921. The senior Holmes operated a series of stores, including the P. K. Holmes Department Store, and a men's and boy's shop run by his two sons.

All three were amazed by, and more than a little envious of, the high-flying Ben Franklin store.

In the late Spring of 1950 P. K. Holmes Senior called at the store to have a business talk with Sam Walton. What the landlord had to say sent a stunned and distraught Sam flying to his lawyer's office.

"My God, what's the matter?" said Fred Pickens Jr.

"My lease! My lease!" said Sam Walton. "It's up at the end of the year!"

"Well, just renew it. You've got an option to do that—I suppose."

The lawyer watched Sam Walton, the thirty-two-year-old merchant "genius" of Newport, lower his head and stare glumly at the rug, shuffling his feet in agitation.

"No," said Sam Walton weakly, "I don't."*

Fred Pickens Jr. rushed to the rescue and began trying to negotiate a renewal of the lease. It was critical for Sam. There was no other suitable and available location for a Ben Franklin store in Newport. If he couldn't hang on to his Front Street location, he'd be out of business.

The lawyer offered Holmes Senior higher rent; he didn't accept. He tried to interest the landlord in vari-

---

*Sam's lease actually contained a renewal option "at terms to be negotiated" which is really no option because the owner could set conditions impossible to meet.

ous different terms but kept running into a stone wall. Then, finally, he grasped the real situation.

"It's no good," he told Sam. "I hope to God the next time you take over a lease from somebody, you check to make certain it contains a proper renewal clause. They're not going to let you keep the store. The plain truth is they want Douglas Holmes to run a Ben Franklin in that building! You've shown the whole town what a money-maker it can be."

Fred Pickens Jr. watched the color drain out of his client's lean face.

"Looks like you're finished," he said.

The lawyer saw Sam clenching and unclenching his fists, staring at his hands.

Sam straightened up. "No, Fred," he said. "I'm not whipped. I found Newport, and I found the store. I can find another good town—and another Ben Franklin. Just wait and see!"

—7—

"$60,000—and No More!"

With its pristine red-and-white-striped awning, inviting "see-in" front windows, big, bold gold lettering, and logos advertising air-conditioning, Dodson's five-and-dime stood out like a prize jewel on East Main Street in Siloam Springs, Arkansas.

Sam Walton parked his car across the street and walked over for a closer look, leading his three sons. Helen, carrying baby Alice in her arms, came too. They were scouting a possible new location. It was late spring 1950, and time was running out. At the end of the year they would lose their Newport Ben Franklin.

"I'd never seen him before," said Jim Dodson. "But they all came in and looked around. Right off, he said he wanted to buy me out."

The store was not for sale. Jim Dodson and his wife, Missouri natives, had "come back home" from a California variety store chain on their parents' promise to help them start their own business. They had come to Siloam Springs in 1940, copied the Woolworth's look, and prospered from the start.

Helen and the children sat at the luncheonette counter and had a soft drink. Sam tried to make a sales pitch—rather a buyer's pitch.

"I hadn't even been thinking about selling," said Jim Dodson. "He was so eager I had to consider it.

We had a real nice store. Ideas I'd brought from California. First in Siloam to have fluorescent lights, air-conditioning, and not boxed-in but see-in windows so people on the street could see the merchandise all the way to the back."

But Sam Walton wanted to buy more than the five-and-dime store. "He wanted our house, too!" said Jim Dodson. "A package deal. He offered sixty thousand dollars."

The Waltons stayed in Siloam Springs for four or five days. They visited the Dodsons in their beautiful ten-room, two-story residence on a tree-shaded avenue in the nicest section of town. Jim Dodson showed Sam his large attached garage, which he used as a vital warehouse for his variety store.

"We kept talking," said Jim Dodson. "Finally I told Sam I'd let him have the house and the store for sixty-five thousand dollars."

The town had a special appeal to the Waltons. It was the right size, only about 3,000 population, located in the beautiful Arkansas hills, amid shady woodlands, with Sager Creek, fed by twenty-eight springs, meandering through its center. Founded in 1881, the town took its name from the biblical pool of Siloam. Siloam Springs was also the home of John Brown University, a privately endowed Christian college established in 1919, which had a student population of 900. All in all, a very pretty community.

What the Waltons liked most was that the town was right on the Oklahoma state line, meaning that Helen could drive just sixty miles to visit her parents in Claremore.

"We couldn't make a deal," said Jim Dodson, who ultimately retired to Springfield, Missouri. "I wanted sixty-five thousand dollars—and wouldn't budge. He offered sixty thousand dollars—and no more."

They parted friends—and in later years their business paths would cross frequently. In fact, Sam Walton eventually would purchase Dodson's five-and-dime. But not in 1950 when he wanted—and needed—it.

Unwilling to pay another $5,000 to close the deal, Sam Walton loaded up his family and drove on—still looking for a new hometown.

About a week later, May 1, 1950, Sam arrived in Bentonville, Arkansas, along with his father-in-law. The sky was overcast and threatening. Sam Walton and L. S. Robson drove downtown to the square, coming in by Highway 71. A downpour was brewing that several days later would flood Benton County lowlands. The men circled the Confederate soldier monument standing amid pin oaks and elms in the center plaza and parked on the west side in front of the Harrison Variety store.

L. S. Robson, in khakis and cowboy hat,* was a spry sixty-four, exactly twice the age of his son-in-law. He gave the store's 25-foot front critical appraisal, made a face, and shook his head. Sam Walton was not the least bit discouraged. "Have to get that store next door—double the size," he said, pointing.

It was another case of a suitable variety store not up for sale. But Butler Brothers, which serviced it as a wholesaler, had thought it could be. Luther E. Harrison had owned it for twenty-six years. He was seventy, and might be thinking of retiring.

Both Sam and his father-in-law were sharply taken aback when they stepped into the gloom of the five-and-dime. The interior was lighted only by three drop-cord 100-watt bulbs. Rickety stairs led up a side wall to a ramshackle balcony "office."

Luther Harrison was, indeed, willing to sell his store. His son, Tom Harrison of Bentonville, said: "My father and mother took it up with us children—my three brothers and three sisters. I told them, 'You've been in business long enough, and none of us are interested in it.' All we ever knew was to go up there and clerk.

---

*Robson wore khakis most of his life, even in the bank, because of dry, sensitive skin.

We might have been interested if we had ever gone to market with them."

Sam Walton, painfully aware of his own impending ouster from Newport, several times reassured Luther Harrison there was "no deal unless you are absolutely certain you are ready to quit business."

They agreed on a tentative price of $15,000 for the stock, fixtures, and goodwill.

"Before we go any further," Sam told Harrison, "I want you to go to the bank and check on my credit." Luther Harrison walked across the square to the Bank of Bentonville and talked to Fred Douglas, the cashier. "He told dad, 'Any check they give you, I'll cash,' " said Tom Harrison.

But it was far, far from a done deal. Sam had two other requirements—and they turned out to be big sticking points. Harrison did not own his building but rented for $25 a month. Sam insisted on buying the building. Also he demanded a ninety-nine-year lease on the barber shop that had a twenty-five-foot front next door so that he could knock out the wall and expand his new store to a minimum fifty-foot frontage.

They called in a real estate agent, Terry Peel, and he immediately ran into trouble. The two widows in Kansas City who owned the Harrison building refused to sell. And the Mrs. Lee of Fayetteville who rented the barber shop to Paul Harris turned a deaf ear to any deal.

Terry Peel still persisted with telephone arguments. The Kansas City widows hung up on him. He drove to Fayetteville to see Mrs. Lee, but she slammed the door.

Sam Walton, never a very patient man, decided the odds were heavily against making a deal here. Disappointed, he and L. S. Robson reluctantly studied the little list of other towns worth considering.

Sam hated the idea of having to abandon Bentonville. It was the seat of Benton County, with a population of 2,900 (virtually the same size as Siloam Springs, which was in the same county and only thirty miles to the southwest). Bentonville would also be an easy drive to

Helen's hometown. Sam liked the people on the streets; being Arkansawyers and Southern, they were polite and friendly. For the most part, too, they were country folk.

Bentonville was even more isolated than Newport. It was 12 miles south of the Missouri line and 18 miles due east of the Oklahoma border, sitting in sight of the Ozark's most primitive wilderness. A few miles to the south on U.S. 71 were larger towns: Rogers, Springdale, and Fayetteville, the latter being the site of the University of Arkansas. No cities were close; Little Rock, the state capital, was almost 200 miles distant, Kansas City was 200 miles to the north, and St. Louis was 300 miles away.

Apple orchards surrounded Bentonville; so many cars were shipped out by train that the town was dubbed the Red Apple Capital of the World. Hundreds of farmers also raised chickens commercially; northwest Arkansas expected to produce 40 million broilers annually, putting $5 million in farmers' pockets. Every year a perky "Ozark Smile Girl" was chosen to promote tourism, which brought hundreds of visitors to the lakes and mountains, especially to Bella Vista resort just north of Bentonville.

By reading government census statistics and talking to the manager of the chamber of commerce, Sam Walton could see just how genuinely this was a country town. Bentonville had only about 900 houses, around 1,000 children enrolled in public school, barely 500 telephones, perhaps 800 registered automobiles, and few black-topped highways. It did have a fine water supply and a municipal electric plant with rates about half what most Arkansas cities paid, and a casual approach to collecting revenues. No monthly bills were sent out—residents simply dropped by or phoned in to find out how much they owed.

This was exactly the kind of community where Sam Walton and his family would feel at home. But not if Sam had to operate a variety store that was only half large enough. Sam and Luther Harrison pressed the real estate agent to keep trying. Terry Peel appealed anew to the owners, but they all still rebuffed him.

This situation put Sam totally in the dumps and made him doubt his judgment. He anguished over losing out in Siloam Springs, but it couldn't be helped—he was underfinanced at that juncture. Counting store profits saved up, sale of his house, and what the Holmeses paid to purchase his Ben Franklin store fixtures, Sam was coming away from Newport with about $55,000. That wasn't enough to pay Jim Dodson's price.

"Siloam would have been a lot better location," Sam explained in an early 1990 reminiscence. "The Harrison store was not doing over $32,000 in yearly sales. But I saw the potential. In Newport I was running at the rate of $225,000, at that time the largest independent variety store in the state of Arkansas. That's what I wanted—to be the leader."

Tom Harrison recalls the nightmare of these complicated negotiations starting on a Tuesday or Wednesday. "Sam was offering everyone excellent terms. But by Saturday it was clear the ladies weren't going to sell or lease. My dad's whole sale was dead."

One who didn't give up was L. S. Robson. Sam's father-in-law slipped away unbeknownst to him (or to Tom Harrison, Terry Peel, or anyone else) and drove to Kansas City. On his own he braced the recalcitrant widows in person.

They still refused to sell their Bentonville variety store building. Robson retreated, but went back next day. About all this, Sam was in the dark. Robson made a new offer to the widows, $20,000. They hesitated, then accepted.

"The deal never would have been done if it hadn't been for L. S. Robson," Sam recalled. "He was a tremendous salesman. I didn't know he was doing it."

That left the still necessary ninety-nine-year lease on the barber shop. Chances of getting that seemed nil. Sam Walton was feeling snakebit. "Bad luck," he remembered reading, "comes soberly, sits by the bed, and brings her knitting." Fortune had turned against him in Newport. And he had struck out in Siloam Springs. How long could bad luck sit and knit?

On Saturday afternoon Mrs. Lee said no for the sixth time on a barber shop lease. "That was the final word," recalls Tom Harrison. "Sunday after church our whole family went to the A. Q. Chicken House* in Springdale for lunch and got back about three o'clock. The phone rang. Mrs. Lee had changed her mind. She would lease!"

Until that phone call, Sam Walton felt himself teetering on the edge of a certain obscurity. In later years he realized that Lady Luck at that time was shooting craps with the individual fate of two Arkansas towns just as much as with his own. Siloam Springs would have been headquarters of the multi-billion-dollar Wal-Mart Stores, Sam Walton said in a retailer testimonial dinner in Dallas in the eighties, "if Jim Dodson hadn't been so darn contrary." He flashed a smile at Jim Dodson, who was in the audience; but the statement was true.

Newport would have enjoyed the same Wal-Mart headquarters bonanza, residents there feel, if Sam Walton had not been kicked out of his Ben Franklin store on Front Street. P. K. Holmes Jr. said he still gets teased about that but believed his family fully lived up to the terms of the lease.

But now it was for sleepy little Bentonville in 1950 that the dice were finally coming up seven-eleven.

Luther Harrison immediately got in touch with William H. (Bill) Enfield, a new young lawyer in town. Sam Walton had chosen Enfield to represent him and write the sale and lease contracts, on the recommendation of somebody from the Presbyterian Church.

Sam and his father-in-law had left Bentonville, but they hurried back. "That lady was tough on her lease," says Bill Enfield. "I remember that Sam was still nervous after getting the shaft in Newport. He insisted on

*A. Q. stands for Arkansas Quality.

multiple renewals almost indefinitely. We managed to work it out. Sam bought the Harrison side and leased the barber shop and arranged to knock out the wall."

The sale of Luther Harrison's variety store was completed in time to make page one of the semiweekly *Benton County Democrat* on Thursday, May 11, under a two-column head reading: "Big Business Deal Is Closed Here." Sam Walton planned, the newspaper said, to remodel and expand the variety store, with Butler Brothers making the new design. His father-in-law was mentioned favorably, and the editor gave the new merchant a typical down-home encomium:

> It is a big accomplishment to have people such as the Waltons come here to live, as this is a fine family, and their progressive plans mean much to the business life of this city.

Luther Harrison handed over the front-door keys. Ironically there was no back door, because the buildings had foolishly been erected butting up against buildings that faced the other street, with no back alley between them for access. When he first stepped inside, Sam looked for places to hang a few more electric lights. Then he mounted the stairs to his loft "office" and nailed an old orange crate on the wall to serve as a shelf for his books.

"He grabbed a couple of saw horses," said Bill Enfield, "and slammed down a piece of plywood on top of them. That was his desk. That put him in business. He used that makeshift desk, I believe, for five or six years."

Bad luck was still stalking Sam Walton. The storm clouds that had hovered over the square on his arrival nine days ago returned malevolently. A violent downpour began May 9—the first day he had taken possession of the Harrison Variety store.

"It was the worst rain in the history of Bentonville," Sam recalls. "Twelve inches in twenty-four hours! Of course, the store's old roof leaked. I had to rush

around covering all the counters with oilcloth and
plastic to keep the merchandise from being washed
away—really!"

As soon as the weather cleared, Sam leveled the
wall, enlarged his store, installed new shelves and
counters, as well as fluorescent lights, and hung out a
big new sign: WALTON'S 5¢ & 10¢." In the *Benton County
Democrat* he announced a one-day remodeling sale for
Saturday, July 29, with free balloons for "all the kids."
Walton's five-and-dime offered a dozen clothespins at
$.09, regular $.25 training pants for $.15, Birdseye
cloth diapers for $1.79, little girl dresses for $1.29, ice
tea glasses at 10 cents a piece, 14-quart gray enamel
dishpans for $.39, and ladies' sheer hose, $.98 a pair.

The newspaper gave him a page one pat on the
back, asserting that the remodeling gave Bentonville
"one of the largest and most modern variety stores in
North Arkansas." The story also named his six clerks:
Ruth Keller, Ruby Turner, Gene Wade, Oleta Ennes,
Wanda Perkins, and Troy Almand.

Sam Walton had pulled off his entry into Bentonville
without any outside help. "I paid $15,000 for the Har-
rison store, $20,000 for the building, and $20,000 for
remodeling the store and the barber shop," says Walton, "I used up all the money I was bringing out of
Newport. I was down to zero again."

Amid the excitement of venturing into Bentonville
came distressing news from Missouri. His mother had
developed cancer and must undergo surgery in St.
Louis. Sam and Bud rushed there. The operation was
performed at Barnes Hospital and within days Nancy
L. Walton died, only fifty-two years old. Her funeral
was held in the Presbyterian Church in Columbia on
Monday, October 2.

Throughout the fall of 1950, Sam shuttled between
his new store in Bentonville and the old in Newport,
having to drive about 250 long miles over curving
mountain roads—each way. That was when he began
to think there must be a faster way to cover ground.

Fortunately, business was booming, and in both stores

cash registers sang a merry Christmas tune. Customers were finding quality merchandise at reasonable or low prices. Sam had laid in a large stock, and the money rolled in.

At the end of the year, the adventures of Sam Walton in Newport were over. P. K. Holmes's sons waited in the wings to take over the flourishing variety store (and later let it fail). The departing owner said good-bye with this two-column ad in the *Daily Independent*:

ANNOUNCEMENT

It is with regret that we are preparing to leave Newport, and our many friends and customers. Being unable to renew our lease, we are moving to Bentonville, Ark., to make our future home.

As of January 1st, the Ben Franklin Store will be under new ownership and management.

We sincerely appreciate your friendship and patronage during the past five and a half years and assure you it has been a pleasure and a privilege to have been of service to you. Once again, friends, "THANKS FOR EVERYTHING."

SAM and HELEN WALTON

—8—

An Aristocratic Country Town

"Neither of us has a blind pig's chance of being accepted by the old guard—the guys who really run this town—till we've lived here at least ten years."

Wes Hunnicutt, new owner of the *Benton County Democrat*, was speaking confidentially to Sam Walton, as one Bentonville newcomer to another, after a board meeting at the chamber of commerce. "They tell me it takes that long. Been so since the Civil War."

If true—and it was—Sam had quite a few years to go; he had just moved his family from Newport on January 1, 1951, and purchased a modest six-room frame bungalow at 401 Northwest B Street. With a friendly smile and proffered hand, Sam went briskly about the streets of his new town. He wanted people to like him, but the atmosphere somehow was not quite the same as in Newport. He figured out, at length, that there was a deeper sense of history in Bentonville. These Arkansawyers were the same plain and honest country folk, merchants and professional people, he knew in Newport, but whereas Newport had only been grazed by the fighting between North and South, this town had felt the searing flames of the conflict—"the Lost Cause," as it was spoken of here.

This new town was, Sam learned, very old.

Originally part of the 1803 Louisiana Purchase, Benton County evolved from Arkansas Territory in 1819, before the first settlers' oxcarts rattled down the old army road between Fort Scott, Kansas, and Fort Smith in 1830. When statehood came six years later, Bentonville sprang up as a sort of capital of northwest Arkansas. Both county and county seat adopted their names as a tribute to U.S. Senator Thomas Hart Benton of Missouri, the forthright lawyer-editor who had so staunchly and successfully advocated statehood for Arkansas. He was a man to be admired, as Benton county schoolchildren were taught in later years. He was the first senator to serve thirty years. And, moreover, he had courage and daring, once asserting in a Senate debate: "Mr. President, Sir, I never quarrel, Sir, but sometimes I fight, Sir, and when I fight, Sir, a funeral follows, Sir."

Bentonville was sedate, aristocratic, and small—and most residents wanted it to stay that way.

"The inner circle here," publisher Hunnicutt explained to Sam, "is our old Confederate families. Terry Peel is supposed to have more money than anybody else, but there are no really rich men. There's Dave Peel, too. And Joe Knott, the insurance man who has a little money, I guess. And his cousin, Gordon Knott, who runs the Eagle feed and grain mill. Fred Berry; Von Lindsey, the lawyer; and the Craig and Rice families."

Most of them lived on what was called Silk Stocking Row—a short section of West Central Avenue that was only a few blocks beyond the business district, which pivoted around the courthouse and the square.

"It was still a Saturday town in the fifties," said Hunnicutt. "Lots of farmers came in. The stores stayed open till nine o'clock. Of course everything was shut down Sunday. But the town was stagnant. Not many people wanted to bring in manufacturing, industry. Still don't. We didn't get our first traffic light until about mid-1970."

The battlefield at Pea Ridge, eleven miles northwest of Bentonville, was a constant and sad reminder to local residents of the struggle between North and South. For four days in March of 1862, Union and Confederate armies fought furiously in Benton County, winding up at Pea Ridge in one of the bloodiest engagements of the war—called "the Gettysburg of the West."

In December of 1862, a Union army stormed into Bentonville, burning the courthouse, a 50-foot-square brick building erected in 1842, which sat in the middle of the square. Fortunately county record books had been taken out and safely hidden, but other downtown buildings were also burned.

(The present $200,000 courthouse was built in 1928, not in the middle but facing the square from the east, two floors and a full basement, with thirty-six rooms and seventy-five windows.)

When Sam Walton came to Bentonville, Silk Stocking Row was dominated by descendants of two distinguished Confederate officers who put their indelible and powerful stamp on Benton County affairs—cultural and political—from the late 1860s into the early 1900s.

Colonel Sam Peel, born in Batesville, Arkansas, September 13, 1831, fought for the South in the battles of Wilson Creek and Prairie Grove, and became a lawyer after Appomattox. He began a distinguished career in Bentonville in 1867, served as prosecuting attorney, 1872–1882, and then was elected to Congress, serving ten years.

Having promised his bride a Southern mansion, Colonel Peel built one in 1875 on a country road just south of Bentonville. Of redbrick and native stone, it was two stories, with walls 18 inches thick and ceilings 12½ feet high, fourteen rooms, and eight fireplaces, with a winding black walnut staircase, stained glass windows, double doors, and a second-floor veranda. It was the showplace of Benton County, but Colonel Peel moved to town in 1903; his mansion—subsequently sold four times—still stands. The present owner, Lee A. Allen, acquired it in 1920. Colonel Peel died in 1924 at ninety-three.

The other Civil War "hero" leaving his mark on the

town was James H. Berry, who, incidentally, fought at Pea Ridge. Born in Alabama, Berry grew up in Yellville, Arkansas, where his father was a storekeeper. In the battle at Corinth, Mississippi, Lieutenant Berry lost his right leg and was captured by the Yankees.

As a struggling lawyer after the war, his father-in-law complained Berry couldn't make a living even with two legs. But Berry came to Bentonville in 1869 as the law partner of Colonel Peel, who had married his sister Mary. He rose rapidly in politics, going to the Legislature in 1872, elected circuit judge in 1878, and governor of Arkansas in 1882. Next he served as United States Senator for twenty-two years, returning to Bentonville in 1907, where he died in 1913.

As Sam Walton picked up on his new town's rich history, he discovered that the real estate agent who had handled his purchase of the Harrison Variety store, Terry Peel, was the grandson of Colonel Peel. Although he had, with Butler Brothers' guidance, installed a modernistic structural glass front on Walton's five-and-dime, something he considered very spiffy and refreshing, Sam later had regrets. It would have been much better to have preserved the character and charm of the square's nineteenth-century atmosphere. He realized that for a certainty when he saw other historic façades being raped by remodelers with no feel for the beauty of the past. While he was sad at having destroyed the old-time exterior of his variety store, Sam was ecstatic over his battery of fluorescent ceiling lights. That made the difference between night and day in his sales volume.

Walton had immediately plunged into civic affairs after his arrival, joining the chamber of commerce, the Rotary Club, and the Presbyterian Church. Before long Sam would be president of the Rotary, as well as the chamber of commerce, a Sunday school teacher, an elder and then a deacon of his church, and elected to the city council and serve on the hospital board.

But in those early days, Sam Walton didn't create much of a stir in Bentonville. "He was just like anybody else up and down the street," said Wes Hunnicutt. "When I came here some of the newer people were active in the chamber of commerce, but the old men—the real insiders—were running politics. This was a strong Democratic county then. Now it's mostly Republican."

Always a remote, out-of-the-way place hidden behind the Ozarks up in the very northwest corner of the state, the modern Bentonville still exudes an atmosphere of isolation, notwithstanding the rumble and thunder of diesel semis shifting loads of brown corrugated cartons in and out of sprawling Wal-Mart warehouses.

Bentonville was left out in the cold before the turn of the century when the railroads invaded Arkansas. And it was an embarrassing episode, according to the tale Sam heard from one of his Rotary Club pals, Charles Craig, a sporting goods dealer and amateur raconteur who delved into local history. Craig, from one of the Silk Stocking Row families, didn't vouch for the episode, but must have written and spoken it 300 times.

"When the Frisco railroad decided to come from St. Louis to the Gulf of Mexico," Craig said, "they started in Monett, Missouri, and built their grade to Bentonville, finishing in 1880. Then the railroad officials asked for a town meeting, and the mayor called it.

"The mayor liked his likker, and he was in his cups. When the vice-president of the Frisco asked the city of Bentonville for six thousand dollars to continue the grade on as far as Cave Springs, which is six miles south, the mayor got to his feet and wagged his head.

" 'You must think we are a bunch of dummies,' said the mayor. 'Why should we give you any money to go on south with it? You are already here and you've got to go south. And there's nothing you can do about it!'

"That was a mistake. The Frisco man was highly angered. 'Oh, yeah! Well, we'll show you!' And he went back to Monett and started building a new grade that went six miles east of Bentonville. There was nothing over there but a general store. But they made a town and named it Rogers—after the Frisco general manager, Captain W. C. Rogers. Then they went on south with the main line.

"That left Bentonville in the soup. Our town badly needed a railroad—we had a lot of agricultural products to ship. Wiser heads prevailed here, and in 1882 the townspeople put up enough money to build a spur to Rogers. Next year the Frisco bought the spur and extended it west to Grove, Oklahoma, to connect with the Kansas City Southern line."

The abandoned Frisco grade still stands, running "for miles and miles . . . I played on that dump many, many times when I was a boy growing up," recalled Charles Craig. The old grade, rising several feet above street level, is today clearly visible from the present home of Sam and Helen Walton on the east side of Bentonville.

Benton County looked to farming for its livelihood since pioneer days. The first cash crops were tobacco, cotton, and hemp; in 1887 Bentonville had four tobacco factories. When disease and insects ruined their tobacco, Benton County farmers put in apple orchards. Apples hit a peak in 1919 when Benton county marketed 5 million bushels at $1.00 a bushel. Disease wiped out most orchards in the thirties. A farm girl at Cave Springs "invented" broiler raising in 1921, selling 324 chickens grown in a heated house for $1.20 each. Her experiment led to Arkansas's present-day billion-dollar poultry industry. Today Benton County is also a big milk producer.

Sam Walton found history a favorite topic of conversation even with his new family physician, Dr. Neil Compton, who later became noted for his activism in the campaign to persuade Congress to not dam Buffalo River but designate it a national scenic river.

Today Dr. Compton's daughter, Ellen Compton Shipley, is in charge of collecting historical papers for the University of Arkansas library at Fayetteville.

"I grew up in Bentonville and was in high school

there when the Walton family came to town," said
Ellen Shipley. "It of course was the county seat and in
a way kind of aristocratic because the leaders of the
county were there, whereas Rogers and Siloam Springs
were railroad towns that came along later.

"So Bentonville was the old capital city. There were
lots of lawyers there, and courts met there. It was a
very stable and prosperous city.

"You could tell that by the buildings. In my opinion
it is culturally connected more to the little towns in
Missouri as you go north, Carthage, Butler, those
little towns going up into Kansas City. They all look
like Bentonville; they all have redbrick buildings around
the square, with the courthouse in the middle. That's
about the only thing that's different in Bentonville—
the courthouse is on the side. In our square stands the
statue of a Confederate soldier."

The windows of Walton's five-and-dime looked out
upon the square, and from atop a 15-foot granite
pedestal the erect figure of a bearded Confederate
campaigner, blanket roll across his shoulders with hands
clasped on the barrel of his rifle, gazed directly into
the variety store.

Every time Sam Walton glanced outside, he was
reminded of a new fact of his business life—old-
fashioned Southern courtesy, and a little chivalry, too,
had to be carefully blended along with low prices and
a guarantee of customer satisfaction in his recipe for
success.

—9—

Airplanes and Hula Hoops

Sometimes hardship can enlighten and inspire. This was the case for Sam Walton as he put in hours and hours of driving Ozark mountain roads in the winter of 1950. But that same boredom and frustration triggered ideas that eventually brought him billions of dollars.

Those countless eight-to-ten-hour commutes between Bentonville and Newport meant slowing to twenty miles an hour on steep dangerous curves that had no guardrail, crawling through village stoplights, dodging fog and stray stock and stalled trucks, and worrying along two-lane blacktops often slick with rain. Usually his trips went into the night, and were thus more dangerous.

The bright side was, however, that he was struck with the realization that if he were competent enough to operate separate variety stores in two towns successfully, why not three, four, or—well, maybe even a dozen? He could see the possibility of his own chain of five-and-dimes, but he groaned at the mere thought of having to endure even more Ozark auto travel to direct such an expanded operation.

But one evening as he tooled along the corkscrew curves on U.S. Highway 62 through Eureka Springs he heard the drone of a small airplane. He glanced at the silver wings in the sky, and a light flashed in his brain.

In Newport he promptly sought out one of the Jackson County farmers who had been in the air force in World War II and now had their own small planes. For a reasonable fee, he chartered a pilot to take him to Bentonville. The eight-hour road trip shrank to a ninety-minute flight.

This gave Sam the answer he was looking for. Without this magic carpet, his Wal-Mart phenomenon never would have seen the light of day.

However, transportation complications became moot in 1951 when the old Ben Franklin store in Newport passed from his hands into the grasp of P. K. Holmes's sons. Sam was down to a single store, but he was thinking, and hard. Quite a bit of capital was needed to open and stock a new store. And profits did not flow in immediately. New ventures would require close managing.

The best place to plant a new variety store would have been Rogers, six miles away, but this location was not open to him, since his supplier, Butler Brothers, had already placed a Ben Franklin franchise there. Sam was now dealing with the Butler Brothers warehouse in Kansas City, 200 miles north of Bentonville. Occasionally he had to drive there, and every time he did he wished he owned an airplane.

Climbing stairs to his balcony office, Sam sat at his sawhorse-and-plywood desk (his lifelong aversion to ornate or even comfortable offices was already set), and doodled with a pencil on a road map, marking possible towns he might invade. One day he drove twenty-five miles south on U.S. Highway 71, the main interstate artery from Kansas City to Fort Smith, Arkansas, to the next county seat, Fayetteville. Sam checked out the square and discovered that luck was with him. The Kroger grocery on the square was moving out. Sam leased the location, a good one between Campbell-Bell and the Oklahoma Tire and Supply Company.

Always in touch with enterprising men with variety store experience, Sam had a manager waiting, Willard

Walker of Tulsa, who was willing to leave the T.G.&Y. chain.* A manager was by no means the last valuable article Sam Walton intended to lift from T.G.&Y. He studied how that chain did things, ready to pounce on any successful little trick they had and copy it.

The Fayetteville store opened on October 30, 1952. It was a Ben Franklin franchise, but the sign read: WALTON'S 5¢ AND 10¢. It was an odd-shaped store—19 by 145 feet, about 2,800 square feet—but at least it had a back door and plenty of storage room upstairs and a hand-operated elevator.

"Sam would come to the store once a week to look it over," recalled Willard Walker. "Once a month he'd look at my books—I kept my own books then—and make a profit-and-loss statement. He was a great help in merchandising, and he helped me deal with the wholesalers. They all knew him.

"Sam demanded that I keep a clean store, that it be profitable, and that the staff—I had no assistant, but did use four girls—be loyal to him and to the store. He gave a good percentage deal to the early managers, to help get that commitment.

"We did a heavy volume in toiletries, with lots of specials on our tables and racks at the ends of aisles. Sam wanted a strong staple program, lots of specials, and a complete assortment on hand."

With two stores now running, Sam staked out the main drag of up-and-coming Springdale, also on U.S. 71, about halfway between Rogers and Fayetteville, as a possible expansion site. But on a trip to the Butler Brothers Kansas City warehouse, he learned that the second shopping center ever to be built in America

---

*An odd coincidence was that T.G.&Y. chairman Raymond A. Young opened his first five-and-dime in 1927 in Sam's birthplace, Kingfisher, and subsequently expanded the chain to include 930 T.G.&Y. stores in twenty-nine states. Young was listed on Kingfisher's famous sons plaque, as were W. C. Coleman, who in 1900 invented his world-famous lamp and stove, and Don Blanding, the vagabond poet. The plaque would later be inscribed with a fourth famous name, Sam's.

was going up in Kansas City's suburban Ruskin Heights. The shopping center scheme captivated him; he couldn't wait to be part of it. He phoned brother Bud to hurry over from Versailles. They agreed to take a Ruskin Heights location and opened a Ben Franklin there, hiring an experienced manager, Henry Dorzab. Once again Sam and Bud were sole owners—50-50 partners.

"We were so spectacularly successful with this variety store," Sam Walton wrote later, "that it just set both of us on fire. We did $350,000 [annual sales] in two or three years and neither of us had done over about $200,000 in any one store before.

"So with that success, I immediately thought, 'This is going to sweep the country!' I thought I was going to go out and find me some property and develop a shopping center."

Before somebody could beat him to the punch, Sam hurried to Fort Smith, but wasn't intrigued by any site there. He moved on to Arkansas's capital city, Little Rock, and found an excellent 40-acre site at Markham and Hays streets, for sale at $275,000. He dug into his bank account for $10,000 and plunked it down for an option to buy, gulping at his own audacity. He had, in fact, bitten off too much, but he didn't know it right away.

The site needed a paved road. Sam snapped some photographs and pasted them in hand-lettered brochures that extolled the advantages of Little Rock having Arkansas's first shopping center. He went from door to door with petitions to get the road paved. "I remember those brochures," Sam recalled. "I just wish we could have kept some of those; they would be priceless today."

This shopping center adventure, undertaken in the mid-1950s when Walton was not yet thirty-four, at least taught the Bentonville tyro several valuable business lessons. At the outset he thought it would be easy. "I was going to develop shopping centers all over the country," Sam said later. "Without any money! And become a magnate. I thought it was a pure cinch."

With his site under option, Sam kept racing around—and writing checks. He finally got the road paved. He signed up the Woolworth people to take some yet-to-be-built space for a store. He took stock one day and discovered he had already poured into the venture between $25,000 and $30,000.

It began to look like a dangerous gamble. It dawned on him that he had nowhere near enough capital to take on responsibility for a site development that would require financing of more than one million dollars.

In the process of pushing his shopping center dream, Sam got acquainted with well-placed Little Rock developer Elbert Fawcett, who also was beginning to think about the possibilities of plazas and malls. He was convinced Sam had at least picked the right location.

Sam struggled on for months. But the burden, especially his lack of capital, was killing. Not even Helen's family could come to the rescue. "Money was so hard to come by in those days," Helen remembers. "We had big ideas," Sam says in a Wal-Mart historical memo, "but no money."

At length, Sam's big dream died. "I got cold feet, ran out of money," he relates, "decided to go back being a merchant and building stores. . . . We were just about ten years ahead of our time with the shopping center concept."

As part of this venture, Sam met millionaire Little Rock investment banker, Jackson T. Stephens, who with his brother, Witt, ran the biggest bond house outside Wall Street. "Jack picked up the pieces of our ambitious scheme," said Sam. "We lost our money, and left town." Later Elbert Fawcett developed Little Rock's first shopping center on Sam's old site.

Years later both Sam and Helen looked on the event philosophically as a learning experience. "We were so glad Sam got out of his mistakes the way he did over the years," Helen observes. It was "the best thing that ever happened" to teach him the fundamentals of expansion, Sam thinks. "I guess the thing that saved us is that we've corrected our mistakes before they became dangerous and really jeopardized the company."

But the shopping center scheme was not a total waste of effort. In the process, Sam leased space for a Ben Franklin store in Little Rock. Also his friendship with Jackson T. Stephens would prove significant. Twenty years later the Stephens bond house would step in and pull Sam Walton out of a crucial money crunch.

Retreating to sleepy little Bentonville, Sam contemplated taking off in another direction—up! On another shopping trip to Butler Brothers in Kansas City, he was again hit with the realization that he had to reduce his travel time somehow, and that meant flying. Why not learn to fly? After all he was young enough—still in his thirties.

"I studied up on single-engine monoplanes," Sam recalled in a recent interview. "I answered ads in the magazines and newspapers. I was looking for something fast, better than a Piper Cub. There was one called an Ercoupe advertised in Oklahoma City."

Sam drove out and inspected it, taking along his own expert, Wesley Dixon, a pilot-instructor and manager of the Bentonville airport.

"That Ercoupe filled the bill because it would fly at one hundred miles an hour," said Sam. "I thought it was a pretty good deal, and bought the airplane for eighteen hundred dollars. Wesley Dixon flew it back to Bentonville, and later taught me to fly."

Bud tried to discourage his brother from becoming a pilot. In a 1987 interview given jointly with Sam and Helen to the editor of the *Wal-Mart World*, Bud said: "He knew nothing about airplanes—and I couldn't believe he was going to buy one. I was real concerned in those days. I figured anyone who drove a car like Sam sure didn't need to be in an airplane. I told him no way.

"I had flown planes before in the war, and I knew the thing wasn't safe. The old radio was a crank job, and it would have been just as effective to open the cockpit door and use a megaphone to communicate. It was well over a year before I crawled in the plane with him. It was a trip to Little Rock and I'll tell you what . . . I was terrified! Not because of Sam—he's a good pilot—but because of the airplane!"

Despite this not very auspicious beginning, Sam Walton would continue to fly planes for the next forty years. His career as private pilot might have ended, not prettily, a number of times. Sam, assert those several with reason to know, has often been a foolish and careless flier, and has had a few very close calls, but his luck has never failed him.

"Sam can't be bothered with the usual sort of pre-flight checking of the plane you're supposed to do," said Bill Enfield, himself a private pilot. "He just comes out there and jumps in the airplane and takes off." Sam's attitude, said Enfield, is that "the man upstairs" won't let anything happen to his airplane.

From his earliest days as a pilot, Sam felt frustrated when bad weather made flying unwise. He flew to Kansas City in the mid-1950s in the second plane he bought, a Tripacer, to check on his Ruskin Heights variety store. Overnight a blizzard hit. Next morning when he went to suburban Stateline Airpark to fly home, he found the runways covered with 6 inches of snow. Nobody could say when the bulldozer would clear them.

Sam decided to take off anyway. He liked flying the Tripacer better than his Ercoupe, even though his newest plane bore the ignoble nickname "The Rock." His lawyer-neighbor Enfield explained: "The Tripacer had very short wings. If you lose power, it won't glide. It falls like a rock."

Sam managed to mush the Tripacer wheels through the snow to the runway, took a bearing, released the brakes, and revved up the engine. The airplane moved slowly; the snow created drag. Sam strained to reach takeoff speed, but it was hard going.

"Sam was in trouble," recalls Enfield, who later got the details from Sam. "Every time he'd pull back on the yoke and try to take off, the nose wheel would just dig deeper into the snow. Finally he had to hit the brakes and try to stop. The Tripacer tipped forward and buried its nose in the snow right at the end of the runway. Fortunately it didn't flip over. If it had, he might have been hurt. But he wasn't scratched."

Watching the take-off attempt was Charles Cate, the Ruskin Heights store manager. "When I nosed my plane over," Sam recalled in a recent conversation, "Charley was bounding across the airport like a gazelle and he was there before I could even get out of the plane."

Sam borrowed Charles Cate's car and drove home, leaving instructions to dig the plane out of the snow and repair it.

"That's the only airplane accident I ever had," Sam remembers, calculating that in forty years of flying he logged more than 10,000 hours as a pilot, covering close to 1.5 million miles. His visitor reminded Sam that he had once forgotten to switch over to his reserve fuel tank and got in trouble at Springfield. "That's right," he conceded. "I did have to make that forced landing."

Learning to fly just added to Sam Walton's hectic day and prompted him to start getting up early and staying up later. He was healthy and didn't miss the sleep. He took Helen to the movies; Deborah Kerr and Burt Lancaster starred in *From Here to Eternity* at the Plaza on the square. The Neta Villa Restaurant offered a special Sunday dinner for $.85! This was true small-town living, but the Waltons liked it. They got out their canoes and went over to the Buffalo River near Yellville, with the children, skimming by sundappled sandbars, camping beneath stark granite cliffs, fishing, swimming, sleeping in tents, and feasting on an unsullied outdoors of crystal water and lush forest. At these times, it was up to his five-and-dime managers to watch the store.

Sam was always on the lookout for merchants-in-the-

making. He thought he knew how to identify good
store locations and to find bright people.

Right in the chair next to him at the weekly luncheon of the Bentonville Rotary Club, Sam discovered
a potential retailing executive. His name was Robert
L. (Bob) Bogle, a young graduate of the University of
Arkansas, who for about a year had been the State
Health Department sanitation officer checking compli-
ance with codes at Benton County restaurants, food
processing plants, and dairies.

In the summer of 1955, Sam tried a round-about
approach. "Bob, you don't know somebody that would
help me in the store, do you? I've got that store in
Fayetteville, and one in Kansas City, and I need some
help over there on the west side of the square."

"Offhand, I don't," said Bob Bogle, "but I'll keep
my eyes open."

In November Sam brought up the subject again.
"Say, did you find me somebody to work in the store?"

"Truthfully I've been so busy," said Bob Bogle, "I
haven't spent much time looking for your manager,
but I'll get right on it."

"I don't guess you'd be interested, would you?"

"Actually, I don't think I am," said Bob Bogle,
"but I'll sure sit down and listen to you."

Sam invited him to come over to his house after
supper that night. Said Bob Bogle: "So we went over
that night, where he lived on Northwest B Street, and
sat down in the living room. He had brought home the
books from the store to show how much volume he
was doing. I took my wife, Marilyn, along and we sat
there a while and listened, and I told him we would go
home and think it over and I would get hold of him in
the morning. We're both early risers so it would be
pretty easy to find him.

"Marilyn and I discussed it. And she was pretty sure
I'd lost my mind. She kept reminding me that I'd won
a U.S. public health scholarship to North Carolina and
had earned my master's degree in public health. So
she felt I would be throwing my education out the

window, but I told her you could work for the State of
Arkansas forever and never build up any equity, and
here was Sam offering me a job and twenty-five percent of the profits of the store.

"I'd have more opportunity, too, he said, because
he wanted to expand to about a dozen stores. Helen,
who was there, got a startled look and nearly fell off
her chair.

"Anyhow, I told Sam I'd give it a try. The salary
was about what I was making, probably four hundred
dollars a month, hardly enough to keep a college kid
over the weekend today. It was all new to me; I was
pliable and willing to learn. I was twenty-nine years
old, and we had two children, and we'd just built our
house. It seemed like a good opportunity, and the
thing that fascinated me more than the salary was the
opportunity to buy an interest in the other stores as we
put them in."

So on December 1, 1955, Bob Bogle became manager of Walton's 5 and 10¢ store on the square—and
began learning the ropes of the variety-store business
from a young master of the trade who figured he had
bigger fish to fry.

Right off the bat Bob learned that if he wanted to
keep pace with the boss, he'd have to practice some of
old Tom Walton's work ethic. The hours were long,
and there was always something to do. Even in 1989,
long after Sam had moved out and his first Bentonville
five-and-dime had gone through other hands as a café
and so forth, on its floor and still serviceable were
green and white asphalt tiles he'd bought for $.11
each. They had been laid, after hours, by Sam and
Bob.

The new manager cheerfully dived into the Ben
Franklin training program, based on a "book" that
actually showed how to order merchandise and display
it. He found the manual tremendously instructive.

Bob Bogle recalled: "We would buy based on what
we thought we could sell. Now you cycle through that
once and you know what you can sell after that. Your

sales may be increasing ten or twenty percent a year. You keep a record—what you sold out of, what you had too many of, the colors, the sizes . . . You do that in every department.

"We would train a girl according to this plan, and you had a checklist. Hosiery was Department H, by the way, and the book was geared to your size, a Class C store doing $100,000 a year, Class B $200,000 or Class A, doing $400,000 and over.

"Your book shows how many a store of your class would normally sell of a certain item, and you learn pretty quick whether pink is better than white or yellow or whatever. So you start training your girls and every time they reorder they check how many items and how many they ordered. Then we circled it in the book that each girl had, so that at any time you could open the book and add the line across by how many sold and divide by the number of months, and you'd know how many you sell a month.

"There's actually not a lot of mystery about it. You just use your intuition about how much to order.

"We were always looking for new items. That is one of the real challenges in this business today." Scouting for new business was a major lesson Sam Walton taught his people by example. According to Bob Bogle: "He is constantly looking . . . wherever he goes. He's doing it today. He's a close observer of people, that's all—what they are talking about, looking at, wearing. . . . He's always looking for a quality item and things that people would be interested in buying and would be pleased to purchase."

In Kansas City helping with the remodeling of the Ruskin Heights Ben Franklin, Bob Bogle demonstrated how well he had adopted that trait. He and his wife stopped by a Katz store at Truman Corners and bought a plastic Halloween pumpkin. At the checkout, he glanced under the counter and saw row after row of baby dolls with layaway tags attached.

"Marilyn, look at that!" he cried. Mrs. Bogle just shrugged but he hurried to the toy counter to examine the 20-inch doll, dressed in cotton shorts and top and selling for $9.95, that was such a hot item. He bought one, went back to Bentonville, and got busy on the phone and eventually located the manufacturer in New York.

"We started placing orders," said Bob Bogle. "I could see that every mama would want that baby doll for her little girl. I had the whole window filled with those baby dolls. I would safely say we sold 5,000—and that's when we had only five or six stores. That was rather expensive; most five-and-dime toys stop at about $2.98. That doll was an enormous seller!"

So were Hula Hoops. But when the craze swept the country in the late fifties, they were hard to come by for small merchants. Sam Walton was not to be denied, however. He decided it was a rather simple plaything; anybody who dealt in small plastic pipe could manufacture Hula Hoops. In Siloam Springs, he found a small company that produced plastic pipe. He got in touch with Jim Dodson, whose variety store there he had unsuccessfully tried to buy in 1950. They were on good terms and both needed Hula Hoops. Sam proposed they go in together and make their own.

"It was a brilliant idea," said Jim Dodson. "We bought all this plastic pipe, and Sam came over and helped. We set up regular assembly lines. Cut the pipe in 9-foot lengths, join the ends with a plug, and staple it, and you had a round Hula Hoop. They only sold for about a dollar but they were so popular you couldn't keep 'em in stock. Us little boys just couldn't buy them from the jobbers.

"We got the pipe in fourteen different colors—red, green, yellow, several shades of pink. . . . We'd make several thousand a night. Sam would haul his off and spread 'em around his stores.

"He didn't have a truck. He had a sort of trailer hooked to the back of his car. Actually it was a boat, a

jon boat* about 12 feet long on a two-wheeler trailer.
But he made do with it. As a matter of fact we would
go in together on some specials I could buy direct
through my membership in Consolidated Merchants
Association. Items like Hershey chocolate, etc., and
we'd be getting that stuff just as cheap as Woolworth
or Newberry, or anybody. Sam would come over with
his jon boat trailer, and haul off his part of the order."

Every nickel and dime counted. Helen Walton wrin-
kled her nose each time her husband started talking
more stores.

"But," said Bob Bogle, "come hell or high water,
Sam was dead set on branching out!"

---

*Known originally on the Louisiana bayous as a pirogue, the jon
boat is flat-bottomed with blunt ends. Sea Nymph Inc., Syracuse,
Indiana, manufactures about 6,000 annually, the 10-foot version
retailing for $500.

—10—

"A Hell of an Idea!"

The wooded slopes of the Mark Twain National Forest had streamed beneath his wings for half an hour. Two thousand feet below a clearing emerged and an odd pattern in it caught Sam Walton's eye. It was his first time flying over the middle of southern Missouri. He banked and went down for a closer look. The tattered highway map on his lap indicated he was approaching Waynesville and the Fort Leonard Wood Military Reservation.

What he saw turned out to be a vast cluster of over-the-road trailers. There were hundreds of them, many parked in neat rows, but others attached to tractors wheeling about, loading or unloading. Sam Walton had never seen such a bunch of eighteen-wheelers.

In his mind's eye this flurry of truck traffic translated into a welcome and intriguing fact of business life—there must be 10,000-12,000 soldiers and their families right around there and somebody could do well with a Ben Franklin variety store at the front door of Fort Leonard Wood.

As soon as he landed in St. Louis, Sam was on the phone to brother Bud, dispatching him to drive about seventy-five miles southeast from his comfortable little home in Versailles to check out Waynesville for store possibilities.

Sam Walton was in an expansion fever. He was beginning to think big, getting ideas so audacious they even scared him. However, he felt confident, sure of his retailing technique—but trying to improve it, pleased that he and his partners now had eleven variety stores in operation.

The latest stores were in Kansas, one in the small town (population 3,000) of Neodesha, Wilson County, about sixty miles west of Kansas City, and another in larger Coffeyville (population 18,000), twenty miles to the south. It was convenient that both stores were only about a hundred miles northwest of Bentonville. Sam liked to keep his stores clustered for convenient supervision and inspection, but having an airplane erased those previously time-consuming auto trips.

Bud Walton drove into Waynesville and got a surprise of his own. It was a hilly town, about as straight-up-and-down as Eureka Springs, Arkansas. Every location that would accommodate a variety store was under lease; he didn't see any ground flat enough for a new building.

But he heard something was going on in suburban St. Robert. There he found a bulldozer cutting into a hillside, while a heavyset man in shirtsleeves stood beside his car and watched. This was a Waynesville grocer who had finally wrangled the hillside out of a badly snarled estate and was erecting a building for a new grocery; it would be close to a new highway interchange.

Once again Lady Luck smiled on the Waltons.

"In no time at all," said Bob Bogle, "Bud had this guy talked into making his building larger, and we leased part of it. It was 13,000 square feet, which was a pretty fair-sized Ben Franklin in those days. But it wasn't big enough—we had to go to 20,000 in less than a year.

"And it proved Sam had a sharp eye for picking locations! Right off the bat that store did $2 million. There was only one other Ben Franklin store in the

nation—one in upstate New York or maybe in Hawaii—
that had a bigger annual volume.

"That St. Robert store was what put the rest of our
chain on the map. It showed what the potential was
for high-volume sales, and probably gave Sam the idea
of just how far he could go. . . ."

Expansion required money, and the Walton brothers then had little capital as they recalled in their 1987
Wal-Mart World interview:

SAM WALTON: All the stores were opened under different arrangements. It was a collection of partner-
ships and individual ownerships . . . including all the
store managers who could raise money to invest.
BUD WALTON: We were basically all financially strapped,
you might say. We put everything we had in the stores
at the beginning. The decisions were made for Wal-
Mart long before the company was developed. Back in
the Ben Franklin days we learned so much. I think
Sam agrees that St. Robert was the originator of the
Wal-Mart stores. St. Robert showed us how much
volume was there if we went into larger units in small
communities and pushed the merchandise.
SAM WALTON: I suppose Bud is right—we became the
first independent variety chain in the country to try
large stores in small towns. After St. Robert, we found
we could do it in towns like Berryville [Arkansas] and
Bentonville as well. We were doing an inordinate—an
amazing—amount of business in a 13,000-square-foot
store, which is totally out of character for a town of
2,000 people. With the trade area and offering the
customers the assortment, we found we could do a
million dollars in a variety store. That was unheard of!

Even so, in this period—the late 1950s—the advent
of the Wal-Mart phenomenon was a considerable distance in the future. Nor was the growth so magical or
certain. And there were temptations for some lieutenants to desert the Walton army.

Bob Bogle, for instance, suddenly got an offer to

take an $11,000-a-year position in North Carolina in the field where he held a master's degree—public sanitation. "I'm glad now I resisted the temptation," he said, "but at the time it was a difficult choice."

The one who had to shoulder extra responsibility and burdens inside the home because of Sam's mania for more and more and better and better store-keeping was Helen.

In the crucial period when Wal-Mart was being born, Helen often had to be both mother and father.

"Sam worked all hours, so it was tough," she recalled in an article written in the late 1980s for the company house organ. "It was difficult in our early years because he worked so much at night. He didn't start getting up as early in the morning as he started doing later. When it came time to put the children to bed, usually I was home alone."

Daddy's spurts of sixteen-hour-days did not preclude regular family vacations, often long motor trips. "We took the children to Yellowstone, and to Grand Canyon, and on just so many, many camping trips," Helen explained to a recent guest, rebutting published accounts that describe their children's growing up as largely father-less. Helen did concede that in the variety store days Sam "probably was more available than when we became committed to starting Wal-Mart."

It was many years later that she learned one dividend of this situation for her was being forced to learn how to make a life of her own. "Well, you have to take it as it comes," said her article. "You have to learn to have your own interests and responsibilities. Otherwise you can get lost and become a nonentity. I'm sure every woman in a similar situation has had to reinforce her sense of value, to be an individual, and be different. Because the husband is so busy, it's easy to lose yourself in the sidelines. You just have to be yourself and know that you're somebody too."

One of Helen's wifely interests in the middle 1950s was characteristically feminine—to build a new house. She had never lived in a new one.

As a family the Waltons did not appear other than
ordinary, modest Bentonvillians. They made no show
of means; in fact, Sam was not then affluent. No
Cadillac was parked in their B Street driveway, not
even a Buick. Helen had a maid, a black woman
named Elizabeth Dishman, but did her own grocery
shopping, ran her own errands, acted as a Girl Scout
troop leader, spent hour upon hour at the Presbyterian Church, and carried in a steaming casserole for
the regular potluck dinners. The Waltons did not boast,
brag, or show off.

However, they had decided Bentonville would be
their permanent home. It was a very pleasant community; they liked the safety and serenity of a small town,
and besides good quail-hunting fields were nearby.
Helen talked to Sam about building a house. At that
time, Walton had only the one five-and-dime on the
square. But Helen had resources.

Sam began hunting for the kind of quiet site they
wanted. He bought a twenty-acre wooded tract strad-
dling Spring Creek on the east side of town, nine or
ten blocks from the square.

Helen and Sam looked at the ages and sizes of their
four children. They were ready for high school, and in
such a short time the boys and Alice would be out of
the nest, and gone who knows where. They decided to
build a new home while the whole family could enjoy
it—now.

They selected a young architect, a professor at the
University of Arkansas, who had spent a year as a
fellow with the renowned Frank Lloyd Wright. He was
E. Fay Jones, and it was love at first sight when he
tramped over the Waltons' twenty acres, where the
slow little creek gurgled across mossy stones and lifted
quiet music into the shade of a dell flanked by a
hundred small, pretty trees. At once Jones was struck
by an idea—to reverse the concept Frank Lloyd Wright
had used when he cantilevered the Pittsburgh area
residence *Falling Water* over a small mountain waterfall. What he would do for the Waltons was just the

opposite, to dam Spring Creek, and wrap their house around the brook. The location was down a private lane, off Northeast F Street, so the house would almost be hidden from view. It would be built of Arkansas fieldstone, glass, and rough cedar to blend into the landscape. "I remember holding my breath for a while to see whether they'd go along with it," said the architect.

Jones designed an L-shaped house with exposed cedar beams that extended over the exterior balconies and walks, with four bedrooms, three baths, and flagstone floors that also extended outside on the upper level. Outside stairs led to a terrace on the lower level, where the dam created a pond and a lively waterfall, beyond which Spring Creek returned to its original form, a meandering stream that Sam and other residents dub "Town Branch."

It crossed Jones's mind that the house, containing about 5,500 square feet of living space, might be too expensive for the Waltons. "He had just one little store on the square," he said. The estimated cost was $100,000.

Helen was enthusiastic about the design. She told Jones to go ahead. Those close to the Waltons feel certain it could not have been built at the time without Helen's financial resources. "It's Helen's house," said Bill Enfield.*

During construction, Helen consulted with the architect and approved the work. "She had to," said Jones. "Sam was gone a lot. He was rarely there."

The Walton family moved in the first part of October 1959, when first-born Rob had just entered Bentonville High School, with three siblings on his heels.

---

*To friends and associates Sam concedes that Helen's equity in her parents' Oklahoma ranch enabled them to borrow money from banks, but asserts business profits paid for their house, which cost exactly $100,000. When they moved in, the house was mortgaged for $76,000.

The house was not air-conditioned; Sam didn't see the need for that. There were many windows, cross ventilation, and it was comfortable.

As it turned out, the Waltons got exactly what they didn't want—a showplace. However, it was largely hidden from outside view in the trees, and while they entertained friends and relatives in their new home, they did not boast about having the prettiest house in town. But for Jones the Walton residence was a creative achievement that deserved attention and recognition. In 1961 the house won him a national honor award from the American Institute of Architects. Later it would be featured in the October 1978 *Architectural Digest*, although the name of the owner was not disclosed.

Over the years, Jones has exhibited photos and sketches of the house in classrooms and architects' seminars. "I look back on that as a prime example of my work," he said. "Architecturally, I was very pleased with the outcome."

For the owners, it meant a wonderful haven for their children through high school and beyond—for it is still the home of Sam and Helen, and there is no indication they want other quarters, though their mushrooming wealth might easily let them replicate the Taj Mahal. (In the 1989 market, Jones estimated the value of the house at half a million dollars.)

Sam's wife didn't play her strong parental role in a vacuum. Her sacrifice and commitment were generally known in Bentonville. Along with scores of other townsmen, Bill Enfield credited her with a large contribution to the family's business success. "Helen is a worker, and she has been involved," he said.

"I don't know to what extent she was directly involved in the business itself, but of course she, number one, raised the family, and number two, she created a [moral and social] position in the community for them by all that she has done for the community. She has made them very acceptable.

"Everybody loves the Waltons, and it would be very

easy for 'em not to . . . be very easy for this town to have a certain envy, that sort of thing. But you don't see that here."

It was not lost on Helen Walton that having stores later in Neodesha and Coffeyville gave her husband other than pure business reasons for visiting Kansas, especially in the fall and winter. The Kansas quail-hunting season started before Thanksgiving, at least two or three weeks prior to its opening in Oklahoma and Arkansas. And she knew that at the Ben Franklin store in Coffeyville the manager made it a point to stock a few boxes of 28-gauge shotgun shells on his sporting goods counter.

Sam, however, was attentive to his family—when he was around. One of Helen's sorority sisters from the University of Oklahoma, Billy Jo Gourley of Oklahoma City, observed: "I like the way Sam will come in, and every time he gets around her he will put his arm around her. It's just that he is a kind of gentle caring fellow . . . doesn't make a big show of it or anything. You can tell it's just natural. He'll come up and ask if she wants to do this or that, and they work out things together."

But his bird-hunting mania did seem to take an inappropriate precedence. Billy Jo Gourley recalled: "A few years ago I called Helen on her birthday and she was home alone—on her birthday! Sam was off somewhere hunting quail with Jimmy Carter."

When an Elvis Presley movie came to Bentonville, it would pack the Plaza theater; and on a night in 1956 when *Love Me Tender* was shown, Sam and Helen were there. He found time, too, to take the family camping.

"We all used to go over on Buffalo River when it was a state park," Tom Harrison told me. "We became friends right from the day Sam bought my father's store. Every summer a whole crowd of us went, about 20 in all, counting the children, and stayed a week or two. It was about 125 miles from Bentonville.

"Wouldn't be over 25,000 visitors a year in the park

in those days because the pavement didn't run from Yellville to the river and people didn't like driving over the old gravel roads.

"We all had rustic cabins, and everybody enjoyed roughing it. It was wonderful over there. You could go down that river and stop and picnic on a rock, or a gravel bar or a sandbar, and only three or four canoes would pass in a day's time.

"That isolation is no more. Today instead of 25,000, I'd guess the park has 2 million visitors a year, and 500 canoes a day on weekends."

As they grew up, the Walton children were mannerly, polite, "churchy" like their mother, but also full of vim and vigor like their father, and active youngsters —too active at times.

They fell out of trees and wrecked their bikes. "Broken arms and legs!" remembers Bill Enfield. "It was amazing the number of casts in that family at any given time!"

Sam and Helen, too, often comment on this. "When Alice was only four," Helen told a recent visitor, "a horse stepped on her foot and broke her ankle. Jim had his arm in a cast at the same time. I just can't count all the broken bones. We kept Dr. Floyd Taylor in business."

As their father had done, the boys earned spending money by delivering newspapers. Starting with Rob, they took turns delivering in Bentonville the *Arkansas Gazette*. It would surprise no parent who has survived the newsboy experience to know that when it rained or snowed, or the kids were down en masse with some ailment, it was up to Sam or Helen, if he was away, to get out the family station wagon, grab the route book, and hurry around town throwing the *Arkansas Gazette*.

In turn, each youngster became a stock boy at Walton's five-and-dime. That included Alice, as well, when she reached her teens, but her main job was popcorn girl. In the summer that meant moving the popcorn machine out on the sidewalk and hawking the delicious-smelling, fluffy treat to any passerby willing to part with a nickel.

Bob Bogle was their mentor and taskmaster, ever watchful, firm but helpful. "Their parents did not allow them to just pick up any article in the store," he said. "They got paid for working, so if they wanted something, they bought it just like any other customer."*

The Walton sons learned to rue the fluke that kept their dad's store from having a back door. Delivery trucks unloaded out front and the boys had to "two-wheel" all the boxes inside to the storeroom.

The manager tried to instill in these youngsters the same concept of customer satisfaction their father had drilled into him. Said Bob Bogle: "I learned early there is no substitute for customers. We would go to any extent to please a customer. I used to tell all the clerks—they pretty well knew I was joking, but in a way they knew I meant it—in order to make this sale, you've got to be willing to carry the item for the customer all the way to Pea Ridge—that's about ten miles out there. If the customer wasn't pleased with an item, you'd give him his money back or replace the item. That was far cheaper than the advertising dollars you were spending to get him in the store in the first place. It would be silly for us not to give him a new item.

"If he goes away mad, maybe he'll knock off a dozen customers. He'll never tell you he was displeased; he goes and tells everybody else.

"That was Sam's philosophy. We both kind of understood the importance of customer satisfaction from the beginning. And we stressed the importance to our clerks. And I hammered it into his kids."

In the late fifties Bentonville was still pretty much a "Saturday town," largely set in its ways, under the

---

*Helen recalls that their Newport store clerks told her—later—that they were amused because every time she visited the store her first stop was behind the candy case. Such family free-loading was passé when Sam's managers became part-owners.

thumb of Silk Stocking Row, and showing remarkably
little growth. Population still was under 4,000. In the
preceding thirty years local school enrollment had increased only about 700, and now stood at around
1,600. The town did go modern with dial phones on
October 5, 1958.*

The Kraft Food Company plant, which had opened
in 1947 to manufacture Swiss cheese, was now buying
milk from 1,500 dairymen in the Benton County area.
But the poultry growers were in trouble; they were
now being paid only $.10 or $.11 a pound, hardly
enough to break even on feed costs.

"Progress" became the slogan of a young clique in
the chamber of commerce. One goal was to get the
Pea Ridge battlefield designated a national monument
in hopes it would bring in tourist dollars. Another
novel scheme was to stress the advantages of retirees
coming to live in Bentonville.

"Somebody figured," explained J. Dickson Black,
"that if we got a lot of retirees moving here, they
would be older folks mainly, no children to speak of.
So the town wouldn't have to be building many new
schools. Older folks don't drive much, so we'd save
money on streets, too. They even figured seniors would
mean fewer big families that run the garbage disposers
a lot and do a lot of toilet flushing!

"That whole idea didn't cut any ice. It was just
talk."

But Benton County did get a "retirement community"
—Bella Vista, a fifteen-minute drive north of Bentonville
on U. S. 71. In the 1920s it had been a log-cabin
summer resort. Developers turned it into a retirement
village with paved streets, a country club, golf course,
swimming pool, condos, and police and fire protection, with small lots for 10,000 homes. Most new resi-

---

*"That was the worst thing that ever happened here," Sam com-
mented in 1990 while telling an associate about olden days. "Before
that I could just call the operator, Rose, and she could know where
Helen was—and just about everything else going on in town."

dents came from the North, incidentally changing the dominant political party in the country from Democrat to Republican.

Toward the end of the 1950s, Sam Walton began having some big dreams about his future. He began scaling down his involvement in town affairs. He became too occupied to attend many public meetings. Nor was he seen so often on the street.

Normally at sometime in the day, morning for coffee or noon for a soup-and-sandwich lunch, leading businessmen could usually be found in the Horseshoe Café on West Central Avenue, in the shadow of the square. It was Bentonville's voice-activated community bulletin board, where you were certain to get an expert opinion on how Congress should have handled its latest dustup, what the weather was doing to business, crops and the water level over at Beaver Lake, and at the lower end of the gossip spectrum a few whispers about ("Don't say I said it!") this or that juicy little minor league scandal around town and bigger tales involving public figures in Rogers or Springdale or Fayetteville, or even Little Rock.

Noticing Sam Walton's marked absence from this usual haunt, J. Dickson Black strolled around to the five-and-dime for a chat. Sam was visible up in his loft office, hunched over his plywood desk adorned with its usual wild disarray of paper clutter. "He holes up there every day," explained Bob Bogle. "He's working on his new plan!"

A couple of weeks later the town ombudsman called again. "He's still at it," said Bob Bogle. Sam indeed had a pencil and pad, writing or figuring, shuffling books and papers. "He acts like it's something big."

It was.

One of the first basic lessons Sam Walton learned in his training at J. C. Penney in Des Moines was not to be so smug you ignored your competitors, especially their successful policies and practices. He was always going around inspecting variety stores—Newberry, Sterling, T.G.&Y., Kress, Woolworth, any he saw.

"If they had something good, we copied it," Sam Walton always said, with total candor.

"I was totally fascinated by the idea of discounting," Sam recalls. "I heard it started up in New England after World War II. So I went up there to see for myself."

His first stop was in Cumberland, Rhode Island, where a former textile-mill owner and plain pipe-rack, clothing merchant named Martin Chase had come out of semiretirement in 1953 and opened a self-service, low-overhead outlet in a 5,000-foot corner of the defunct Ann & Hope* weaving mill.

"I thought he invented discount retailing," Sam says. Martin Chase was trying to set up his son Irwin in business, and copied the new scheme from Korvette's in New York and two other discounters in New Jersey and New York, who had launched the idea.

"Sam talked to my father," says Irwin Chase, "and I think got a little help. Dad told him if he had low enough overhead, he could sell very cheap. Dad helped a lot of them, including Harry Cunningham, who made K mart what it is." Irwin Chase is president of Ann & Hope Inc., which still has six stores in New England with annual sales of about $250 million.

"There's no one in the world I respect more than Sam Walton," Irwin Chase told me. "He's a great retailer, a great motivator, always asking questions and trying to learn. He never talks about himself; he tries to get you to talk. I'd like to see him in Washington; he's the outstanding kind of person we need in government."

As the 1960s began, Sam Walton had absolutely no interest in government service; what he wanted was to find out all about how to successfully run discount stores. For two years he prowled New England, looking over stores with a true merchant's eye and some-

---

*The building was named for wives of two Brown-Ives textile executives, from families closely associated with Brown University, Providence, Rhode Island.

times interviewing home office executives. He kept a low profile. "He introduced himself as a little country boy from Arkansas," said William F. Kenney, president of the now-defunct Kings department stores.

The "amazing amount of business" being done in the Ann & Hope operation impressed Sam, but there probably was no discount store in existence in 1960-1962 that didn't get a visit from Sam: Spartan, Zayres, Mammoth Mart, Giant, K mart, and a few others.

But it was not Ann & Hope that set the pattern for the yet to be born Wal-Mart discount operation. It was a Pennsylvania-born, fiftyish former newspaper reporter turned merchant named Harry Blair Cunningham who was picked by aging S. S. Kresge to investigate the field and see if Kresge stores should branch out into discount retailing.

"I didn't know Cunningham until much later," says Sam. "He went to see the Ann & Hope people just as I did. He was much more organized than I was. He came up with the K mart concept. What a guy! I have always had the greatest admiration for Harry Cunningham because when he threw that vehicle down, that thing was ten or twenty years ahead of its time, and he did it better than anybody else.

"What I did later was take pieces of it and make our Wal-Mart as much like it as we could. It was a copying proposition. Now [1990] they are coming back and copying us—but making some mistakes.

"At the start we were so amateurish and so far behind! We had our merchandise priced right, and it worked in small towns. K mart just ignored us. They let us stay out here, while we developed and learned our business.

"If they had jumped us . . . I hate to think of that. But we were protected by our small-town market. It would have been unthinkable for them to have tried to put a competing store in a small town. They gave us a ten-year period to grow, and finally we were able to hold our own.

"K mart stayed with it too long. They were self-

satisfied with what they had accomplished. They thought
they could roll over everybody. And they woke up one
day and found out the world had changed, retailing
had changed. They were behind."

Of course, Sam Walton was speaking about what he
had learned by the seventies. But as 1961 began, he
was toying with the idea of buying stock in the Bank
of Bentonville, urged by his attorney, Bill Enfield. He
finally did, and on March 23, 1961, the *Benton County
Democrat* carried a page-one story stating that Sam
Walton had been elected a director of the bank. The
newspaper pointed out that he and his partners operated thirteen variety stores in three states, and listed
all his city council, Rotary, chamber of commerce, and
Presbyterian church credits.

However, the Bank of Bentonville was in serious
trouble. A young Arkansawyer—who was then a
stranger to Sam Walton but would be destined to play
a tremendously important role in the rise of the coming Wal-Mart empire—stepped forward to bail out the
bank.

He was a "barefoot whiz kid" at one of the most
powerful banks in the Southwest, Republic National
of Dallas, thirty-year-old James H. Jones. Born in
1930 at Alpena, a tiny railroad junction fifteen miles
out of Harrison, Jones graduated from the University
of Arkansas, and received banking management degrees from Southern Methodist University and Harvard Business School.

Just out of college, Jones joined Republic National
Bank in 1954 and rose quickly, becoming a vice-
president in 1960. He spoke with an Arkansas twang,
had a pleasant good-ole-boy manner, and made friends
easily. The Dallas bank assigned him to travel Arkansas and Missouri, soliciting business from banks and
companies.

Just how he got involved with Sam Walton in August 1961 is best told by Jones himself in an interview
with me:

It's a long, interesting story, a
had been traveling Arkansas and Mi
three years. The bank in Bentonville h.
and one-half million in total assets, a
was in trouble. It had some loan problem
guy controlled the bank—he's still alive and
him and we're still friends—but I got an option
him to buy control of the bank.

Two bankers over in Fayetteville, Arkansas, Buck
Lewis and Ellis Shelton, ran and controlled the First
National in Fayetteville, the biggest bank in northwest Arkansas. The three of us were going to buy
the Bank of Bentonville as an investment and run it.

At the last minute Buck and Ellis decided they
didn't want to do it. They were afraid it might hurt
them with other banks in the area doing business
with their bank. I said, "Well, hell, I'm not gonna
do it alone, and so forth and so on, but I wanted to
keep control of the business. So I said, "Do you
know anybody up there you think would be interested in buying the bank?"

I think it was Buck who said, "Well, we don't
know anybody right now, but there's a guy over in
Bentonville named Sam Walton we hear has some
Ben Franklin stores who is interested in expanding."
They hadn't met him, but they had heard about him.

So I'll never forget as long as I live the time I
picked up the phone and called Sam Walton from
the bank at Dallas and told him who I was. I said,
"I've got an option to buy the Bentonville bank, uh,
if you are interested and your financials are all right,
and this that and the other, I'll loan you one hundred percent of the money at three and a half percent and a lifetime to pay."

Back then if you owned a bank, you could use the
balances to support your other businesses. That was
a common thing done then, and I explained it all to
him.

We talked quite a while, and he said, "Aw, I
don't think I'm interested."

"You think about it overnight," I said, "and call
me back."

e next day the phone rang, and he said, "I've
een thinking about this, and talked to my wife, and
I'd like to talk to you about it."

So my wife and I got in the car and drove up to
Bentonville and went out to his house.

We sat outside and talked about the whole deal
and he decided to buy the bank. I asked him for a
financial statement, and he didn't have one.

He grabbed a brown paper bag and started making some numbers.

"Hell, Sam," I said, "you haven't got anything I
can loan money on except your reputation!"

So I asked Helen if she had anything, and I learned
that her father was a lawyer and a banker over in
Claremore and bought all through the years about
20,000 acres of land starting at Tulsa and going east.

She had some nice things, you know, in her trust
so I had Helen endorse the loan.

I had them both sign and I loaned them $350,000,
we hired the management, and I made out the financial statement, made out press releases, and he owned
the bank!

Back in those days under Fred Florence, who
built our Republic Bank, we were training bank
people first, and everything else fell into place. Today, you know, it's computers first and to hell with
people. . . . That's what's wrong with the banking
business, in my opinion.

But that's how I got acquainted with Sam Walton.
Then I started financing his expansions of Ben Franklin stores, one at a time, and he finally got up to
seventeen or nineteen. He kept talking about the
discount business like K mart had really going back
then, and Gibson's.

The old Gibson stores—that's really what he was
looking at. So I did a little research and looked at it
and told him, "I think you've got a hell of an idea,
going into these little towns. I think it will work."

And I agreed to loan him money and back him.

Of course, as any old-time Benton County rustic
might put it, it does take money to make the old mare

go, and now Sam had it, but the buggy needs four tight and sturdy wheels, and plenty of grease on the axles, or you ain't gonna get a very fur piece up the road.

And the truth of the matter was that at that time, Sam Walton hadn't got hold of his necessary wheels or enough axle grease.

—11—

Watermelons and a Donkey Mess

Trucks rumbled and taxi horns blared on the streets of Chicago, in the winter of 1962 outside the headquarters of Ben Franklin Stores, Inc. Inside, Sam Walton leaned on the board room's polished table and made an offer that startled the top corporate executives.

His proposal was audacious, perhaps impertinent—certainly unacceptable! He suggested that the variety store franchisers leap into the frontline of the booming discount business.

"I think that kind of store will fit in the rural markets just as well as in the major metropolitan markets," said Sam. "You should franchise them. I'll be your guinea pig."

The Ben Franklin brass exchanged sour looks. Sam went on: They'd have to cut their wholesale prices. Instead of making 20 to 25 percent profit off the merchandise they sold their retailers, the Ben Franklin warehouses would have to be satisfied with about 12.5 percent.

"They blew up!" said Sam Walton.

To these sophisticated and experienced businessmen in natty tailored suits and custom shoes, it looked like the tail was trying to wag the dog. What was that Arkansas country fellow's experience with only a dozen

116

or so stores compared to their thousand outlets and nearly a century of retailing know-how?

The Ben Franklin outfit was cannonading its field anyhow, making tremendous strides forward. Butler Brothers had gobbled up 128 T. G.&Y. stores and then merged with City Products Corporation of Chicago. And further consolidation involving 110 Scott Stores was in the wings. Finally there were plans for Butler Brothers to come under the parental umbrella of the money giant Household Finance Corporation.

Sam Walton was trying to toss two bits on the crap table where the big boys were casually flinging down $10,000 chips. But he was undaunted by their rebuff. He held on to his dream; he would find another way.

The next day one of the Ben Franklin executives, Donald G. Soderquist, went out for a close look at the first of the new K mart discount stores to invade the Chicago suburbs. He got a surprise; Sam Walton was there ahead of him.

Said Soderquist: "Here he was, twenty-five miles from our office, and he was talking to a clerk. He was writing in a little spiral notebook, and at one point he got down on his knees to look under the display cabinet. I said, 'Mr. Walton, what are you doing?' He said, 'Just part of the education process, Don. I'm still learning.' "

That episode made an impression on Don Soderquist, to such an extent that a decade later Sam Walton would be able to woo him into taking one of the highest posts in the Wal-Mart hierarchy.

But now, in 1962, Sam had to return to Bentonville no further along in his quest for a toehold in the discount store business than when he had gone to Chicago. He knew whom to blame for this failure—himself. He had slowed down, taking life too easy.

"At that time," Sam said, "Bud would go fishing

and Helen and I went camping, played a lot of tennis, and we had a lot of time for our kids.*

"We could see that this discount concept eventually would lead to warehousing, buyers, the whole commitment that was required to run a chain. We'd been spoiled by working out of the Ben Franklin warehouse, their program. We had their book, the regulations and everything was laid out for us—all we had to do was be good readers and execute. So I thought Ben Franklin had worked pretty good so why not go up there and ask them to do the same thing for our new discount operation?

"They would do the buying and the warehousing and we'd execute and run it for them. . . . But to do that they'd have to make a commitment to buy real low and sell it to us at a very low margin—not nearly what they had been charging us at Ben Franklin. We in turn could pass on the savings to our customers—give them the prices I knew we'd have to give them.

"Well . . . they just went straight up in the air!

"They just couldn't see the philosophy. It might not have worked with somebody in between. It may not have been the logical approach. But we thought it was. When they turned us down, that left Bud and I to swim on our own."

The drubbing in Chicago might have vanquished a man less strong than this Arkansawyer. It only made Sam think deeper, and try harder. "I was threshing around for the right way to go," he remembers.

Sam had been watching a new store that had opened

---

*To what extent Sam can be characterized as an "absentee" father is subject to interpretation. Helen, and her closest friends, say the day-to-day parenting of the four children as they were growing up fell largely to her. However, John, as an adult, told the author they never felt neglected by their father. He came when he could to their school events and served as leader of their Boy Scout troop. Each child, at least for a time, rejected the idea of a lifelong career as a merchant, if that meant emulating their father's workaholic ways. Regardless, there exists no strife or rancor today inside the family. It is solid and unified.

in Fayetteville. It was a discount store called Gibson's. It sold mainly appliance-type items, not really Walton's style, since he preferred a variety-store line. But he had driven often to Fayetteville to see how this new breed of cat was behaving and whether Gibson's had any tricks he could lift. Not only was he investigating their techniques used to attract customers and move merchandise, he was also looking for their mistakes.

The Gibson slogan was "Stack It High and Sell It Low." Their stores stretched all across Texas, Arkansas, and a few nearby states. They were no-frills, warehouse-looking outlets that lived up to their motto.

It occurred to Sam that he might somehow piggyback on the Gibson juggernaut—either by getting some of their franchises or by buying merchandise through their general offices.

The man from Bentonville found much to admire, and perhaps envy, in the founder of Gibson Discount Stores. He was a gruff, suspender-snapping Arkansawyer named Herbert R. Gibson Sr. Born in the little Ozark mountain town of Berryville in 1901, he worked as a barber, wrestler, streetcar conductor, and merchant in Missouri and Arkansas. He left Little Rock in 1935 for Dallas, where he set up as a wholesale distributor for health and beauty aids.

Gibson jumped in early on discounting and helped introduce Americans to buying marked-down goods off shelves of minimally decorated, barn-like stores. He opened his first store in 1957 in Abilene, Texas—and at its peak the chain would operate 550 stores in 33 states.

Getting excited about Gibson possibilities, Sam abruptly decided to beard the lion in his den. He went unannounced to Dallas and marched into Herb Gibson's headquarters, arriving about noon, and asked to see the head man. Sam was told to be seated, and Gibson would be informed he was waiting. Sam thumbed through trade magazines, using his idle time to look for new ideas. He was patient; this mission was important.

About five o'clock, according to Jim Dodson, who later heard about the episode, Herb Gibson finally summoned Walton to his office and let him explain his mission.

"Do you have one hundred thousand dollars?" Gibson asked.

"No."

"Well, we buy in carload lots. Takes a lot of money to do that."

"But, I—"

"You're not fixed to do business with us. Good-bye."

Sam took the sting of a fresh rebuff in stride. He had faith he'd somehow get on the right track. He'd just have to keep plugging and grow big enough to command both respect and carlot prices.

What already was happening in the variety store industry made him shudder. He saw the power—and the menace—of Sebastian S. Kresge's giant company. Founded in 1899, it grew so swiftly that by 1912 it comprised eighty-five stores with annual sales of $10,325,000.

Now, even though Kresge was ninety-five years old, he had directed Harry Cunningham to lead the company in 1962 into discounting. The first K mart store was opened in a Detroit suburb. By 1966 Kresge sales would top $1 billion with a total of 915 stores, of which 162 would be K marts. And ten years later it would become the second largest retailer in the United States, with sales of $8.4 billion at 1,647 stores, the majority of which, 1,206, were K marts.

This was the retailing tidal wave on which Sam Walton hoped to ride the crest, with very limited resources, and swim all the way to a fortune.

He was already wrestling at home with a large challenge. He discovered that the banking business was no piece of cake. The new president he brought in from Urbana, Missouri, Larry W. Meier Jr., didn't work out. The bank also was in the process of erecting its first new building in thirty years and moving to the northeast corner of the square.

In the midst of this banking turmoil, Sam was in almost constant consultation with his new financial mentor, the personable James Jones at Republic National in Dallas, about his scheme to plunge into discounting. One condition written into Sam's bank mortgage was that Jones would have to give approval for opening additional stores, since Republic National would be financing them. Jones was present for the February 9, 1963, opening of the new bank building; he helped find a new president, Ed Buck, who had put in twenty-five years as an executive in Springdale and Fayetteville banks. Buck proved to be a wise choice, a man who understood Arkansas manners and mores; he would run the bank for fifteen years and increase assets to $51,800,000. (Likewise Jones would help Sam expand his banking horizons by buying control, on March 7, 1963, of the Bank of Pea Ridge, which had been founded in 1911 by W. T. Patterson.)

But in 1962 the main thing on Sam's mind was getting started as a discounter. It was not easy.

"Republic Bank basically controlled [Sam's expansion ambitions] for the first few years," said Jones. "I had to approve everything, and I was up there all the time. We decided to put the first store in Rogers. It took us about a year and a half to agree on the site. Sam wanted one and I wanted another, and we finally agreed on a site and that's where we put the first store."

Initially, to launch his new venture Sam tried to team up with the holder of the Ben Franklin franchise in Rogers, Max Russell. Said Bob Bogle: "Sam went to Max and suggested they go in together and put up a new building that would have parking and be large enough to serve the needs of a growing community.

"Well, Max was in the real estate business and he had a real nice comfortable living and he was well up in years and he just didn't see the wisdom in that. So Sam went to Larry Larimore [a Rogers real estate dealer] and he put up a building for us at West Eighth and Walnut Streets, not too large, only about 16,000 square feet."

Shortly before the building was completed, Sam was flying to Fort Smith, taking Bogle along in the plane, to interview a prospective new employee. While they were in the air, said Bogle, Sam pulled a card out of his pocket.

"Bob, we've got to figure out what to call this thing," he said. "We can't call it Ben Franklin." He handed the card to Bogle. On it were scrawled three or four prospective names for the new discount store. "Which one of those do you think we should call it?"

Bogle studied the list for a few minutes. All were long names, each made up of three or four words.

"Well, Sam," he said, at last, "you've had me buying the letters to go up on our Ben Franklin stores and I know how much they cost and how much they cost to repair, and how much to light. It's expensive to put that many words in a name.

"As Scotch as I am, I'd keep our Walton name. . . . Listen, I've got one idea." Bob Bogle took his pen and wrote below the boss's list: WAL-MART. "I'd make it just like this; that keeps the Walton name and adds a place to shop."

Sam glanced at it briefly, grunted, and stuck the list back in his pocket.

"He didn't make any comment," said Bob Bogle. "And the subject wasn't discussed after that. We went on to Fort Smith, and we talked to a guy down there who later came to work for the company.

"A few days later I went over to Rogers to check on the store and see when we were going to set the fixtures. Mr. Jacobs was our sign painter, and he was there in front of the building with a ladder. He already had the *W* and *A* and *L* in place and he was going up the ladder with the M. So I could pretty well figure out what this thing was going to be called. But Sam—he never said boo to me about it."

Years later when Wal-Mart was having Wilson Sporting Goods manufacture tennis balls branded Wal-Mart, the question of trademark copyright came up. Rob Walton was by that time the company lawyer. Said

Bogle: "Rob raised the question of whether we'd ever got a copyright or trademark on the name. I told him not that I knew. 'I'll get on that right quick,' he said. We'd gone along for years using the name Wal-Mart without really owning it. Anyway, Rob got busy and got us legal."

In spite of Sam Walton's detailed planning, hard struggles, and rose-colored confidence, the birth of the first Wal-Mart Discount Store did not rock the town of Rogers to its very foundations. To begin with, it was very small, only 16,000 square feet. It opened with no fixtures except tables, according to Clarence Leis, who became manager six months later. He told me in an interview: "That's what Sam Walton was unhappy about. It had tables in about two-thirds of the floor and a few racks. Nothing was put together and nothing was categorized, just put in there like a big sale.

"When I came in the first thing I began to do was put things together and categorize the departmental items. And then in 1964 we remodeled it the first time. We added 4,000 square feet, giving us our first stockroom. My wife and I and her three sisters and their husbands and three other men totally relaid that store in one night. We moved every table and every counter in the store. We didn't have end caps as such, and we stacked a lot of merchandise on the floor.

"And we didn't have time to do anything further before Thanksgiving so that's the way we left it. And from that day, that store for fifteen years had about a 30 percent annual increase in sales. The first year the volume was $700,000. And when it was moved across the street in 1974 as a 60,000 square-foot store, it did $5.4 million.

"The clerks got $.50 or $.60 cents an hour, as I remember. Not many years later that went to $1.00 an hour, which was about twice what I thought they were worth."

Said No. 1's manager: "That store made a profit from the beginning. It wasn't as much as Mr. Sam wanted, or what it should have been. But we got that worked out.

"We didn't have a lot of direct sources [manufacturers] —especially in the health and beauty aids [H&BA] department—but we did have a direct source for toilet paper and the like. We'd order carloads of sanitary goods, and stack 200 cases on the floor.

"Right from the beginning, we had a whole wall of H&BA. And we had auto [supplies] and oil in the back. Oil sold by the truckload at five quarts for a dollar."

From his vantage point, James Jones remembered "tough times" starting up Wal-Mart. Jones said: "In the beginning a lot of big manufacturers wouldn't sell to us. There's some that still won't today. For instance, Levi's. They just wouldn't do it. . . . Because we're a mass merchandiser or a discounter, some excuse like that.

"Starting out we had merchandise that you wouldn't believe. A lot of it was low quality, or medium quality. We had to buy where we could. But that was all right. Every year we kept upgrading it, as we got into these manufacturers, but at first it was real tough."

And the boss haunted his infant Wal-Mart store, looking for flaws, praising clerks for what they were doing right, poring over the manager's monthly report.

In late fall he phoned Clarence Leis. "I've just looked over your report, Clarence. You're twenty thousand dollars over inventory! Don't buy anything else until you get back in line."

"Yes, sir," responded the store manager. He was young, eager, and loyal to the boss.

Around Thanksgiving Sam came prowling through the Rogers Wal-Mart No. 1. In the men's department, he stopped at the shirt counter, and exploded when he found it totally empty.

"Clarence! Where are your shirts?"

Leis gave him a woebegone look. "I'm still overstocked. I didn't order—"

"Use common sense," interrupted Sam Walton. "Don't ever run out of shirts and things you need.

What I meant was when you're long on inventory, don't load up with useless odds and ends."

Highway 62 from the south into Harrison descends a long hill, turns sharply across a bridge, and reaches the town square just two blocks beyond the banks of Crooked Creek. The traditional redbrick Boone County courthouse sits in the middle of the square. The town is larger than Bentonville, around 10,000 population, even more imbued with Confederate heritage, with strong and active ladies in the U.D.C., and decidedly more aristocratic because some of its old families are quite well-to-do.

From the square, hills rise on every side, and a few streets climb at a 45-degree angle. Crooked Creek gurgles over gravel shoals so shallow that in times past a horse and buggy could ford it. Every ten or twenty years when cloudbursts assaulted the Ozarks, Crooked Creek would rise and flood the square, lapping at the courthouse door. Sam Walton remembers the tragic damage of the 1964 flood.

Harrison was a prosperous town with old-fashioned traditions built on integrity and word of honor among its merchants and professional people. Sam Walton discovered the intrinsic and binding power of a Harrison handshake when he picked this town, eighty miles east of Rogers, as the location for Wal-Mart No. 2. He came to Harrison in the early summer of 1964 and found on the north edge of town, near the Highway 62 bypass, a suitable vacant building. The owner was Rex Younes, who put up a row of store buildings on acreage he had used for a cattle auction yard until the city zoned that out of existence.

"I want this building," Sam told the owner. "And your terms are agreeable."

"Then I suppose we ought to draw up a contract," said Younes.

Sam looked him in the eye. "Your word is good enough for me, Mr. Younes, if mine is good enough for you."

"Perfectly fine," said the landlord. They shook hands, and the deal—amazing in view of the fiasco of a non-renewable lease on the Newport Ben Franklin store—existed in perfect harmony for at least four or five years, before it was put into writing.

Grace McCutcheon, a middle-aged Harrison house-wife, was the first salesperson hired for Wal-Mart No. 2. The second week in July she walked in and found the place a shambles, with the opening set for mid-August. Carpenters were at work, several boys were running around, there was a jumble of corrugated cartons helter-skelter in the corners of the bare concrete floor. No shelves or tables were in place.

Grace McCutcheon remembers:

> Those boys were trying to get the counters in place. We didn't have any rest-rooms. The manager, Don Whittaker, made arrangements with Mickey Pace who had a beauty shop next door to let us use hers.
>
> The first thing they put me doing was checking Dr. Scholl's foot products. I'd never heard of Dr. Scholl's. I'd never had any foot problems, except putting mine in my mouth.
>
> But anyway Mr. Whittaker was a rough-talking man. If you didn't know him, he would scare you to death. After you got to know him, you liked him. He was yelling at this boy and that boy; he didn't say much to me and I didn't say *anything* to him.
>
> I took my copy of the invoice, and this wasn't prepriced, and I had to figure it out and mark it up so much and hope I got it right. Next thing they put me on was some imported china and pretty glass-ware, and a dozen little figurines. They were scattered among all the boxes and I had to dig until I found them.

The shelves, salvaged from a defunct five-and-dime, were brown-painted boards flecked with white. "We thought they looked pretty spiffy," Sam reminisced not long ago. But they were a challenge to the crew setting up store No. 2. The shelves were not fastened to their upright brackets. When Grace McCutcheon and the others stacked merchandise on one end, the other would fly up. "We solved that," said Grace McCutcheon. "Just started stacking in the middle, and worked out to the ends. Anyway, we finally got the store ready to open."

That proved a memorable day—perhaps some kind of seriocomic highlight in the entire history of Wal-Mart Stores, Inc.

Sam Walton was on hand. James Jones came from Dallas. Clarence Leis arrived from Wal-Mart No. 1 and assisted in the final preopening days. Other Walton hired hands were brought in to work the opening show.

Notably present was a skeptic from the Little Rock office of Cranks Drug Company of Springfield, Missouri, which was in the process of being sold to a New York concern. His name was David Dayne Glass: he had been the whiz kid top financial officer of Cranks. He was well acquainted with Sam Walton, who was urging him to take a job in Wal-Mart's main office. Glass thought Sam might have lost his marbles with all this discount store foolishness. It would surprise him if this kind of store had any future in Arkansas, or anywhere else.

"It was the worst retail store I had ever seen," said David Glass. "Sam had brought a couple of trucks of watermelons in and stacked them on the sidewalk.

"He had a donkey ride out in the parking lot. It was 115 degrees, and the watermelons began to pop, and the donkey began to do what donkeys do, and it all mixed together and ran all over the parking lot.

"And when you went inside the store, the mess just continued, having been tracked in all over the floor.

"He was a nice fellow, but I wrote him off. It was just terrible."

Like so many before him—and since—David Glass was guilty of snap judgment on unorthodox merchandiser Sam Walton. The skeptic from Little Rock didn't have a clear perception of where Walton was heading in retailing, or how he would get there, and—more important in David Glass's case—who would be laboring mightily at his side when he hit the big time.

That very point was addressed—after Sam became a phenomenal success—by *Fortune* magazine in a 1989 article by John Huey:

So how—from there—did Sam Walton get to be America's most admired retailer?

The theory here is that he willed it through sheer force of a complex personality. As the donkey-watermelon episode illustrates, he is an old-fashioned promoter in the P. T. Barnum style.

But he is more than that. He's a little bit Jimmy Stewart—handsome and halting "Aw, shucks" charm. He's a little bit Billy Graham, with a charisma and a persuasiveness that heartland folks find hard to resist. And he's more than a little bit Henry Ford, a business genius who sees how all parts of the economic puzzle relate to his business.

Overlaying everything is a lot of the old yard rooster who is tough, loves a good fight, and protects his territory.

On that torrid August day at the birth of Wal-Mart No. 2, David Glass had no idea that twenty-six years later Sam Walton would make him chief executive of the nation's miracle discount empire.

Said Glass, when he knew quite a bit more than he did in 1962: "The thing that I underestimated about Sam is that he has an overriding something in him that causes him to improve every day. That's not difficult when you have something as bad as he had in Harrison, but sometimes you achieve success and say, 'Boy, now I got it like I want it. Now I can lay back a little and enjoy it.' Sam has never done that. As long as I have known him, he has never gotten to the point where he is comfortable with who he is or how we are doing."

Grace McCutcheon, proud of having played a sweaty role in the birth of the Wal-Mart No. 2 store, had a more charitable view of the Harrison "disaster."

"We opened at nine," she said. "Nine till nine. Those watermelons hadn't burst when we opened—that was later in the day, and some of it was the next day. They had this little donkey out there for the children to ride. It was free. That was Mr. Sam's idea. He came over for the opening.

"He is a wonderful person. He may tell the managers that the store looks awful, or this and that, but I never in my life heard him tell one of the employees out on the floor that they wasn't doing a good job. He'd meet 'em and shake hands with 'em and say, 'You're doing a good job. . . . Looks good.' If it could be a little better, he'd say, 'You can do this or you can do that.'

"He makes you feel good. I'm sure he did tell the managers things they ought to do. I always liked to see him come because he made me feel like maybe I was important."

Grace McCutcheon, who started at $.95 an hour, felt important enough to stay in the Harrison store until she reached retirement age, and then came back for a few years part time as a front-door greeter. "I enjoyed my years at Wal-Mart. It wasn't all pleasant. There were some days when I'd get so mad, I'd want to just walk out. But I didn't. It wasn't anybody's fault anymore than it was mine."

With the Harrison store off and running—under that astounding hand-shake rental agreement—Sam Walton was already on the lookout for a new town in which to open another store. But he felt the fledgling Wal-Mart general office was woefully strapped for experienced merchandisers who could help him expand.

—12—

Finding a Few Key Men

Sam Walton sipped a cup of coffee at the F. W. Woolworth lunch counter in Memphis. On the adjacent stool sat the assistant manager from McCrory, another five-and-dime across the street. Sam had flown down to try to hire him. This was just one of Sam's many recruiting forays in the early sixties to get new managerial talent. He needed promising men for his expanding Ben Franklin variety store chain, and to help achieve his dream of a discount store empire.

But this early-morning interview in 1960 wasn't going well. The McCrory man was doubtful he could give up Memphis's excitement for uneventful small-town life. Sam, sensing it was going to be "no sale," glanced around the Woolworth store and saw its manager, Claude Harris, strolling the aisles. Sam wondered about him.

Obviously it is best to fill managerial and executive positions with experienced individuals brought up through the ranks of your own organization. Sam Walton understood this, but he didn't have the time to invest in this process. Being in a rush, he decided to see whether the competition had anybody he wanted. His tactics later prompted *Discount Store News* to describe him as a modern-day combination of Vince Lombardi (insisting on solid execution of the basics) and General George S. Patton. ("A good plan, violently executed now, is better than a perfect plan next week.")

Having struck out with the McCrory man, Sam called the Woolworth manager over to the lunch counter for a talk; he has always been credited with a rare knack for seeing inside people and expertly analyzing their talent and character.

Bill Enfield, who has been an intimate of Walton's since 1950, has long marveled at this trait of Sam's. He told me: "I've thought about it quite a bit, and I think one of the principal reasons that Sam was successful is because of his ability to motivate people. He is a tremendous motivator. He also has a peculiar faculty for being able to evaluate people. Not all of us are that good at selecting someone who then does a great job, but he invariably can see into people well enough that he could get out of them what he really wanted."

Did Sam Walton measure a prospective employee by some sort of mental yardstick, looking for certain standards of morality, education, honesty, ambition, aggressiveness?

"I would think so," said Enfield. "He absolutely would not have anything to do with anyone who would be satisfied with what's now. Sam just absolutely insists that people that he uses, the people that work for him, must have that drive, that ambition to do something better, to do something more—because that's the way he is and always has been. If they change, then he gets rid of them.

"There's no 'standard' type. I'm sure Sam has a sixth sense about hiring. If you got together one hundred of his Wal-Mart managers and executives, you'd have one hundred different people. There's no pattern."

But getting back to the Woolworth story, by the end of his second cup of coffee, Sam was offering the Woolworth manager a job.

"I told him no, real quick," said Claude Harris. "I had a good job, and I didn't even know him. But Sam followed up. He seemed to know in advance every

time my wife and I visited her grandmother in Bentonville. I was finally convinced when I was at Sam's
house one day and Bob Bogle's kids ran in and jumped
up on Sam's lap. That little touch helped convince me
that Sam Walton was everything he appeared to be."

It was a lucky day for both Claude Harris and Walton. Sam got an excellent retailer to come in at the
very start, an executive so talented he would rise in
the Wal-Mart corporate structure to senior vice-
president of marketing, one of the most critical positions in discount store operations.

When Sam Walton turned forty-eight on March 29,
1966, he was still caught in the throes of business
expansion. By this time he and his partners had in
operation four Wal-Mart discount stores and eighteen
Ben Franklin variety stores. Wal-Mart No. 3 opened
in Siloam Springs, and No. 4 in Springdale. Fortunately, the flaws in the Rogers store had been ferreted
out and corrected, and from the start the profit margin
of the Harrison store was very satisfactory. Sam was
building a good base on which to move ahead.

To fellow merchants around the Bentonville square,
Sam showed no visible change these days. His struggling Wal-Mart chain, still in its infancy, demanded
more of his time, but he remained pretty much a
regular in his old haunts. When he didn't join the
early breakfast crowd at the Horseshoe Café, he usually dropped in later for coffee and a chat with friends.
He was cheerful, friendly, talkative—no change.

The men envied his good health, tennis-trim figure,
and athletic stride, the obvious byproducts of his discipline as a youth, when his motto had been work,
work, and more work. Sam wasn't changing with the
times; none of the "mod" trappings beginning to in-
fect masculine fashion rubbed off on him. Long hair,
sideburns, and beards were commonplace—even among
his own sons and many employees. His fairly thin hair
was still kept close-cut and combed back. He shaved
regularly, and his attire was conservative, though often casual. In the main, he looked old-fashioned. He

could crack a smile, but he was usually sober-faced, with good reason.

Getting launched as a discounter was almost too much for one man. He needed help. It was necessary to achieve two things—and rather quickly if he was to go on. First, he needed to buy merchandise at lower prices than the Butler Brothers' Ben Franklin warehouses offered. Second, and equally important, were the smart and aggressive retail executives Sam needed to bring into the Wal-Mart headquarters to help him expand his new concept of big stores offering low prices in small towns. The awkward Wal-Mart opening in Harrison caused experienced, prospective hires like David Glass either to shake their heads in disbelief or voice downright scorn and ridicule. Sam would have to work hard to change the industry's perception of his Wal-Mart outfit.

Although frugality was essential, he had finally given up his plywood desk, orange-crate shelves, and loft office in Walton's five-and-dime. Bill Enfield and his partner, Clayton Little, surrendered their second-floor suite on the south side of the square and took ground-floor space in a former Western Auto Supply store. Sam rented the old law offices plus an additional upstairs room and moved in his small staff of Wal-Mart merchandisers, buyers, and supervisors.

At this juncture he began his most intensive head hunting. Now he sorely needed, if he were to continue branching out in discounting, two first-class executives. He put out feelers with trade sources in several states for both a variety store executive who grasped the potential that discounting offered and a certified public accountant to do the necessary creative financing.

Walton heard impressively of Ferold G. Arend, the regional manager in Omaha for the J. J. Newberry chain of variety stores. Sam and Helen went to see him. Luck favored the Waltons. Arend was already piqued with his treatment by the Newberry company, which had just changed ownership.

But Arend was not at all certain he should jump to

Wal-Mart. It was only an infant concern, with the look of a shoestring operation that had a highly problematic future. Wouldn't an executive in a good, established job be a fool to leap into such a gamble with some country-boy dreamer who might get quickly washed out by K mart, Gibson, and the other big guys?

Sam started trying to make Arend see the light. Helen worked on Mrs. Arend.

Arend already knew something about discounting. He had experimented with such cut-rate pricing in his region, and got called down by the company. He listened closely to Walton's job offer.

"Finally, I could see Sam Walton had a future," said Arend. "He believed in discounting into smaller communities. I was experimenting myself and trying to get our company enthused about this. All I caught was heck for trying something. Anyway, I could see a future with him, that was the main thing."

Sam remembers that his argument in trying to lure Arend, and others, from a larger company had two main prongs: "I guess we were able to sell them on the good quality of life in Bentonville. And the opportunity with a young company. . . . It took some selling. Ferold probably took the biggest gamble at that time."

Sam's ace recruiting backup was his wife. "Helen was with me lots of times when we went to talk to managers," he said during a joint interview they gave *Wal-Mart World* in 1987.

"Yes," said Helen, "we usually took the wives out, too. I'm sure lots of people weren't doing that in those days."

The national chains seemed to pay little heed to the Walton raids. "They didn't worry about us, not until much later," said Sam. "They would just tell their guys at that point that they'd made terrible mistakes. Newberry's had just changed hands and the people were shaking out—so it was fair ground to work on."

Making the switch from bustling Omaha to a small rural town in Arkansas was a jolt for both Arend and his wife. He almost had second thoughts, saying: "It was really tough coming from a city, living in a nice home. . . . There weren't many nice homes down here at that time, and our Wal-Mart offices were very preliminary—primitive, I should say. Anyway, it was quite a change!"

Tom Harrison, a neighbor of the Arends, once asked Ferold why he decided to leave Newberry. "He said, 'Well, Sam came up and talked to me. . . . You couldn't help but believe he was telling you what was what, and what he had in mind, and what he was looking for. And he convinced me it was an opportunity.' At Ferold's age—he was in his forties—if he was ever going to make a change now seemed the right time.

"He said he went around with Sam. 'Whatever he told me, it was exactly that way. We'd go into his stores and walk around. Somewhere the manager or assistant manager would be doing an exceptional job. Sam would say he ought to do something a little extra for that manager. That stunned me! Newberry would never have said anything like that. Newberry cared less for the people that helped. In Newberry's they never would have made a statement like that.' "

Helen Walton's role in the search for talent to complete the transition from Ben Franklin five-and-dimes to Wal-Mart discount stores was considerable. She often helped her husband interview and evaluate prospective hires. She held a sort of tacit veto power, says Clarence Leis, who was running a McCrory variety store in Vinita, Oklahoma, when Sam first got interested in him. Leis explained: "My friend Willard Walker, who managed the Walton five-and-dime at Fayetteville, phoned me and asked if I might want to come and work for Sam. I thought about it for a while and then called Sam and said I was interested. He and Helen came to Vinita to interview me—at that time Sam and Helen didn't hire anyone unless they both saw him."

Two weeks later Leis went to Bentonville to talk some more. Sam and Helen put him up in their home during several days of negotiations. That wasn't unusual, as Leis explained: "Many a night I've spent in one of the Waltons' guest rooms. If you were in Bentonville, Sam wouldn't tolerate you staying anywhere else." Before going to Rogers to manage Wal-Mart No. 1, Leis put in about a year as manager of the Walton five-and-dime in Coffeyville.

Through mutual friends, the Waltons heard of a CPA in Harrison named James T. Henry. Sam and Helen looked him over, were impressed, and asked him to become Wal-Mart's financial and accounting officer. Jim Henry was dubious about leaving his partnership in a CPA firm that had six offices in Arkansas.

But the Waltons wouldn't give up. They wooed him for a year.

"At that time discounting was in its infancy," Jim Henry said in our interview. "The looks of the stores and some of the types of merchandise in the beginning, quite honestly, were not up to what they very quickly became.

"It was a new innovation as far as retailing was concerned. I was skeptical of being able to operate on such a low margin. But it was a challenge, and of course Sam has the type of personality that is pretty convincing."

Even so, Henry did a little on-the-scene investigation, carefully examining the Harrison store and questioning employees. He had lived in Fayetteville for eight years and knew the Ben Franklin there. As he had done audits in Bentonville, he could check on Wal-Mart with some of his clients. "They told me Sam was the type of individual that was willing to take chances and try new ideas, and that he seemingly treated his people well."

So in October 1966, Jim Henry moved into the Bentonville headquarters. He was more than financial chief. "In those early days all of us had to do several jobs, and I had many other responsibilities besides the financial and accounting function—such as helping with store locations and being involved in working leases and the legal part, since we didn't have a legal department at that time."

Not only was the work piled on, so were the hours on the job. Sam Walton typically worked a sixteen-hour day, and expected his top executives to put in plenty of overtime. Arend and Jim Henry made a game out of trying to outsmart the boss. They found his work habits rather amusing—but only in the beginning.

"Ferold and I came to Wal-Mart about the same time," said Jim Henry. "We laughed about the situation —we could never outguess Sam as to when he would be back in the office.

"Ferold and I met together many a morning at the Horseshoe Café at five o'clock, or whenever it opened, and we'd schedule our day, and do our planning. Sam would take off and do whatever he needed to do during the day, either visiting stores, or bird-hunting, or playing tennis.

"Then Ferold and I would try to leave the office around five-thirty or six, somewhere about that time. Almost invariably as we started down the stairs Sam would be coming up. He'd say, 'Boys, we need to have a little meeting.' We'd turn around and go back with him. The little meeting might last two or three hours.

"We knew it was one of those things that was necessary at the time. There were only a few of us to do all of it."

In his entire history of bringing in partners or executives perhaps no business relationship is more of an anomaly than Sam's partnership with "kid brother" Bud.

From the inception of Wal-Mart Stores, Inc., Bud was listed as J. L. Walton, Senior Vice-President and Director. That designation never changed.

In the early days, Bud Walton was heavily involved in real estate operations, acquiring leases, getting buildings erected, helping to expand the chain physically. For many years he maintained his home at Versailles, doing a lot of commuting to Bentonville. That shut-tling back and forth later took a toll on his family life. His wife Audrey and two daughters remained in their Versailles home; Bud eventually bought and restored in Bentonville a landmark colonial mansion built around the turn of the century for Judge Greenwood, just a few blocks from the residence of Sam and Helen.

Bud was a quiet presence in Bentonville compared to brother Sam. He was just as friendly around town but not as apt to be seen on the street. Sam's friends and business associates acknowledge Bud's fundamen-tal contribution to Wal-Mart success. So does Sam; otherwise Bud would not have wound up with 10,197,591 shares of Wal-Mart common stock (based on May 2, 1990 proxy statement) easily worth $500–$600 million.

Clarence Leis has observed: "Bud has always been a behind-the-scenes type of individual. If he wants to say his piece, he does, and Sam listens to him. Bud would always attend meetings and listen. He wouldn't say much, but he always listened, and he always put things together. I'm sure Sam listened to him a lot over the years. I think Sam wanted him to be a little more involved, but he was always kind of laid back."

When a store manager showed imagination and ap-titude, Sam promptly tried to make room for him on the executive staff in the general office. Don Whitta-ker quickly got his Wal-Mart No. 2 in Harrison in excellent shape and was moved to Bentonville as vice-president of operations, and later shifted to vice-president, real estate and construction. Whittaker's gruff style was in evidence on his visit to the Wal-Mart at Morrilton, Arkansas. Billy Hugh ("Bud") Hendricks, who was then manager there, recalled: "He was very good as vice-president of operations. He was like a bear, but he had a heart of gold. He talked rough. I can remember him coming into the Morrilton store; he'd have you walk down the aisle with him and he'd tell you to change this end cap or do that. You'd make the changes while he was in the store, and you'd ask him, 'What does this look like?' He'd back up, and cock one eye, and say, 'It looks like hell but I guess it'll do.' But if he said that, you knew it was in good shape. That was his normal comment of approval."

Not only did Sam seek centurions in the enemy camps, he also closely inspected his own ranks for lively soldiers who looked like future corporals, captains—even generals. He took an interest in Ron Loveless, the eight-year-old son of the Walton housekeeper, and kept tabs on him. Ron was a good high school baseball player and Sam offered to help him go to college. Instead Ron went into the Air Force and came out in 1964 to take a job in a garage.

Sam offered him a chance to learn retailing—from the bottom up. Ron went off to St. Robert, Missouri, to work as a stock boy in the Ben Franklin there. He moved up fast. By the time Loveless was forty-two he was senior vice-president and general manager of Sam's Wholesale Club division of Wal-Mart, with a six-figure salary.

It is a wonder Loveless survived his first promotion— from stock boy to head of the pet department at the St. Robert variety store. Two pet orders he filled were incredible, perhaps unbelievable. But, in a long feature on his career, the *Arkansas Gazette* said, August 24, 1986:

> In his youthful enthusiasm, Loveless, then in his early twenties, said "Why not?" when a customer from nearby Fort Leonard Wood asked for an elephant. Loveless cheerfully placed the order.
>
> He found out why not. The elephant arrived dead.
>
> "Some of the ideas I had were costly," Loveless said. "It took a few years to laugh about it."
>
> But it was a different story for the baby leopard. It arrived alive—far too alive, as it turned out. The customer took it home, only to return it after his home had been shredded.
>
> While those efforts may have been expensive, they demonstrated two qualities that Walton wanted— imagination and aggressiveness—while he was building his Wal-Mart discount retailing empire.

Ron was promoted to manager of the Wal-Mart in Mountain Home, Arkansas. His magic touch failed him. He kept running out of stock over the weekends. Sam threw a fit.

"It got awfully touchy," said Ron Loveless. "If you don't produce, you'll be gone. Mr. Sam is a very demanding individual."

The Mountain Home problem was solved, and Ron Loveless went on to be district manager, regional operations manager, and assistant to the president and general merchandise manager before Sam picked him to head the new Sam's Wholesale Club division, which by 1990 has grown to 123 stores with annual sales of over $5 billion.

When he retired at age 42 in 1986, Loveless blamed burnout: "I was feeling the stress. Mr. Sam hated to see me go. But he pointed out whenever anyone took their money and ran, it had the beneficial effect of creating more opportunity for other ambitious executives to move up."

This one-time stock boy quit work with retirement and stock benefits giving him a six-figure annual income.

—13—

The Courtship of Ron Mayer

On an Indian summer day in 1968, Sam Walton crossed
the Bentonville square and climbed the stairs to the
second floor suite into which was jammed the total
Wal-Mart executive corps. His two top lieutenants
greeted him with dazzling smiles. With obvious pride,
they displayed their sketches for a company innovation and milestone—a 72,000-square-foot combined
warehouse and general office.

At that point the company had only twenty-four
stores in four states doing an annual sales volume of
$12.5 million, but Wal-Mart was growing fast. Ade-
quate office space and a merchandise distribution center were needed immediately.

For a few minutes the boss pored over the architect's floor plan. His face began to get tight. He shook
his head and grumbled as he handed the blueprints
back to Ferold Arend and Jim Henry. The incident is
still vivid in Jim Henry's memory.

"Nope," said Sam. "You-all are trying to get about
twice as much office space as we need. Cut down on
that. Put more space in the warehouse end. That's
where we get our revenue."

The elusive "secret" of Wal-Mart success has been
pondered and debated in recent years in corporate
boardrooms across America. Sam Walton's "magic" is

141

a combination of parts—basic and few—but frugality in the extreme always has been a principal element.

The frugality inherent in the rebuff to Ferold Arend and Jim Henry is just as elemental in the Wal-Mart organization today as it was in 1968. Sam's CEO in 1990 had only a cramped ten-by-twelve-foot "private" office and worked at an ordinary mahogany desk whose top had been seriously scratched by its fifty-nine-cent wire in-basket. The CEO's private secretary sat outside in a bull pen. He got her attention by hollering through his open door. Sam does the same thing.

No less essential an ingredient is, of course, customer satisfaction. Hardly a day has passed without Sam reminding an employee: "Remember Wal-Mart's Golden Rule: Number one, the customer Is always right; number two, if the customer isn't right, refer to rule number one." But the boss actually wanted to go beyond that. For example if a customer brought back a pair of shoes whose soles had started coming off, Sam reminded his stores that not only should the shoes be cheerfully replaced, but "the salesclerk should throw in a pair of socks or stockings for the hassle" of having to bring back the defective merchandise. In this August 1989 communique, he said the store's message should be "We really regret your inconvenience and want to make you happy."

When Sam bought 12½ acres—with a railroad siding—about a mile from downtown Bentonville on which to erect his new headquarters, he was far more interested in creating a distribution center through which those thousands of cardboard cartons containing appliances, hardware, shoes and dresses, and the like could move out expeditiously and efficiently on his own trucks to his stores.

So Ferold Arend and Jim Henry cut the office space down to 12,000 square feet and put the other 60,000 into warehouse space.

It also is axiomatic that to create the eventual Wal-Mart miracle, Sam went at distribution backward. Traditionally retailers build warehouses to serve existing outlets, but Walton built the warehouse first, then the stores were spotted around it. Initially Sam only opened stores within a radius of 300 miles from Bentonville headquarters. That meant that his trucks could deliver fresh inventory to any Wal-Mart within five or six hours. And if he knew anything about running a store, he didn't show sales growth when what the customer wants to buy is not on his shelves. Grudgingly, Sam later extended the radius to 350 miles, perhaps 400. But when the stores began to spread out all across the Sunbelt, he insisted on building a flock of new distribution centers to keep the truck travel within the five- to six-hour drive time.

Arend and Jim Henry proved to be pretty good designers in the first place; within three years Sam was forced to double the initial office space at his Bentonville complex. Naturally, at the same time he had to add 64,000 more square feet to the original warehouse, which would now cover an area as large as three football fields. The Wal-Mart distribution operation was already unloading two to three railroad cars a week, and four or five full trailers a day.

Bentonville remained the sleepy little town that was so appealing to the Waltons. The 1970 census would put the city population at 5,508, and 50,475 for Benton County. The Bank of Bentonville opened Arkansas's first drive-in window "outside of Little Rock." The average income of a Benton County family was $6,505 (as compared with a state-wide average of $6,273). Wal-Mart was not, however, the only show in town. The Bear Brand Company's Bentonville plant employed 500 with an annual payroll of $2.5 million, and every week turned out 40,000 dozen pairs of panty hose, and 13,000 dozen pairs of regular stockings.

Still it was a small town, with small-town ways and small-town problems.

But that was at the heart of the Wal-Mart chieftain's oft-quoted explanation to business journalists and stock analysts about why he has kept his headquarters in Bentonville. As he told *Forbes*:

Move from Bentonville? That would be the last thing we do unless they run us out. The best thing we ever did was to hide back there in the hills and eventually build a company that makes folks want to find us. They get there sometimes with a lot of trepidation and problems, but we like where we are. It's because of the work ethic, because of the chemistry of the people up there and the support we get. We're much better off than if we'd gone to Chicago.

In those days in the late sixties when Wal-Mart had only 2,000 employes and 30 or so stores, doing around $12.5 million in sales, not even Sam Walton, the biggest dreamer of all, could foresee the astounding explosion of growth that would propel Wal-Mart into the 1990s as a merchandising giant employing 250,000, with 1,500 stores in 22 states, ringing up sales of almost $26 billion a year!

It is staggering to realize that this remarkable success is the direct result of the bright idea Sam tried to sell to the sophisticated honchos at Ben Franklin Variety Stores headquarters in Chicago back in 1962. Of course, the key ingredient turned out to be Sam's masterful execution of the idea and in creating a "major competitive advantage" in his "low-cost structure." Those are characteristics that would be identified down the road by the stock analyst for A. G. Edwards, St. Louis-based national brokers, who also wrote in 1985:

Wal-Mart continues to be among the most efficient retailers in the country. As tangible evidence, for over a decade, WMT's expense structure (measured as a percentage of sales) has been the lowest among the discount department store companies included in the annual Cornell University study on retailers. The company's shrinkage (i.e., theft, inventory shortage, etc.) runs 1 percent of sales, about half the industry's average of roughly 2 percent. . . .

WMT's people are also highly motivated and productive. This valuable intangible is part of Wal-Mart's corporate culture. High productivity lends itself to lower overhead. Personnel operate in an environment where change is encouraged. For example, if a WMT store associate makes suggestions regarding: 1. merchandising ideas which lead to significant sales gains for that item, or 2. the implementation of improved procedures which result in meaningful cost savings, these ideas are quickly disseminated. Multiply each suggestion by over 750 stores and by over 80,000 associates* (who can potentially make suggestions) and this leads to substantial sales gains, costs reductions and improved productivity.

They were talking again about Sam Walton's waste not–want not mentality, or put bluntly, Spartan frugality. On the other hand he was known for encouraging his store-front troops to be flexible and innovative. If he said this once, he said it a thousand times: "Do it. Try it. Fix it." Translated, that meant he'd welcome seeing a store manager take a gamble on something new, then if it didn't work, tinker around with changes that might help it to succeed.

Even with all his enthusiasm and personal conviction that he was hitting on all four cylinders and right on target, the astounding success of his merchandising miracle caught even Sam Walton by surprise. As he told *The New York Times* in 1984: "I had no vision of the scope of what I would start. But I always had confidence that as long as we did our work well and were good to our customers, there would be no limit to us."

More than that, he wasn't operating in a vacuum. Other retailers were out there trying to do just what he was doing. Only he did it better than nearly anyone. Particularly, Herb Fisher of Secaucus, New Jersey.

The same year that Sam launched Wal-Mart No. 1 in Rogers, Fisher opened his first Jamesway discount

*These are 1985 statistics As of 1990, Wal-Mart has in excess of 250,000 associates.

store in New York State. Reporters from *Forbes* made
a comparison of the two, out of curiosity, in 1989. The
magazine said, in part:

> Both founder-chairmen sport no-frills headquar-
> ters, call employees by the more dignified term of
> "associates," and promote the same "we care" mot-
> toes in the stores. Over the years they have even
> borrowed a few merchandising concepts from each
> other.
> But they part company rather quickly when it
> comes to growth and profits; Wal-Mart Stores Inc. is
> 26 times the size of Jamesway Corp., yet it still racks
> up profit margins three times as high as its smaller
> rival. Each square foot of Walton's stores generates
> $210 of sales, nearly twice as much as Jamesway . . .

Getting out of cramped quarters on the Bentonville
square into the new general office-warehouse building
a mile away provided more elbow room, but did not at
all ease the pressure cooker strain Sam put on his top
executives.

Rushing pell-mell into new store openings and the
"grand" reopenings that Sam savored, his officers often had to resort to stopgap tools. "Sam remembered
how I came unglued," Jim Henry told me in a 1989
interview, "because we were using cigar boxes for cash
registers because we didn't have enough registers rented
for some of those openings we had in the early days."

Walton's hard-driving pace finally got to Jim Henry.
Sam watched this financial officer begin to seemingly
struggle under the enormous load that went with the
job. Never out of his mind was the thought that the
man he really needed was Ron Mayer. He decided to
try again to snare him.

Today Jim Henry says: "I have nothing but praise
for Sam and his work. Usually he was more competitive than other companies. I think the key to his
getting the people he wanted was that he paid well.
But he also expected one-hundred percent effort. Again,

I feel like all the associates from the very beginning felt they were part of the organization. Back at that time it was fairly innovative that some of the managers were able to invest in store locations. That was certainly tying them to the organization. There were several that borrowed money to put in."

In this crucial period Sam knew he needed a battle-tested, innovative executive who could work some of the magic needed to shore up his weak financial underpinnings, and who likewise already had front-line experience in creating distribution center efficiency.

Sam knew where that man was—working away at A. L. Duckwall Company in Abilene, Kansas. Sam had thoroughly checked out Ron Mayer, was enthusiastic about his business background and discount store achievements, and finally determined to spare nothing in the attempt to bring him into the Wal-Mart general office.

Ron was born November 5, 1934, in the tiny hamlet of Dwight, Kansas, forty miles west of Topeka. As an only child, he grew up in Dodge City, where his mother, Mildred, was treasurer of the city school system. Notwithstanding its colorful history dramatized in the television series "Gunsmoke," Dodge City in the thirties and forties was a quiet town of 20,000 in the heart of wheat and cattle country.

At Dodge City High School, from which he graduated in 1952, Ron was remembered as a *B* student, and as a player on Coach Fred Day's tennis team. When he arrived in Wichita to major in accounting at Wichita State University, he suddenly came into his own.

"Ron was tremendously bright," recalled Fran Jabara, former dean of Wichita State's business administration school. "Smart guy. Hard working. Had what it takes."

Ron Mayer was graduated from Wichita State in 1956 with a bachelor's degree in accounting. He completed examinations in 1961 to become a CPA.

In his courtship of the Duckwall executive, Sam

Walton steadily upped the ante and made his employment offer so alluring that at length Ron Mayer had to succumb.

His photograph—with thick dark, wavy hair and smiling movie-star good looks—appears for the first time in the January 31, 1973, annual Wal-Mart report. Not only was he vice-president for finance and corporate treasurer, he also was one of the four-man executive committee.

Ron Mayer moved into the Bentonville general offices eager and anxious to climb higher—as quickly as possible.

His grasp of the intricacies and potential of the discounting business impressed both his fellow executives at headquarters and the associates on the frontlines in the stores. "He was probably the right guy for that stage of the company," recalled Bob Bogle.

Jim Henry agrees: "Ron succeeded me. I thought he had tremendous potential. We had—I wouldn't say difficulty—in our infancy in trying to set up our data processing department and so forth, but there were a lot of new things we were trying to do with computers. Ron was working on that."

When Ron Mayer visited the Harrison Wal-Mart, he immediately won over manager Bud Hendricks. "He was a real nice guy, real down-to-earth kind of guy. You could sit down and talk to him and explain your problem to him and he'd listen and he would do something about it if it needed to be corrected."

Hendricks heard from Mayer the story of his close brush with death in Sam's Beech Baron. "He told it in a meeting. He wasn't mad. He was telling a story for it to be amusing."

It was still largely the seat-of-the-pants instincts of Sam Walton that guided his Wal-Mart expansion. He did not believe in hiring market surveyors. He felt he could eyeball a small town, count the cars whizzing along Main Street or parked on the square, and determine all the factors that would either recommend or discourage the opening of a store.

Most of the time it was Sam's snap judgment that determined the next location. But there were family councils, too. Helen was not as enthusiastic as her husband about branching out so vigorously. Nor did Sam and James Jones always see eye to eye.

"I'll tell you the one location we debated the longest," Jones told me, "and Sam resisted and I just stayed after him and after him. That was Berryville, Arkansas. He said, 'It's not big enough,' and I said, 'Sam, now our concept is so many people, they don't have to be in the town, but you look at that county, Carroll County, and Eureka Springs and Green Forest, all that population around you, and so forth and so on.' It took me a long time to convince him but we finally went into Berryville and it has been a very profitable store."

In the early and midsixties, Jones and his wife became close friends of Sam and Helen and often visited them in Bentonville. Said Jones: "We were up there all the time and we would sit down and debate whether we should go into this town or that town, and how many more we should put in. Helen would say, 'Aw, ten's enough, Sam. Let's don't do any more.' Or something like that. And we'd talk about it and then we'd go out and do ten more. And we kept doing it. The thing was working."

Working, yes, but not without a lot of rough edges and some reckless activities in the stores. Bud Hendricks of Harrison, who managed several Wal-Mart stores between 1967 and 1981, recalled the opening of the company's eighth store in Morrilton, just off Interstate 40 between Little Rock and Lake Dardanelle:

"The Morrilton store was in an old Coca-Cola plant that had closed. It had a lot of pipes sticking out of the floor. In the stockroom you had to stack your excess freight around the pipes and the drains and all that.

"We didn't have air-conditioning in that building. We had twenty-eight window fans. Big windows with a bar you unlock and push out. Two fans for each window and plywood with holes cut for the fans to sit in, and that would pull air through the building.

"Ferold Arend came in one day. He was standing in the breezeway between two sections of the building. He said, 'Bud, it's not very hot right here. What is the temperature?' I stepped around the corner and I said, 'It's a hundred and five right here right now.'

"It was a hundred and five in the building. It had a metal roof, no insulation. If you stood in the breezeway, it was pretty cool. But if you got out of the breezeway, it was pretty hot.

"Of course, we couldn't stock any chocolate or bulk candy like we should have. It would all melt and run together."

Sam Walton was a frequent visitor to his stores, hopping around in his airplane, making four or five stops a day. He was checking up not only on what his own stores were doing, but the competition as well.

"Competitive situations create your profit structure," Bud Hendricks said. "You have a standard markup you're going to get on an item and if there's no competition you'll make extra profit. But if you have an Alco [Duckwall Company discount store] or a Magic Mart*, and they're going to sell a particular item fifteen cents below you, you've got to reduce. You sell at or below. You meet or beat your competition.

"Mr. Sam would come in and say, 'Bud, let's go to Magic Mart and look around.' We might spend thirty or forty-five minutes in there. He'd ask, 'How much are we getting on Aquanet, or this other hair spray?' He'd ask about anything we had featured.

"It depended on the seasons, of course. In the spring we might be checking how they're pricing their peat moss and their potting soil or fertilizer.

"And you'd better know what your cost to sell was. You did that by taking your total sales for the week

---

*A division of Little Rock's Sterling Company against which Sam competed in Newport.

and your week's payroll. Divide your total sales into the payroll to get your payroll percentage. He always wanted to know that."

On every visit, Sam would roam the aisles and talk to all the clerks—whom he referred to, as did J. C. Penney, as "associates." Bud Hendricks was an hourly employee when he first met him.

"He was always asking what was the best-selling item, what kind of markup percentage was on the item. We made sure we had plenty of panty hose and his kind of socks out on the counter—he had favorite brands. In fact, nearly every time he flew in he'd bring two or three cases of panty hose with him. They sold fast."

Even with several Wal-Marts in operation, Sam Walton was still learning the ropes as a discounter. His first store in Rogers had the necessary sales volume, but not a sufficient profit margin.

"Mr. Sam was still in a learning stage as to what costs he had to control the most," said Hendricks. "That was payroll. That was the big expense. He was paying minimum wage, and you didn't get raises back then like progressive raises now. That was unheard of in the sixties. You gave raises on merit, not by mandatory quarterly or biannually meeting with your associates."

Some of the more improvised Wal-Mart activities occurred when winter snows hit the Ozarks and made highways impassable. That proved a formidable obstacle to getting store employees paid, because Walton didn't use the U.S. mail to send correspondence between company headquarters and the outlying stores. Instead, it was cheaper and faster to send all general mail on company trucks, which make trips from Bentonville to each store up to three times a day. If that heavy volume had to be shunted down to Fort Smith for sorting and dispatch, at least a day's time would be lost.

"We had to sign for the mail sack," said Bud Hendricks, "and put our mail going to the general office back in that bag and put a new seal on it. I think Fort Smith was already the busiest mail exchange in Arkansas, just on account of the outside correspondence between the company and vendors, with invoices and the like."

When roads were impassable for the company's eighteen-wheelers, Bud Hendricks would get out his four-wheel drive truck in Harrison and plow through to Bentonville and pick up all the payroll for his district.

"When I got back to Berryville, I would drop his payroll off, and call the Mountain Home manager and tell him to meet me in Harrison. I'd keep my payroll and he'd take the rest for Salem and Ash Flat and one store across the line in Missouri, West Plains. Before he left my store he'd call ahead and have those men meet him at Mountain Home. They all had four-wheelers. That was still going on in the late seventies when I quit."

Things did not always run smoothly between the managers and the boss, as Bud Hendricks related: "One thing sticks very vividly in my mind—the day I upset Mr. Walton. He called the Harrison store one day and asked me to pick him up at the airport. We were starting a modular program trying to get our basic items in certain spots on the shelf. For instance if a case of hair spray was packed in twelve cans, you had a modular sticker showing where it went on the counter, with an IBM reorder number. It was one of the best things, merchandise-wise, that ever happened to the company.

"Before that we just went down the aisle and if we were out of Style hair spray, or Bayer aspirin, we'd just order a case and when it came in scoot everything down to make room. This modular system gave everything a definite home, and if Bayer came packed thirty-six to the case, when you got down to fifteen you reordered so the thirty-six would come in before the fifteen sold out. You had to know your rate of turn, how many you were selling a day, a week. . . . That was the whole point of the modular system.

"I went down and picked him up at the airport and the first thing he said was, 'Bud, what do you think of this modular system?' I said, 'Mr. Walton, it's a great thing, getting all your related items together, and giving them a definite home. But there's got to be a point where it's used with common horse sense.' He gave me a sharp look, and I said, 'If the modular calls for twelve units on a shelf, why I may sell twelve in two days, so I may need twenty-four. So after you set your modular, you've got to merchandise your store by the way items sell.'

"He didn't act like he liked that. He apparently didn't understand what I was trying to get across to him.* The subject just ended. He didn't ask any more. I always felt like I hit a sore spot."

Sam may have been miffed, but he didn't hold grudges and got along well over the years with Hendricks. In fact, they shared one episode that has become a Walton quail-hunting legend. It happened when Bud Hendricks was managing the Wal-Mart store in Conway, Arkansas.

The telephone rang at Hendricks's home at 3:00 A.M. Bud got up and answered groggily.

"Bud," said the voice he recognized as Sam Walton's, "I'm socked in. It's too foggy. I can't get out."

Bud Hendricks mumbled something, and waited for the boss to continue. "Don't leave your house to go to the store until I call you back."

"Yes, sir," said Bud.

The episode had started the afternoon before when Sam had called and asked if Bud could pick him up early next morning at the airport. "I'm coming down to go bird hunting."

At 5:00 A.M. Sam again called Bud's home. "The fog looks like it's going to flat lift. Why don't you meet me at the airport at seven o'clock."

---

*Hendricks was actually criticizing the parameters of the modular concept, which povided an insufficient number on the allotted shelf space for fast selling items.

Around 6:30 Bud Hendricks arrived at the store, checked the parking lot for stray shopping carts, then unlocked for the assistant manager and headed for the airport. He was there by 7:00, but Sam had not arrived.

Fifteen minutes later Sam flew in. The Cessna's cabin door swung open and Ol'Roy and another bird dog sprang onto the wing, with tails wagging and eyes flashing. They leaped to the ground.

"Can I borrow your car this morning?" asked Sam. "I'm going to Damascus to hunt with a friend and I don't have any way to get there."

"Yes, sir. You'll have to drop me back at the store first."

Bud handed over the keys to his 1967 Chevelle, and Sam put his two dogs in the backseat. They drove to the store and then Walton headed for Damascus.

It was after dark when Sam Walton returned. "Bud," he said, "I filled your car up with gas. It's making a little bit of a racket. I don't know what really happened. But here's twenty dollars, take that and go get it fixed."

"Okay, that's fine."

At the airport Sam and the bird dogs alighted. Bud Hendricks started home. He recalled: "Well, I had to leave all the windows down on the way home going up the interstate to air it out because of the smell from the dogs inside my car. It was bad. Apparently they had got sick and vomited inside the car.

"I got about five miles from home and my eight-track stereo quit working. I couldn't figure out what had happened. I fooled with it a little bit and then turned on the radio and listened to it.

"Just as I pulled off the interstate I smelled something burning. I looked down and saw there was a big hole burned in my carpet. I stopped and jumped out and put out the fire. Then I drove home and looked under the hood. Sam had run over a rock or something and tore the whole exhaust system loose.

"That let the exhaust from the manifold blast right back against the firewall. First it burned the wires to my eight-track, then it had set the carpet on fire.

"Fortunately I was able to get another set of Chevelle pipes at a wrecking yard, and fix the car. I got a new floor mat. It cost me more than twenty bucks, but it's been worth the money to tell a good one on Sam. He still laughs every time he hears me tell it."

—14—

"I Need Money—Quick!"

Sam Walton was in Dallas, and he was frantic. He needed money—lots of money—immediately. He had a $1.5 million line of credit at Republic National Bank, but they wouldn't give him a dime. Wild-eyed with worry, he rushed to the phone.

He dialed New Orleans, trying to reach James Jones, who had helped him buy the Bank of Bentonville and with whom he regularly consulted on financing his expanding discount store chain. Jones had set up the line of credit before leaving Republic in Dallas to take over as president of National Bank of Commerce in New Orleans.

This crisis came in August 1969, when Jones had been on his new bank job a little over a month.

"The phone rang and it was Sam," said Jones. "He had flown down to Dallas to draw on his line of credit and they were hassling him around and wouldn't give him the money. He had to have it that day. I knew he had to have it because we talked every day, I mean every day we talked.

"The one fellow at Republic who would have taken care of it—one of the senior officers—happened to be out. And nothing was happening.

"When Sam called he was almost in tears. He said, 'What do I do?'

"When I left Republic I told the guys there that I was not going to take any business with me, but I said, 'If you foul up, they may come to me or something.'

"So on the phone I asked Sam if this happened, and that happened, and he did so and so. He said, 'That's right.'

"I said, 'You're at Love Field?' He said he was. I said, 'Well, get back in your Baron'—he was flying that little Beech two-engine job—'and fly on down to New Orleans. I'll wait in my office. Doesn't make any difference what time you get here.' "

When Sam landed in New Orleans, the bank's limousine picked him up and whisked him downtown to the National Bank of Commerce.

"It was a little after six o'clock when Sam came into my office," said Jones. "We visited for a while and I calmed him down. He said, 'You going to be able to help me?'

"I said, 'Yes, Sam.' And I pushed a note across the desk, an unsecured note, and told him to just sign it. He did. I said, 'You've got the money.' I'll never forget that as long as I live. I look back and see what a big mistake they made in the bank at Dallas, but, you know, they're just people. . . ."

By that time, the Wal-Mart chain had grown to thirty stores, all within 300 miles of the Bentonville distribution center and warehouse, and Sam wanted to add more locations, at least fourteen a year. The financial hurdle he faced was that it would require almost half a million dollars to build or lease and stock each new store. Wal-Mart didn't have that kind of capital, but that didn't stop Sam from dreaming big dreams.

"Our plan is to grow internally," he explained. "Our growth potential lies within the magic circle—an area that encompasses northern Arkansas, southern Missouri, southeastern Kansas, and eastern Oklahoma. This area has had an excellent economic gain over the past ten years—increasing substantially in population as well as per capita income.

"This has been due primarily to the development of tourism and the influence of a large number of industries that have moved into this area. We have a balance of tourism, industrial jobs, and agriculture that should encourage a healthy growth in this Ozark region for years to come."

It worried Sam Walton that his discount store network might be unable to keep pace with the growth of his "magic circle" simply due to lack of capital.

Jim Jones had stepped into the crisis to rescue Sam from a desperate cash crunch, but it was a one-time deal. They couldn't do business permanently because Arkansas-based merchandising did not fit the New Orleans bank's lending pattern. As for the Dallas bank, Sam felt it was kicking him around with Jones no longer on the scene.

So somehow creating a solid financial foundation on which to expand his Wal-Mart empire, and with a lot of speed, remained Sam's number one priority. Ron Mayer, charging like a fire truck into his new Bentonville job on July 1, 1969, immediately joined the boss in brainstorming to find the answer to the permanent financing question.

Jim Henry was moved aside. Sam recently observed: "Jim did a good job. I began to see he was not the talent we needed long-term. He didn't think like we do." At the end of 1969 Jim resigned and returned to the CPA business.

"Ron was the right guy at the right time," Sam says. His previous success in organizing and directing Duckwall's distribution center, trucking, and retailing was an immediate boon for Wal-Mart. "He was fantastic! He developed systems that stayed with us almost to today [1990]."

The new financial officer virtually became the boss's shadow. Ron Mayer hopped in the Beech Baron with Sam and flew all over the territory, spurring on store managers and associates, tossing out fresh retailing schemes, scratching and clawing along with Sam to get a better toehold on their race to become America's number one retailer.

That was Sam's goal, and he wanted people who believed Wal-Mart could reach it. Ron did. They made a good team, Sam recalls. "We flew up to Kansas and signed leases for three new store locations in a single day—Junction City, Manhattan, and Leavenworth."

His cash registers were ringing a merry tune. But it was not until Lady Luck waltzed—the word Sam uses in telling this episode—into the Bentonville offices in the form of a young bond salesman named Mike Smith that his long-term financial-base aspirations began to turn rosy.

Mike Smith was from Little Rock's Stephens, Inc., the bond house owned by "Mr. Witt" Stephens and his brother Jack—the latter being the "angel" who twenty years earlier had rescued Sam from his abortive venture when he tried to start the Little Rock shopping center. The closest contact they'd had since was Sam borrowing a substantial sum from Union Life Insurance Company, then owned by Jack Stephens, to build the new Wal-Mart general office-warehouse.

Mike Smith climbed the stairs to the Wal-Mart headquarters, which were still located on the south side of the square.

"I hear you want to go public, sell Wal-Mart stock," he told Sam. "Least that's what the Union Life comptroller tells me."

Sam looked at him. They'd met a time or two, when Smith had called on Sam's bank to sell municipal bonds. Mike was a graduate of the University of Arkansas, always a good recommendation in Sam's eyes.

"That's right," Sam said. "We've talked about it— Ron Mayer, Jimmy Jones . . . and Helen. Do you think the Stephens folks would like to handle it?"

"You bet," said Mike Smith, and immediately started talking business.

Mike Smith remembers it well. "Sam wanted to show me some of his Oklahoma stores," the bond man told me in a recent interview. "We got in the plane and we took off heading west, and started looking for Tahlequah [Oklahoma]. I recall we'd fly around and he'd say, 'Is that Tahlequah over there?' I didn't know Tahlequah from anywhere, you know. We finally found the airport. That was the first of my many exciting plane rides with Sam."

After spending the day with Sam and Ron Mayer, Mike Smith returned to Little Rock and "we really got fired up about it." And when the Stephens brothers got excited about a project, Sam Walton would soon discover, the fur flew. They were most unusual, and successful, entrepreneurs.

Wilton Robert Stephens, known as Mr. Witt, was described by the *Arkansas Gazette* as "one of Arkansas's great characters. He has made and broken governors, congressmen, and legislators through his financial backing and network of political and business friends."

His brother, Jackson T. Stephens, sixteen years younger, graduated from the United States Naval Academy, but was unable to pursue a military career because of poor eyesight. Mr. Witt brought him into the Stephens, Inc., bond house in 1946, taught him the trade, and in 1957 made him top man in the organization.

When the Great Depression caused Arkansas to default on its millions in municipal bonds, Wilton Stephens, a jewelry and Bible salesman in his early twenties, saw a golden opportunity for a poor-boy hustler such as himself. He bought up bonds at $.20 on the dollar, because his father was certain they "had no place to go but up." With a confident pitch Stephens peddled them at a handsome profit to other believers in the ultimate solvency of the Razorback state.

Stephens began establishing a "market" for all types of Arkansas investments. His tiny Little Rock office, opened on a borrowed $5,000, eventually would become the biggest banking investment house off Wall Street, with a $320 million capital base, underwriting as well as trading in government and corporate issues. His confidence in Arkansas municipals was confirmed in 1943 when they became redeemable at face value in money markets throughout the nation. In 1954 he enhanced his wealth by buying a majority interest in the mammoth Arkansas Louisiana Gas Company. Soon he had trouble counting his millions.

The Stephens brothers came from the river bottoms of Grant County, off the family farm near Prattsville, sixty miles south of Little Rock. Their father, Albert Jackson Stephens Sr., was a proud farmer, a power in the state legislature, and a stern family disciplinarian. He used to tell his sons: "Don't be ashamed of your poverty, and don't be proud of it. Just get rid of it as quick as you conveniently can."

In 1988, when Mr. Witt was eighty but still going every day to the Stephens building in downtown Little Rock to visit old cronies and sell a few more bonds, he told an *Arkansas Gazette* reporter:

"Jack and I never departed from what Dad told us and drilled into us that the Lord's way is the best way. He taught us, don't ever make money out of whiskey, don't ever make money out of prostitutes or gambling.

"Because it won't pay 6 percent."

The 1988 *Forbes* magazine tally of America's 400 Richest included the two Stephenses, listed as each having $350 million. By that time they had expanded worldwide with banking investments in Hong Kong and Paris, and had purchased a 500-mile-an-hour corporate jet.

That was the same list that had Sam Walton at the top, as America's richest, with a fortune of $6.7 billion.

But he certainly did not have that kind of money in the fall of 1969 when he arranged for Stephens, Inc., to underwrite an issuance of Wal-Mart common stock.

Jack Stephens shared Sam's vision and enthusiasm. His people pitched in to quickly assemble the mountain of paperwork—reports, statements, business and personal histories, etc., etc.—required by the Securities and Exchange Commission and by the New York Stock Exchange.

Stephens, Inc., proposed to offer 300,000 shares over-the-counter at $16.50 a share, which would raise

somewhere around $5 or $6 million new capital for
Wal-Mart expansion.

But there were hitches and glitches. The Wal-Mart
road was usually bumpy—Ron Mayer had already discovered that in his first few months on the job.

Everything was in place in the spring of 1970 for the
stock offering. The registration had been filed with the
SEC in Washington. Just then the stock market went
into a mild tailspin.

Mike Smith went to Bentonville in early May to
attend the annual Wal-Mart owners' meeting, which
turned out to be a fishing trip at Bull Shoals for Sam
and Helen and the managers; no one else had a Wal-
Mart stake at that time. Mike and Sam and his partners talked over the stock offering.

"It is not the time to go public," Mike Smith told
them. "Wall Street is just in terrible shape. There's no
market for new stock now. We must wait."

They waited. But Sam still needed money. He
couldn't open more stores without capital. And he was
dying to open more stores.

It would be helpful, Walton reasoned, to get a Wall
Street investment house to join up with Stephens,
Inc., in selling the stock. He had read in the newspapers
about White, Weld & Company, Inc., successfully introducing stock in an Iowa discount firm called Pamida.
In New York on a buying trip, Sam looked in the
telephone book and got their address.

He walked into White, Weld & Company cold and
approached the receptionist.

"I'm Sam Walton from Arkansas. Who can I talk
to?"

The girl, fortunately, was pretty sharp.

"Why," she said, beaming, "our senior vice-president
is from Arkansas. I'm sure he would be glad to see
you. Let me ring his office."

Harmon L. "Buck" Remmel, who had Little Rock
roots, shook hands with the visitor—and it was an
instant, lifelong partnership.

Buck Remmel had relatives in Newport and a lot of

questions to put to Sam. They hit it off. White, Weld & Company joined Stephens in handling the stock issue. Buck Remmel went on the Wal-Mart board and served for many years.

But the market was still in too much turmoil, Mike Smith remembers, to think of bringing out the Wal-Mart issue. It might fall on its face. "Things were so terrible even IBM didn't do an issue. There was just no market." Now they decided to try in the fall.

More waiting, which, of course, Sam hated. He took the bull by the horns and decided to go to the big life insurance companies and make a pitch for a $5 million loan to tide him over until the Wal-Mart stock could go on the market.

He got an appointment at Prudential Life Insurance Company and flew accompanied by Ron Mayer to New York. His request a few years earlier for a $1 million Prudential loan had been rejected. This time the executives again frowned deeply, and did not seem overly impressed with the country merchant from down in the Ozarks.

"You show," said one official, "that your sales volume is now at an annual rate of around twenty million dollars."

"Yes," said Sam Walton. "Our business is really growing. Our sales for fiscal year 1969 were $21,365,081. That's quite a jump—the year before we did only $12,618,754."

The life insurance man considered that a moment.

"What would be your projection of sales volume, say five years from now?"

Sam Walton consulted with Ron Mayer. "Our calculation is that for fiscal year 1975 our sales will be two hundred thirty million."

"What! From twenty-one million to two hundred thirty million? In five years!"

"Yes, that's what we estimate. I'm pretty sure we will make it."

The atmosphere on the insurance company side of the table grew chilly and decidedly skeptical. They said they would give their answer in a few days on his loan application. (Sam Walton, however, was right on target; total sales for 1975 came to $236,209,000.)

But the man from Bentonville was in a pretty big hurry. He went on to Springfield, Massachussetts, to appear before the loan committee of Massachusetts Mutual Insurance Company. They listened avidly to his story and offered to lend $2.5 million.

Sam considered their terms. The interest was okay. Mass Mutual wanted warrants to buy thousands of shares of Wal-Mart stock at the initial price. At the moment the warrants were worthless because Wal-Mart was still a private company. Meanwhile, Prudential said okay, and set their terms.

Walton weighed all the factors and consulted with Ron Mayer and others involved. He took the Mass Mutual deal. Mike Smith chuckles about that. "Good lord, over and above their interest, Mass Mutual made a ton on that stock!" Sam Walton told a friend: "Yeah, but remember then we needed money—bad!"

In October 1970 the stock was ready to come out on the over-the-counter market. Sam and his crew started what he calls a "road show" to encourage interest. He flew to Los Angeles, San Francisco, Chicago, Little Rock, New York, and Boston to hold meetings to which investors and money managers were invited. With him went Ron Mayer, Mike Smith, and Jack Fraser of White, Weld.

In all these meetings Sam was pleasantly aggressive and showed off his tremendous gift of memory for names. Telling about that remarkable recall trait, Mike Smith credits Sam with a bit of masterful bunkum.

"In Los Angeles, for instance, one hundred people showed up. Sam always got there ahead of the crowd. He shook the hand of the first to arrive and chatted with him. He shook hands with all one hundred and tried to remember their names.

"He mixed and mingled. When he got up to talk, he'd say something like, 'Bill, that table right there' —pointing—'wanted to know so and so.' And he'd give the answer. Hell, the guy's name might have been Joe. But everybody thought he had it right, and marveled at how he could do it. And he was right a lot of the time. But it shows you how Sam works every angle. Bill or Joe or Bob, whoever—they loved it, too."

The four relaxed from their road show—which traveled by airline, not Sam's plane—playing tennis doubles. Mike Smith remembers Sam and his partner usually won.

So the stock finally came out, and the public gobbled it up. By 1972 it was so widely held that it left the over-the-counter market and began trading on the big board—the New York Stock Exchange, where its symbol is WMT.

The Wal-Mart stock turned out to be hot, very hot. Vernon Giss, a Stephens official, told me he remembers selling one hundred shares to a Little Rock couple. "Over the years there have been seven or eight two-for-one stock splits. It wound up that [in 1989] their one hundred had grown to twenty-five thousand shares." (That investment of $1,650 in 1970 would be worth more than a million dollars in 1990.)

Wal-Mart was now off and running, with no limit on how far it would zoom as long as Sam Walton was exercising his imagination and muscle.

The year 1971 came to a close with the opening of fourteen new Wal-Mart discount stores*, bringing the total to fifty-one, located in five states: Arkansas, Missouri, Kansas, Oklahoma, and Louisiana.

Sales volume for the year was $78,014,164, having jumped 77 percent in a single year and risen in five years from the $12,618,000 level when he operated twenty-four Wal-Marts. In the same period the corporate profit leaped from $481,750 to $2,907,000.

Proud of these gains, Ron Mayer gave the impres-

---

*By comparison, on a single day—January 31, 1990—Wal-Mart opened thirty-six new stores, in a geographical sweep from Arizona to Florida.

sion of a fast-rising business star—but not to everyone who closely followed Sam's fortunes. Something was slightly off. Bill Enfield, the Waltons' closest neighbor and Sam's former lawyer, put it succinctly: "Mayer's style wasn't in tune with Sam's."

George Billingsley, a Bentonville travel agent who is a long-time friend of the Waltons and a Wal-Mart director, saw some early signs of a problem. Billingsley is so close to the family that they selected him on two important occasions to act as press spokesperson. From him *Financial World* got much information when the magazine selected Sam as "CEO of the Decade" and featured him in the April 4, 1989 issue. Billingsley also supplied anecdotes to *Ladies' Home Journal* for an article in the May 1989 issue that included Helen as one of seven wives of billionaires.

"Sam was very fond of Ron Mayer," Billingsley told me. "Ron was very, very brilliant and very, very aggressive, and Ron was an excellent person. But his life-style was different from the Wal-Mart life-style. This is my opinion. I like Ron very well, but any person who knew the structure of Wal-Mart and had observed it would recognize that Ron didn't fit the normal mold of Wal-Mart people.

"Ron was not necessarily a materialistic person. But look at the life-style of the normal Wal-Mart executive. He is in there [his office] at 6:30 or 7:00 Monday morning. Tuesday he's in a small airplane checking out store sites and looking at locations as well as present stores around the countryside, perhaps Tuesday and Wednesday, as well. Thursday he's back in meetings all day. Merchandise meeting on Friday. He may sit on the real estate committee. He may serve on the finance committee. He may serve on personnel committees. Saturday morning meetings and interviews perhaps on Saturday afternoon. Sunday morning he's in church and Sunday evening he's with his family, and Monday morning he's back at work.

"That's a pretty hard life. And if your life-style doesn't fit that mode in any form or fashion, you're not very comfortable. And if you're one who doesn't have a forgiving and understanding family, you have problems."

More than anyone, Sam was aware of the Wal-Mart life-style. He was alert to its dangers, the risk of burnout. In fact, he had just witnessed that in the case of Jim Henry, who left because the demands of his job began to tear him apart and sap the boss's confidence in him. Sam had seen others resign or get fired because of the rigors of working in a pressure cooker for a boss some staffers inelegantly called "that old slavedriver." He expected there would be others, too, down the road.

But in the early seventies Sam was watching closely the performance of Ron Mayer. The boss liked how Ron dived right in—and had a tendency to take charge in aggressive fashion and get things done.

Ron looked like he was growing in stature and expertise. He exuded an air of confidence and became something of a flashy dresser, given to crimson shirts and colorful ties. He had a strong chin and a darkeyed, direct look that could make laggards squirm. He wore modish sideburns, as did quite a few Wal-Mart men, and his curly hair occasionally loosed a ringlet that fell over his wide forehead.

Sam, striding up and down the corridors of his barebones general office and warehouse complex, constantly took stock of progress and personnel. He had been under the gun himself for twenty-nine hectic years, and Helen and his children had been urging him to retire—or at least take it a little easier. So he began mulling over possibilities. Who could take over command and keep Wal-Mart humming?

He gave a lot of thought to Ron Mayer.

Sitting down to assemble his chairman's message to stockholders for the 1974 annual report, Sam was decidedly impressed by the growth of his creation. Sales and net earnings had reached all-time highs. There were now 78 Wal-Mart stores with a sales volume of $169,365,623 and a net income for 1974 of $6,158,520.

Sam wrote that twenty-four more stores would be added in 1975 and forecast total sales in excess of $225 million. The growth of Wal-Mart, he explained, "is a remarkable story of achievement and people . . . and therein lies our Wal-Mart 'secret.' " He added:

> Wal-Mart is obviously a company which is concerned about its people, its customers, its suppliers, its communities, and for honesty and integrity of service.
>
> Perhaps the key factor that makes our Company unusual is this quality of total personal concern on the part of our people. This must be listed as our "number one" asset and must be the "number one" reason for Wal-Mart Stores' success.
>
> We're all proud of our record to date, and we're confident this is just the beginning of our Wal-Mart story.

If in truth this was just the beginning of the Wal-Mart saga, should Sam Walton remain in command? Or should he finally step back now that everything was solidly in place and let a younger leader take over?

Should he hand over the reins to Ron Mayer?

Sam watched his protege from Abilene bustling around the office, going out on the road, making critical decisions—and arriving at brilliant and correct solutions to monumental problems.

At this point Sam did not himself detect any deficiencies in the financial officer, or any lack of his commitment to the yeoman life-style that Wal-Mart demanded.

In his heart Sam Walton already knew in 1974 that he had reached a decision. He was going to put his healthy, rapidly growing discount baby into Ron Mayer's hands.

Not just yet. But soon. Very soon.

—15—

Stylus Virum Arguit

In trying to characterize Sam Walton, one thinks of a line from Shakespeare's contemporary Robert Burton (1577–1640) "It is most true, *stylus virum arguit*—our style bewrays us."* Or as a wise nobleman proclaimed in 1753 on admission to the French Academy: *"Le style est l'homme même."* The style is the man himself. Sam Walton is what he is—no more, no less; no fake front, no cheating changes, nothing concealed.

Many of his successful policies have been brazenly and openly scavenged from retail competitors and then given Walton's personal spin. That is not to say he hasn't generated his own original schemes and stunning ploys, dozens of which are now accepted as industry standards. He has also always lent a ready ear to brainstorms from his lieutenants. Their bright ideas have added significantly to the Walton, or the Wal-Mart, style. Actually, there can be no distinction between the two: The company is the man. Absolutely.

Sam's principles come straight from the whiphand of Thomas G. Walton. They are rock hard and lifelong. They are his heritage and his faith. They are the old-fashioned virtues of hard work, honesty, fair play, courage, truth, courtesy, faith in God, kindness, and,

*The archaic bewray is defined: To make known; reveal; disclose.

importantly, discipline—for himself and for every last person involved in Wal-Mart.

Stubbornness against the odds—any odds—has been an asset rather than a hindrance to success. If Sam believes in anything, he will exhaust himself—and his troops—in a valiant effort to make it work. Generally thought to be muleheaded and often blind, Sam can, in fact, be quite flexible and open to change. An executive who has labored beside him almost thirty years, Clarence Leis, had this to say about Sam:

"Everyone talks about Sam's luck. Funny thing about that. I've thought about it many times. He's got a crazy intuition that probably not another man in the whole world's got. I mean he could have us all going one way today, and have second thoughts. And have us all going another tomorrow. And he still does that. He probably did it five times a week for twenty years." Leis punctuated his recollection with a hearty chuckle.

Another man eager to disabuse the public of the notion that the Wal-Mart chieftain pigheadedly sticks to a predetermined course is George Billingsley, a longtime Walton family intimate. He also claims that the public conception of Sam as a good ol' country boy wearing a soft velvet glove misses the fact that there's an iron fist within.

"Sam Walton is not one to stay still," Billingsley explained. "He'll shake the roof every once in a while. He's not hesitant to make changes and sometimes you wonder why. But he makes 'em, and he very seldom makes an error."

The boss himself candidly agrees. "I guess I can get a little tough if I see things I don't like," Sam told an interviewer. He stressed that he knew his business from bottom to top. "I used to do it all, sweep the floor, keep the books, buy the merchandise. . . . One of my assets is my willingness to try something new, to change. I think that is a concept we carry throughout the company. We have a low resistance to change. We call it our 'RC Factor.' "

With all his sterling qualities, Sam Walton has over

the years demonstrated quixotic tendencies and an occasional contrariness that has left observers with the notion that the Wal-Mart boss was riding north and south at one and the same time.

Perhaps the greatest puzzlement about his personality is that he accommodates a high degree of ego—the source of his drive to overtake his rival discounters, especially K mart—and yet can appear so humble that he almost seems to be apologizing for taking up space on the earth.

"Ego, in my opinion, is one of the worst things that can happen to a company," Sam said. He denies that he has ever run a one-man show. But Ferold Arend, retired Wal-Mart president and one of a little band of keen-eyed retailers who early on helped steer the company to success, offers a different opinion. Talking to a *Business Week* reporter, Arend said he always knew it was time to stop arguing a point when Walton thundered, "By golly, I still own most of the stock in this company, and this is the way we are going to do it."

Some business writers accustomed to big-city sophistication and briskness admit they had a hard time believing the fellow in Bentonville was for real. One is Stephen Taub, senior editor of *Financial World*.

"I've been to Bentonville and I've done a couple of pieces on Sam," Taub told me, "and I find him an interesting character. . . . It's funny . . . when I was down there working on my story, he came across almost as sort of this stereotypical absentminded chairman who played no role in the success of the company. He's very soft-spoken, apologetic.

"Then our magazine made him CEO of the decade [1989] and he comes to New York and he's playing the same role, you know, working the crowd. Then they introduce him and he gets up to the microphone and all of a sudden that big, powerful, booming voice comes out.

"And at that moment—that was the first time I realized why he gets his boys in a trance. It wasn't until then; I was really puzzled until that moment. He was just so powerful at the microphone!"

Intimates recognize "the ego thing." But it does not really emerge in Sam's public persona. In evidence, although in a rather unobtrusive way, are typical signs that mark the upward path of the rich and famous. In their Bentonville parlor hang oil portraits of Sam and Helen. Likewise, portraits hang on the wall of the fine arts center at the University of the Ozarks, Clarksville, Arkansas. This building was paid for by a gift of $5 million from the Waltons; the university put their name on it and awarded both honorary doctorates.

Consider also Sam's grasp on Bentonville, still a small town—only 10,800 population in 1989. Thirty-five hundred of its residents get their paychecks from him. He could buy and sell the whole community, but he has no desire to do that. His company officials get involved as normal citizens in community affairs, not with a sledgehammer approach. He doesn't permit anyone to throw around Wal-Mart's weight. Perhaps "Silk Stocking Row" does not exercise the rigid control it once did in the 1950s, but the new number-one citizen is sympathetic to the old nesters' heritage and traditions. It is clear to all that Sam remains devoutly small town in value, decorum, and life-style. He hasn't changed since the days of his five-and-dime on the square.

Testimony to his old-shoe commonness comes from his Kingfisher friend Irvin Bollenback, who flew to Bentonville in the mideighties with the multimillionaire Oklahoma City publisher Edward Gaylord. "I would say this to anybody," Bollenback confided. "I don't believe there is any successful man that kept the common touch as much as Sam Walton. . . .

"I went down to Bentonville with Ed Gaylord, and Sam was just going to show us around his place and all the deal down there. He came out to meet us at the airport in an old car that had cuts on the dashboard. I got in the backseat and there was a dirty old carburetor back there on the floorboards and I mean it was just something you'd expect from some Okie that they always talk about here [Kingfisher].

"Sam Walton, as wealthy as he is, would drive an old car, never put on airs. . . . I rode the front seat sometimes because I wanted Gaylord to see that back there. That was kind of interesting."

Something similar—but much more gauche—occurred when an important business couple flew in from London to discuss some aspect of Wal-Mart's "Buy American" campaign. Sam was waiting to greet them at the Rogers airport.

"They were sort of royalty," said Burton Stacy, president of the Bentonville bank. "He was a lord or something and she was Lady so-and-so. When Sam picked them up, he was driving his pickup truck. And she didn't appreciate it worth a damn. He doesn't get too worried about things like that. It's just transportation to him."

More seriously, Stacy is an eloquent advocate of his boss's humanistic concepts. "I was just driving along the other day and I was reflecting. I was thinking, you know, if we could all truly adopt Sam Walton's philosophy, and that's everything we do, we do for others . . . Everything he does is directed towards other people's benefit, and look at the reward he's gotten back. Getting rich has been the last goal that man has."

Has Sam Walton given up too much of himself?

The banker shakes his head. "You got to understand that's his pleasure. That is truly his pleasure. I say the man is totally generous. . . . He has got to be the best example of entrepreneurship, of achieving it through hard, dedicated, intelligent work. Completely honest and completely ethical—completely. I know. I cannot think of one single instance where Mr. Walton has ever demonstrated anything less than perfect ethics. Period. Not once."

Any serious student of this unorthodox man is quickly inundated with remarkable Sam stories. Like flagging down one of his own eighteen-wheelers and climbing into the cab to ride a hundred miles with the driver to gain firsthand experience that might improve Wal-Mart transportation. And getting up at 2:30 A.M., buying a sack of doughnuts, and taking them over to his warehouse loading dock, where he solicited, between bites, ideas to upgrade their effort. Right off the dockers said they needed two additional shower stalls; they immediately got them.

One incident that gave Bentonville a chuckle is related by historian J. Dickson Black:

"A few years ago somebody spotted the old car that Sam used for hunting parked over in front of the high school building that then was directly behind the old Presbyterian Church. On the front seat were Sam's hunting clothes and his guns, but he was nowhere in sight.

"They called the police. A squad car came and the first thing the policemen thought was that somebody had kidnapped Sam! The cops hightailed it down to Sam's house and rang the doorbell.

"Sam answered the door. The policemen asked about his abandoned car. Sam broke out laughing. 'I just forgot it,' he said. 'I went hunting early this morning and ran down here to the house to let the dogs out, and drove back up to go to church. I had my suit in the car and just parked there by the school and changed my clothes and went to church. Helen was, of course, there. And after the service she asked if I wanted to ride home with her. You know I just forgot I had left my car over at the high school.' So the policemen drove him up to get his car."

Sam's record as a motorist has several blemishes. In write-ups in several out-of-town newspapers, the Bentonville police boasted they've handed America's richest man at least two traffic citations. "We treat him just like anybody else," said one officer.

The worst traffic accident Walton had was largely due to his persistent curiosity about how his competition is faring. Tom Harrison relates: "Sam was driving through Rogers on his way to some kind of a meeting down in Springdale. He was going along and he looked over at the Safeway store, counting the cars in the parking lot. He's always doing that—he calls it research. Right in front of him was a Wal-Mart tractor-trailer and right in front of that eighteen-wheeler was a stop light. It turned red, and the truck stopped. Sam didn't.

"Sam ran into the back of his own truck. Pretty good smashup. Those Waltons have a guardian angel, because Sam just got a little scratch or two. Could have been hurt bad. The thing that upset him most was that it was a Wal-Mart truck and the driver had just received a ten-year pin for safe driving."

But there was considerably more to the crash than that. Historian Black provides the interesting aftermath: "Naturally somebody called the police and the only woman officer on the force, Carol Connor, responded. Sam started explaining who he was and that he had a very important business meeting in Springdale, and since he owned both the car and the truck, he'd take care of everything, and if they wanted papers filled out he'd drop down to the police station next day and do it.

"She informed him that she knew who he was, but that he would be treated like anybody else who had an accident in the city limits of Rogers, and he would stay there and fill out a report or she would call for a backup and they could handcuff him and take him down to the police station and take care of it. And he decided that he had plenty of time to stay there and fill out the form and sign it for her.

"But the next day he realized that he might have seemed a little pushy, and sent some flowers to the police station."

That wasn't written up in the local newspapers, since nobody had been injured, but news of the episode traveled pretty fast on the Bentonville grapevine. It also was remembered and highlighted as a parade float when Bentonville staged a mammoth "Appreciation Day" in 1983 for the Waltons.

Some of Sam's company cronies stuck a brand-new

blue-and-white Wal-Mart eighteen-wheeler smack in the middle of the parade, with attached to its rear end a smashed-up car that resembled Sam's. Behind the vehicles strolled a uniformed policeman. No explanatory sign was necessary. As the float rolled by, Sam and Helen in the reviewing stand laughed merrily.

His impromptu visits to Wal-Mart stores have made him a much-loved boss. He wears his own "Sam" badge, and first-names as many "associates" as he can. He is friendly, approachable, and he listens. Tom Harrison recalled stopping at a store near Memphis. "Lady clerk there asked if I knew Mr. Walton. I said yeah. She said he came in the store once and called her by name, and she said it was like the Second Coming. . . . Sam tells me the main thing he hated was when they got so big he didn't know all the people any more."

Newspapers all across the country have referred to him as "rich but corny" and brand him as down-to-earth as homegrown tomatoes. He was unorthodox enough to delay a Wal-Mart press conference at a Little Rock hotel when the University of Arkansas basketball team was tied in the closing minutes of a tight game. "Come up to my room," he told the reporters and cameramen, "and we can watch the Hogs win." Everyone hovered around the TV. In the last four seconds the Razorbacks' Charles Balentine sank a one pointer that won the game, 65–64.* Sam exploded in a cheer and told the press both he and Balentine started out in Newport, Arkansas—Walton with his first variety store and Balentine as a standout high school player.

Walton hops in his airplane and attends as many out-of-town Arkansas University football and basketball games as he can—combining each trip with store visits. "I've flown to several ball games with Sam," recalled Bob Bogle, "and I usually see six to eight

---

*After graduating, Balentine joined Wal-Mart and is called by Sam "one of our best" regional supervisors for new store openings.

Wal-Mart stores. If it's a night game, he goes in the daytime and you're going to see all the Wal-Mart stores between here and College Station, Texas, or Jackson, Mississippi—or wherever the Razorbacks are playing. And maybe some on our way back."

Bill Enfield found one bit of amusement in flying around the country with Sam in their search for a new bank president. "Every time we'd land somewhere, Sam wanted to call back to his office to see how things were going. He never had any money for the phone. I got in the habit of carrying a roll of dimes." Tom Harrison said: "He's always broke. He stopped up in Missouri at a gas station and wanted to get a check cashed. The service station man asked if he knew so-and-so who was head of the bank there. Sam said, 'Oh, he's a real good friend of mine.' The station operator said, 'Yeah? He's been dead two or three years.' The Waltons are down-to-earth. I've never had better friends."

His hula dance down Wall Street in 1984 was a startling and bizarre performance—a totally uncharacteristic exhibitionist stunt he tricked himself into, and felt honor-bound to carry out.

Rashly, in an effort to fire up his associates all along the line, Sam vowed that if the Wal-Mart stores made a pretax net profit of 8 percent for the year 1983, he would hula down the heart of the New York financial district. He didn't expect to lose the bet. Three percent is a normal retail profit. The best the company had ever done was 7 percent. But Sam lost. The profit was a little above 8 percent. So on a windy March morning in New York, he wrapped a grass skirt around his blue pinstripe suit, donned a flower lei and the weak smile of a man undergoing total public humiliation. Then with three authentic grass-skirted Hawaiian dancers and two Hawaiian ukulele players, Sam shimmied—or sort of—down Wall Street to the cheers of reporters and photographers.

Looking on, Wal-Mart's David Glass observed: "We'll never get him to do something like that again." And

Glass was right. Sam still makes all kinds of outrageous bets—all extravagantly publicized in the *Wal-Mart World* and calculated to keep high spirits buzzing among the troops. But the stakes are very ordinary—betting Glass a steak dinner, or somebody else a $1.00 can of peanuts. Sam Walton henceforth is allergic to grass skirts or making a total fool of himself in public.

When Sam discusses his management style he is dead serious about identifying it as MBWA, "management by walking around." It's a term he admits he borrowed, probably from author Tom Peters, and it rarely fails to appear somewhere in any issue of the monthly *Wal-Mart World*. It represents his tactic of haunting stores—his and the competition, as well—on the lookout for methods and means, finesse and fault, the winning and losing tricks of mass merchandisers. He obviously has made MBWA work.

Unleashing his personal magnetism like a movie star or a politician, Sam leaps up on a Wal-Mart checkout counter and grabs the public address mike. Then comes a high-octane, happy-face performance he has repeated hundreds of times. It is his attempt to be an inspirational leader. It is behavior he is perfectly comfortable with—and very, very good at.

A typical scenario is the opening of a new store, the "grand" reopening, an anniversary, some special event. Hanging from the ceiling is a tricolor banner, as if ready for a high school homecoming. Sam has already worked the crowd, shaking hands, remembers several longtime employees by name and tells them, "Thank you." As *Financial World* observed, "He employs large dollops of eye contact. It is as traditional as a Bible Belt revival meeting, as silly as a high school pep rally. It is show biz. It works."

Mike in hand, Sam croons: "Have you only just begun?"

"Yesssss!" The store is electrified, and the "associates" shriek their affirmation.

"Are you taking care of your customers? Are you going to keep doing that?"

"Yessss! Yessss!"

"Give me a W!" Sam shouts.

They are eager and ready. The "W" comes in a throaty roar.

"Give me an A!"

Another explosion from his enthusiastic clerks. . . . And Sam works his way through W-A-L-M-A-R-T!

Robert Buchanan, the analyst at A. G. Edwards & Sons, Inc., St. Louis, who follows Wal-Mart stock, told *Financial World*: "Walton does a remarkable job of instilling near-religious fervor in his people." His observation was echoed by David Banks, a native Arkansawyer who is president of the California nursing home concern, Beverly Enterprises, and has served since 1985 as a Wal-Mart director. "He makes people feel good," Banks said. "He is willing to get out there and do that. They all know he is the richest man in America and he is out there with them on the floor and that gives them pride. There is a feeling that it is a success that begat success, and once he got it started he could maintain it."

The other side of the affability coin is Sam's toughness in dealing with merchandise salesmen—whom he calls "vendors"—and likewise with his own buyers, who are charged with never failing to obtain rock-bottom wholesale prices. At Sam's insistence, his buyers have demanded price concessions—promising high-volume sales—from the biggest names in manufacturing, including Procter & Gamble, General Electric, and the Sony Corporation. Even the regional manager of a cosmetic firm felt exhausted after emerging from an afternoon session at Wal-Mart's general offices. He told *Arkansas Times* business magazine: "I got an order. These people are folksy and down-to-earth as homegrown tomatoes. But when you start dealing with them—when you get past that 'down home in Bentonville' business—they're hard as nails and every bit as sharp. They'll drive as hard a deal as anyone anywhere."

Not even a hometown "vendor" is exempt from getting caught in Sam Walton's hard-driving purchas-

ing style, as one of the "Silk Stocking Row" merchants, Charles Craig, discovered. He told me: "When
I was in the wholesale business here—tackle, sporting
goods, and the like—I sold Sam some flashlight
batteries—four gross of Ray-o-Vac. Three months later
I figured he needed more, so I went around. Sam
grinned when I walked into his office. 'You here to
talk batteries?' I said yes. 'How many do you want?
I'll sell 'em to you right now.'

"I said, 'Come on, Sam!' He said, 'With you I
thought I had the best deal on batteries, but after you
left, I got in my plane and flew up to Ray-o-Vac, and
we had an understanding—and now I do have the best
deal!' And he did, too!"

Company policy prohibits Sam's buyers from accepting any sweetheart treatment from salesmen. It's
to be all business—no gifts or gratuities of any sort,
not even a free lunch. In large black letters, Wal-Mart
policy is posted in the lobby of the general offices. It
says: "When dining together, the vendor and the Wal-
Mart associate must pay for their own meals."

One candy salesman handed the receptionist a one-
pound box. She handed it back. "No, thank you, it's
against the rules." He said, "It's a little box. You can
open it up and eat it right here." She gave him a look.
"It makes no difference. We accept nothing."

A few years ago a Wal-Mart buyer thumbed his
nose at the rules by taking his wife along to a sporting
goods marketing show in Las Vegas and letting a
manufacturer pick up her trip tab.

After he got back, Sam found out about it, called
the man in and gave him two weeks off without pay,
and said he would be reassigned out of buying. Downtown at the coffee shop the man started yelling and
screaming that he was going to quit Wal-Mart, that he
wasn't going to put up with that kind of treatment. If
somebody wanted to give him a little gift, that was his
business, not Mr. Sam's.

But two weeks later, he was packing to go to a

Wal-Mart store as assistant manager. The point was driven home—for all the buyers to see. He was a good man, and later Sam made him manager of one of his new stores.

An interview J. Dickson Black had to have with Sam to meet publication deadline for his history of the Bank of Bentonville illustrates the tycoon's down-home way of operating. As Black tells it:

"The receptionist told me he was running behind and I'd have to wait maybe ten minutes. She apologized. I had come from refinishing furniture, and I had on pretty ratty-looking clothes. It was the day salespeople were waiting to see the buyers—men with $300 and $400 suits.

"Those people stared at me. Jack Shewmaker wandered through and he stopped and shook hands, and so did a couple of other important officers. All the visitors just gaped. Finally I was led in to see Mr. Sam, who had said I'd be limited to twenty minutes. But we got to talking about this and that and I was in there maybe an hour. I stopped by another office to check on something, and Sam comes running after me. 'Black! Black! Don't go—we haven't finished talking yet!'

"He'd thought of something else to tell me, and we stood right there at the entrance to the waiting room talking for a few minutes. Those salesman out there just gaped at us. They couldn't believe the chairman of Wal-Mart was chasing down and calling back such a scroungy, long-haired character!"

Those whose ideas of the opulence of corporate executive suites come from movies, television, or magazines are stunned by the bleakness of Wal-Mart's general offices. The exterior of the rambling redbrick structure that quickly becomes a mammoth warehouse, all surrounded by black asphalt parking for several thousand autos and trucks, is decent enough. But the interior is as stark and functional as a Midas muffler waiting room. Even President David D. Glass described the decor as "early bus station." This is how the *Kansas City Star Magazine* depicted the lobby in 1984:

> Conditions inside the waiting room are not exactly palatial, either, inexpensive paneling, plastic stack chairs. Inside waiting their appointments, salesmen wearing "Visitor" badges pick lint from their lapels. Occasionally, they rise, get change from a boxful of nickels on the receptionist's desk and head for the pay coffee machines. Everyone, from the receptionist to the company president, goes through this routine. Everyone pays.
>
> On the walls are various declarations of gratitude from retail companies for Wal-Mart business such as a shiny, ceremonial record from Kenny Rogers and a plaque from Van Camps for the world's largest order of pork and beans ("the Beaning of America"). Behind the receptionist's desk is a painting of Ol' Roy.
>
> "That's him. He's famous now," the woman says in response to my question. "Mr. Walton just loves that dog." She pauses. "Or did."
>
> Several varieties of mounted fish gape in another part of the room, testimony to the fact that brother Bud devotes much of his time these days to the sport, much of it with fishing authority Howard Ensley. . . . This is the type of personalized frugality that has resulted in the lowest overhead costs for a discount department store in the industry.

I sat in that lobby in 1988, in 1989 and in 1990. Nothing much had changed since the Kansas City reporter saw it. On my last visit, however, the polished floors glistened, everything appeared freshly painted, and the men's room was spotlessly clean. Probably the waiting room would not get much shabbier for another five or ten years. You couldn't help reflect on the contribution this type of headquarters makes to a Wal-Mart boast that their total administrative cost amounts to 2 percent of revenue, far below industry norms.

In everything connected with business, Sam goes

bargain basement. Once Stacy was delegated to rent a car while they were traveling. Sam made him take it back; he wouldn't pay for anything bigger than a sub-compact, Stacy said. "He is not going to be seen in anything better than what his people are allowed, you see. Sam Walton is not going to stay in a better hotel than his people are allowed, nor eat in a better restaurant, nor drive a better car."

When he travels by commercial airline, he flys coach. George Billingsley said Sam had a fit on a South American trip; there was only one available seat—in first class. "That's the only time I've heard of him flying first class."

There is something "inspirational" about the Wal-Mart frugality in the opinion of Jack Stephens, the multimillionaire Little Rock investment banker, who served two hitches on the Wal-Mart board of directors, retiring finally in 1987.

"How did it inspire you?" I asked.

"Well, I was on another corporate board also at that time. I used to try to explain the differences between those board meetings. At Wal-Mart, we never knew where we were going to meet. We'd take any room that was available. The chairs were kind of rickety. Our sandwiches were cold, but we had potato chips. And if we brought our own quarter, we could buy a Coca-Cola for lunch. That's the philosophy of the company. That's what makes it lean and strong.

"Now the other board I was on—linen, proper china, cocktails before lunch, and jets taking people home after the board meeting. And I've been on other boards like that. Now Sam Walton—he lives and breathes efficiency."

"Do you believe that's part of the key to his success?"

"No question about it!"

At Stephens's office in Little Rock, during a discussion of Walton's thriftiness, Mike Smith, a vice-president who has spent a lot of time with Walton observed: "My shoes cost more than everything Sam Walton is wearing today, I'll bet you!"

Sam has been no more prejudiced against women in executive roles than perhaps was the norm in corporate America until recent years. Now he has one woman board member—Hillary Clinton, a youngish, pretty, high-powered, articulate Little Rock lawyer, who also is the wife of Arkansas Governor Bill Clinton. Wal-Mart's 1988 annual report listed as vice-president and divisional merchandise manager Harryetta Bailey. For years the signature on proxy statements and stockholder information has been Bette Hendrix, assistant secretary.

The rise of Clara Slater from hosiery-lingerie manager in the Wal-Mart store at Moberly to a district manager of a group of nine or ten company stores in northeast Missouri was extolled by none other than the chairman himself.

"I remember well reviewing her lingerie department," Sam recalled, "and asking her what her best-sellers were in the ladies' panty section. She impressed me then by her knowledge and capacity, by getting out her order books and showing me that she ordered regularly by rate of sale; she knew and took pride in what she was doing.

"Soon we were discussing how to develop a promotion and a VPI [volume-producing item] program on her best number at that time—a 100 percent, full-cut cotton brief. She did it well and continued her journey through Wal-Mart as in-store assistant and manager at Macon, Missouri, until today she has become one of our most respected and capable district managers.

"My hat's off to you, Clara, and your entire Wal-Mart team," Sam asserted in his June 1989 *Wal-Mart World* column. "We're very proud of you all."

Then he continued in a vein that must have lifted women's hearts and spirits in every quarter of the whole concern. He wrote:

In fact, thinking about the development of our company, I'm so pleased to see us beginning to recognize and promote women to responsible positions of management throughout Wal-Mart. For years, retailing management was considered the exclusive province of men. That's not so today. Wal-Mart's Executive Committee realizes that we have a tremendous pool of future management talent in the ranks of our women associates and has made the commitment to train and develop them to the fullest.

I'm convinced that our Wal-Mart women associates have unlimited opportunity to advance and assume top management responsibilities in our Wal-Mart organization. In my opinion, there is not a single management job in our company that can't be handled effectively by women who have the training, determination, ambition, and capacity to do it.

Despite those fine words, Walton has not always been so sensitive to women's pride for he began Wal-Mart with a company policy intended to discourage romance between the men and women in the stores and offices. Unless "approved," one Wal-Mart employee could not date another employee. That was spelled out in the employees' handbook.

Sam apparently felt that if some stock boy or clerk started mooning over a pretty girl in the store, he might handle his chores in a slipshod or careless fashion, and business efficiency and customer satisfaction would suffer. And vice versa; some pretty girl in housewares might devote too much time to setting her cap for a handsome fellow in electronics or the paint department. In the face of this harsh and outdated policy, it would seem that Wal-Mart men and women would have stormed the barricades to get Walton to lighten up.* But nobody wanted to challenge the boss.

When an employee sought company "approval," his proposed in-store courtship was put under scrutiny of not the store manager, but the district supervisor. It was a strict rule.

"I mean dead serious," said Shirley Cox, a twenty-

*I tried to get the views of Hillary Clinton, as the sole woman on the Wal-Mart board, on this issue but she did not respond.

year employee in the Harrison store. "They looked at which departments were involved in a romance—that sort of thing. If it wasn't approved, one of them would have to quit. You absolutely couldn't date an assistant manager. He might, you know, show favoritism."

Jim Dodson, Sam's former business associate, said Walton believed in high standards: 'No fraternizing in the store. . . . The men and women, no hanky-panky. I believe he'd fire a man quicker for that than he would for stealing."

"It was a pretty stiff rule," said Clarence Leis. "Unless there was approval of going with someone in the company, it was not to be done. Some probably violated the policy. But I would imagine they did that on the QT."

After more than twenty years trying to control the love bug, Sam had second thoughts about in-store romance. He decided to ease off—but only partway.

When the new edition of the Associates' Handbook was distributed in late 1989, the old rule was dropped. Instead, on page twenty, the handbook said: "Good management directs the necessity of avoiding even the appearance of favoritism among our associates, therefore no management will be allowed to date or become romantically involved with another associate in his/her department or store. No one will be permitted to date anyone under his or her supervision."

The handbook also probibits two members of the same family, such as husband and wife or mother and daughter, working side by side in the same department, although supervisors may make exceptions in certain situations.*

But Sam did not back off in the slightest about sin and cheating in the workplace. The latest handbook

---

*The strict policy against accepting any gift or gratuity, even a lunch, from anyone doing business with Wal-Mart is reiterated in the handbook. Another rule warns that any associate who issues hot checks or whose paycheck is garnisheed is subject to review and possible dismissal.

Sam distinguishes himself as "Most Versatile Boy" at Hickman High, Columbia, Missouri.

Sam and Helen cut the cake after their Valentine's Day wedding, 1943.

The Walton family, Christmas 1949. *Left to right:* Sam with Jim on his lap, Rob, John, Helen and baby Alice on her lap.

Sam Walton's first store—a Ben Franklin 5¢ and 10¢ franchise in Newport, Arkansas.

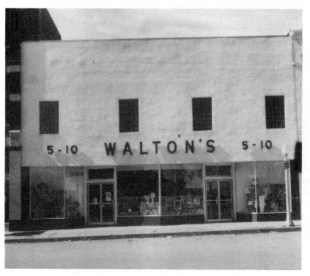

Sam's first Bentonville five-and-dime.

WAL-MART, Sam's chain of discount stores, takes off and signs like these pop up in small towns across the South.

A key factor in Wal-Mart's success was that merchandise could be trucked into stores from distribution centers no more than one day's drive from any store.

Sam initiates the "Buy America" campaign in the mid-80s. He's pictured here holding up U.S.-made washcloths at a press conference.

Recent family photo. *Left to right:* Alice, Rob, Sam, Helen, Jim, and John.

Sam and brother Bud relaxing on a hunting trip.

Sam's first HYPERMART USA, opened in
Garland, Texas in 1987.

Interior view of a typical cavernous Sam's
Wholesale Club.

Sam and Jimmy Carter on a 1987 quail-hunting trip.

says unequivocally: "Wal-Mart strongly believes in and supports the family unit. A dating relationship between a married associate and another associate other than his or her own spouse is not consistent with that belief, and is prohibited."

—16—

To Crown a New King

As he approached his fifty-seventh birthday, Sam Walton was reluctantly trying to change his life-style completely—by surrendering the day-to-day command of his Wal-Mart empire. But he found that difficult, almost impossible, to do.

Helen was after him all the time to let up, to quit scrambling to open more and more stores. Sam started to think maybe she was right. He had been a variety store merchant and mass merchandising discounter for thirty years. And for thirty years Sam Walton was in charge, responsible for most of the corporate thinking and decision-making, and now the future of Wal-Mart would go into somebody else's hands. It had finally sunk in that none of his three sons had the desire or ambition to reign over the Wal-Mart empire, although he was still working on Rob to become more active in corporate affairs. And he couldn't count on Bud taking charge; Sam's brother was much too laid back.

Even the thought of stepping aside nettled Walton. But he had to think seriously about it, because of mounting pressure from one his foremost underlings. There was no threat from Ferold G. Arend, Wal-Mart's savvy and dedicated chief operating officer; he was happy in his executive role.

But Ron Mayer, the boy-genius financial officer,

was making noises. His attitude and hints dropped in conversation told Sam all he needed to know. Ron Mayer had been with Wal-Mart five years, he was about to turn forty, and he thought he ought to be the number one man. He made it known that he could do a great job running Wal-Mart, or some other big retailing operation.

"I am going to lose Ron," Sam confided to one of his closest friends, "if I don't step aside and let him be chairman. And I don't want to lose him. He's a talented guy."

In the fall of 1974 Sam had a heart-to-heart talk with Ron Mayer. Then he carried his files, pictures and desk set into Ron's office, and had Ron move his things into Sam's chairman's office. It was official. Sam had retired; Ron was the new chairman and CEO of Wal-Mart, and the old boss was just a big stockholder, director, and chairman of the executive committee.

Ron Mayer tackled his new top job with gusto. He was quick and effective and had new ideas. He was a people person, friendly and well liked down at the associate level. These qualities pleased Sam. Even so, he kept a fairly close watch on his successor.

Their offices were on the fringes of the central bull pen that accommodated the secretaries for top executives. Everyone kept his office door open. There was a lot of hollering back and forth to relay messages. Everything was very informal. Sam liked it this way. Wal-Mart—from the very top down—was "family." Sam wouldn't tolerate formation of any cliques or the creating of patches of exclusive executive turf, which he thought would foster secrecy, jealousy, and suspicion. All hands in the corporate general offices were equal—in the family fold. They called each other by first names—especially Sam. There were no secrets. Profit-and-loss figures were posted in plain view—even in stores' stockrooms so associates could see them. In such an atmosphere, one of the great "family" strengths was trust.

The Wal-Mart company was still on a growth binge. At the end of January 1975, there were 104 stores, doing annual sales of $236 million, with $6 million net income and not quite 6,000 employees. And everyone predicted more growth—much more.

Sam, serving as chairman of the four-man executive committee of the board of directors, was mainly watching out to see that nothing went wrong, that there would be no slipups in his dream of one day making Wal-Mart the biggest mass merchandiser in the United States.

He remained a total skinflint. It became necessary to double the size of the general offices, but he insisted upon frugality. The offices were still bleak, functional, "early bus station." The rooms occupied by Sam, Ron Mayer, and Ferold Arend were no more elaborate than perhaps that of the owner of a successful small-city lumberyard, or the job applicant office in a Sears, Roebuck and Company district office.

Tulsa attorney Henry Will, who works on Wal-Mart employees' pension and trust matters, sniffs at the Bentonville offices. "Nothing fancy at all. Want to get through your business as quickly as possible. Not comfortable, crowded, gerrymandered offices. Walk in the front lobby—salesmen and telephones out front, a sheer workroom. Not at all the usual style of a big corporation."

With his new-found freedom, Sam Walton found it easier to pay close heed to the affairs of Bentonville, which remained very much a small town over the years. Merchants endeavored to retain in the town the rustic charm of still being somewhat of a "Saturday town." They sponsored a provincial "fun fair" to be held on the courthouse square. The first fair featured a Maypole dance, chicken barbecue, performances by the junior and senior high school drill teams, a pet show, and arts and crafts booths. It was an instant hit. Started in the midseventies, it has been held every other Saturday from spring through fall, even into the late eighties.

Sam and associates purchased the First National

Bank of Rogers on April 2, 1975. His Bentonville
bank had $29 million on deposit, and, under a new law
enacted after Wal-Mart lobbyists had worked on the
legislature, was permitted to open a branch at nearby
Bella Vista retirement community. Sam and Helen
had cut the ribbon in late 1974 for Wal-Mart No. 100
in Bentonville, and he found time to sit on a public
"Trust Forum" at the Holiday Inn to educate investors.

In this period the new $2.5 million high school
opened, work was begun to expand U.S. 71 from the
Missouri state line to four lanes through Bentonville,
and fire gutted the historic Massey Hotel—which would
be later taken over by the Waltons, its second floor
converted into Walton Enterprises, Inc., offices, and
the downstairs rebuilt as a new home for the public
library. On the square there was the wry comment
that Bentonville had just seen a sure sign it was about
to become big-town: the postmaster announced stamp
and mail windows would be closed on Saturdays.

Across the U.S., citizens were still reeling from
Watergate and President Nixon's resignation. U.S. civilians were evacuated from Saigon. Motorists were
queuing up because of the gasoline shortage. The FBI
captured Patty Hearst, the kidnapped heiress turned
gun moll bank robber. Legionnaires disease stunned
Philadelphia, and America began celebrating its bicen-
tennial.

But nothing on the national or local scene could
slow down the full-steam-ahead Wal-Mart juggernaut.
Smiling from the glossy pages of the annual report, a
curly-haired Ronald Mayer, in a maroon shirt, reported to stockholders that the fiscal year ending January 31, 1976, was the "most successful year in the
history of Wal-Mart with sales and net income both
reaching record levels."

In the new total of 125 stores, manned by about
7,500 employees, the cash registers rang up $340.3
million (44 percent gain), earning $11.5 million net
profit. Ron Mayer called the last half of the year
"surprisingly strong in terms of our customers' willing-

ness to purchase high-ticket items." The chairman's message said:

> We look forward to our continuing challenge of developing Wal-Mart as the leading regional discount chain. We plan to emphasize the same priorities that have contributed to the success of this company. To reach our sales goals of approximately $440 million for fiscal year ending January 31, 1977, we have set the following objectives. . . .
>
> —We will continue our program of opening new stores prior to November 1, thereby enabling us to concentrate on the Christmas season. We plan to open approximately twenty-five new stores and to relocate two existing stores to larger facilities for a net increase of 1,200,000 square feet.
>
> —We will accelerate our training and development programs for all Wal-Mart associates to effect an even stronger organization.
>
> —We will continue to maintain our leadership in competitive pricing and expense control.
>
> —We will fine-tune our inventory control program and continue to improve our inventory turnover and sales per square foot.

There was nothing in those fine words, aggressive and optimistic, to disturb the mind of Sam Walton. But he was clumping around the headquarters building with an uncharacteristic frown. Loretta Boss, who had been his personal secretary for years, and could read him like a book, was concerned about the change in his mood. He developed a tendency to snap at trifles; the old affability was no longer there. Something was bothering the boss. Perhaps it was that he no longer was boss.

Sam's personal secretary knew that under Ron Mayer there had been a lot of changes—and not necessarily for the better. She didn't complain or run to Sam. She knew Sam Walton was not blind. Whatever she saw, Sam would see; it just might take a little longer, since he was flitting in and out of headquarters, doing his best to back off and give Ron Mayer a free hand as chairman.

But it never has been Sam Walton's nature to dilly-dally or back off. He hadn't changed his habits; he was on the scene every day, haunting headquarters and still hopping in his plane to visit stores spread across eight states. His role was now supposed to be unofficial. But he couldn't keep hands off. When he saw something—anything—he didn't think was right, he'd just step in and correct it on the spot. "That's the way I've always been," he remembers. "I guess I was getting in the way of Ron's *authority*."

In the spring of 1976 Sam was brooding a great deal, sitting in his office chair, rattling around in his old pickup, or with his head bowed in the Presbyterian pew. He looked at the good side. Based strictly on the numbers—sales and profits, etc.—Ron Mayer was doing a magnificent job as number one man. He thought of how Ron, a great systems person, had put together Wal-Mart's first data processing program. It pleased the boss that this was done efficiently and at low cost.

It bothered Sam's conscience that he personally had made a mistake. He discovered, as he told Helen, that he really wasn't ready to retire. He missed his old job. "I'd hate to have anybody cut Ron down," Sam confided to an intimate, "and make it look like he's not an effective management person. He really is."

Even so, Ron Mayer's personal characteristics rattled Sam. It became generally known in the office that Ron Mayer was romancing a woman in Wal-Mart headquarters and that his wife was talking divorce. Strait-laced Walton couldn't condone that behavior—also, ironically, a direct violation of the company code.

More troublesome was that under the new chairman, cliques of executives had formed, driving a wedge of disharmony between Ferold Arend, the COO, and Ron, the CEO. That made Sam Walton see red and swear.

By early June Sam was making up his mind what to do. He had to either get back into it or leave com-

pletely. He did not want to leave, so he called in Ron
Mayer and asked him to step down as chairman and
return to his former position of vice-chairman and
financial vice-president.

He bluntly refused. Sam Walton had always said
Ron Mayer could make up his mind quickly—and
seldom changed a decision. Sam tried to talk him out
of leaving, but found him adamant about going. "He
wasn't fired," Sam has said. "It was awkward and
some outsiders wanted to turn it into a good story, and
tried to make it look a little sinister."

Thus after a "vacation" of twenty months, Sam
Walton was again chairman and issued an announcement to all Wal-Mart personnel giving the bare facts
on June 26, 1976. Three days later the news was
published in the *Wall Street Journal* as a six-paragraph
story on an inside page, containing a considerable
amount of double-talk about Sam not being able "to
assume a passive role" and causing friction by bugging
Mayer with criticism or suggestions.

Old hands in the general offices and out in the
stores undoubtedly were glad to see the founder back
on top. But such a cataclysmic headquarters rupture
did shake the company. Wal-Mart stock stumbled on
Wall Street but not for long. In fact, the strength of
the discounter righting itself may be the most remarkable element of this unhappy episode.

Critical events that take place behind these corporate doors rarely leak out in Bentonville. Not that the
townsfolk wouldn't relish gossip, but it's such a small
place that company tattletales might be easily tracked
down and suffer the fearful retribution a straight-arrow
like Walton would deem appropriate.

So it was almost three years before any gossip about
Ron Mayer leaving gained much circulation in town.
Some whispers were wild and outrageous; of course,
none of these fanciful innuendos made their way into
print. Some outsiders read a lot into the fact that Ron
Mayer's marriage was breaking up just about the time
he left Wal-Mart. In fact, the departure of Ron Mayer

and the return of Sam Walton to Wal-Mart's helm was handled by the national business media in a rather blasé way—not totally ignored, but barely speculated about. Truth is in the midseventies, Wal-Mart, regarded as just a little company down in Arkansas, was not hot copy in the national journals.

Talk about Ron Mayer died down in Bentonville and lay dormant for ten years or so—until local residents were interviewed in 1989 and 1990 for this book. Several people made reference to the episode, principally in discussing how Sam once tried to give up his chairmanship, but felt forced to come back and reclaim the king's crown.

"Sam is pretty straightlaced," said Clarence Leis, "and apparently something was going on—and he wasn't going to put up with it. I never really paid a lot of attention to that stuff. I knew what happened and when it happened and how it happened. I was never one that talked."

Another Wal-Mart insider said Ron Mayer began developing "little cliques" in the general office, totally in violation of Sam's belief in the company as "one big family."

George Billingsley, a Walton family intimate, said: "Sam was very fond of Ron Mayer, very fond of him . . . I think I've indicated Ron thought he was going to take over . . . I imagine Ron was very ambitious. And most young, aggressive executives want to go to the top perhaps quicker sometimes than they deserve or perhaps the chairman or owner would like to stay in. . . . It all happened rather quickly."

"Ron Mayer was smart," said Tom Harrison, "but he wasn't one that mixed around with people a lot. I don't know what happened. Next thing you knew he was just gone."

In the course of time it got back to Sam—not surprising in such a small town—that his friends and associates were giving interviews about his life. Sam had twice agreed with me to be interviewed, but canceled both appointments. We had talked once briefly in person, and chatted a few times on the phone. But when he heard that people were giving different versions of Ron Mayer's departure, he was disturbed enough to phone me from Bentonville on August 9, 1989. He was friendly and pleasant, as always. This is part of our conversation where he discussed Ron Mayer:

SAM: If you are going to do this thing, I want you to be accurate with it—

VT: Sam, I want to be accurate.

SAM: Yeah, because I understand that you had gotten some information from some of our folks that Ron Mayer, uh, we kicked him out and he left. He didn't have anyplace to go. I think a term was used—"a midnight massacre" of some kind. Well, you'd better sure get that straightened out because that's about 180 degrees from being true. . . In a nutshell, Ron Mayer did a fantastic job for this company and I thought I was ready to retire at age fifty-five, and you ought to know me better, well enough, to know that was a mistake.

VT: Yeah.

SAM: And I moved Ron in as chairman and CEO.

VT: Yes.

SAM: I got in his hair constantly. I was just always meddling with things, and I thought I was ready to quit, and I wasn't. In spite of that, he still did a good job. I told him I wanted to come back in, and I wasn't ready to retire, and I wanted him to continue as vice-chairman and chief financial officer, which is what he was before.

VT: Yeah.

SAM: And, in fact, if he had said, "Well, I'm not ever going to work another day for you, Sam Walton," to me he would have been worth paying the rest of his life for what he did for this company.

VT: Is that right?

SAM: But he chose at that moment to leave because he didn't want to be . . . step down, and he felt like it was time for him to move on, and it was his decision and no one else's, so you need to understand—

VT: Yeah, I need to understand.

SAM: And you need to get the facts on that deal—

VT: I want to get them.

SAM: And too many folks in the company know that's exactly the way it was, and I don't know how you could have . . . you know, how it could have been misconstrued. But I'm sure that with as many mistakes as we have made—I'm sure we have made mistakes, we've made a lot of mistakes— we've had to let people go . . . Some of them are going to try to take the dark side of everything and build up a case of being mysterious, or being this or that . . .

VT: I'm not looking for that. What I'm looking for is the straight, honest story.

SAM: There ought to be some folks that can give you the . . . Just all I'd like you to do is just tell the truth—and that's all you want.

VT: That's all I want.

SAM: And you're that kind of a guy; so I was real concerned when I heard that, and I knew that wasn't accurate, and somebody just didn't give you the right poop at all.

VT: Well, see the thing about it is, Sam, when I find out something, I just lay out what I have heard and ask for the truth. I don't know how else you could do it.

SAM: Well, that's true. There will be various perceptions, too, of situations, and—

VT: Don Spindel [market analyst at A. G. Edwards, St. Louis] told me, for instance, that you said after Ron left, you told the stock analysts [at a meeting in Bentonville] that it was one of the most crucial times for your company.

SAM: It was. It really was. It was critical because Ron took about four, five, or six that he had hired and brought on stream [into Wal-Mart].

VT: And you've got Bill Fields back with you— and he was one who left.

SAM: Bill came back later on, and that's when Jack Shewmaker came in and picked up and did a good job and Al Johnson and a lot of other folks. You know, I have always maintained that none of us is indispensable.

VT: I sure appreciate you helping me get the story straight.

SAM: Well, I haven't helped you much . . . The damn thing bothers me, if I'm fretting about, uh, uh, not, you know, having it be like it really was . . . I don't want you to flower it—

VT: I'm not going to flower it . . . Well, you have helped me a tremendous amount.

SAM: Thank you a lot. Thank you, Vance. Have a good day.

Now shift the scene back to the summer of 1976, because there was an explosive aftermath to Ron Mayer's departure. . . . His sudden and abrupt exit would be expected to send a jolt through the Wal-Mart ranks. To the associates out in the stores, and even to the underlings in the general offices, the event carried a certain aura of mystery. But its aftermath triggered more sensational and surprising (even to Sam) events.

The key player in the new Ron Mayer chapter about to unfold was Jack Stephens, the self-made millionaire Little Rock investment banker who had helped take Wal-Mart stock public, and was in 1976 serving on the Wal-Mart board of directors, as he had since 1971.

Jack Stephens looked on Ron Mayer as a very bright and aggressive merchandiser, with an excellent grasp of finance, and plenty of down-to-earth experience. He knew that a discount store chain named Ayr-Way, operating about forty stores principally in the Midwest, was on the market. It might be a good idea, he reasoned, to seize the opportunity and buy Ayr-Way and put it in the hands of the newly available ex-chairman of Wal-Mart and Stephens did just that.

Ayr-Way had been founded in 1961 by the big department store chain L. S. Ayres and Company as a subsidiary in the discount field. When Associated Dry Goods purchased L. S. Ayres in 1972, the FTC ruled that this deal threatened to eliminate competition in Indiana and Kentucky, and ordered Associated to sell Ayr-Way to a willing third party. That is where Jack Stephens entered the picture.

For a published price of $19.9 million, Stephens, Inc., and a few other investors, bought Ayr-Way. The deal was finalized in January 1977, and Ron Mayer moved to Indianapolis to become Jack Stephens's hand-picked chairman.

As Sam Walton mentioned in his telephone conversation, several Wal-Mart executives left Bentonville and joined Ayr-Way under Ron Mayer. One was the Wal-Mart controller, C. Ray Gash, and among others, Bill Fields and Royce Chambers, as well as top men in warehousing and data processing.

In an interview with Jack Stephens, I raised that point, along with the question of ethics in his becoming a competitor in the discount chain field while still serving as a Wal-Mart director.

"If you just put it down on paper, it doesn't look very friendly," I said.

"Well, but it was very friendly," he said. "Nobody came to Ayr-Way directly from Wal-Mart. Ron Mayer retired, uh, long in advance. He was just doing nothing. . . . My people here, Mike Smith and Jon Jacoby, said that Ron Mayer was available and that we could buy Ayr-Way at what we thought was a good price from Associated. And since we had Ron Mayer it was something that we should do. I never would have participated in anything that took directly from Wal-Mart."

"Now do I get it straight that you had already stepped off the Wal-Mart board when it took place, or as it was taking place? After you bought Ayr-Way, then you got off the board?"

"Yes. Wal-Mart was expanding and I just felt like being on the Wal-Mart board I might be privileged to inside information, and I explained to Sam, and he understood."

However, the fact is that Jack Stephens did not officially resign as a Wal-Mart director until about two years after he made the Ayr-Way purchase. His smiling photo was published in the list of directors in the annual report, as of January 31, 1979.

In his Ayr-Way gamble, Jack Stephens and his partners threw snake-eyes.

"Ayr-Way didn't materialize as you expected?" I inquired. "It was not a successful operation?"

"That's when we had the first of the great automobile slumps," Jack Stephens responded. "Automobiles went to hell, and so forth. Bad, bad economic times."

"So you decided to sell Ayr-Way?"

"Yes."

"And sold it to Target [one of twelve companies owned by Dayton Hudson Corporation] after three or four or five years—what was it?"

"Oh, God, it seems longer than that," he said. "I don't think it was that long. . . . I guess two and a half years." [Actually, the sale went through on October 10, 1980.]

"Well, do you still have the same high regard for Ron Mayer as a merchandiser, retailer as you had when you put him in charge of Ayr-Way?"

"I think Ron Mayer is a super, uh, individual," Jack Stephens said.

The failure of Ron Mayer to replicate at Ayr-Way the hard-charging success he had achieved in less than two years in Bentonville was commented on by George Billingsley in our interview. He had observed the event firsthand and feels Ron Mayer failed to recognize that Wal-Mart's growth was the result of team, not individual, effort.

"He just couldn't walk away with that Wal-Mart concept and by himself make it work somewhere else," he said. "You will not find people in Wal-Mart today—least of all Sam—who feel they are solely responsible for its success. Most recognize they could step aside tomorrow and the ball keeps right on rolling."

My telephone interview with Ron Mayer in the summer of 1989 at his office in Indianapolis was not too successful. He talked freely about his close brush with death in Sam's Beech Baron in 1969, but, in response to my first question about his Wal-Mart days, he said: "Really, I'd just as soon cut this off. No offense meant, but . . ."

The next question quoted the *Wall Street Journal* article about his reasons for leaving.

"I don't think it was because we couldn't see eye to eye," Ron Mayer said.

"Well, he apparently couldn't keep from wanting to run things, which I think he still does."

Ron Mayer laughed.

"Several people in Bentonville told me your resignation was requested."

"Yeah? Well, that's not true."

Ron Mayer operates two gift shops and two golf and tennis equipment and apparel outlets in Indianapolis. He would not respond to questions about his Ayr-Way experience or comment on a remark that he seemed to now occupy a rather minor position for an executive who today might still be head of the giant Wal-Mart enterprise.

"You were chairman of Wal-Mart. What do you do now?"

"I just take care of personal investments."

That comment effectively ended our conversation.

The A. G. Edwards analyst Don Spindel talked to both Sam Walton and Ron Mayer about their parting. Spindel told me: "Sam told me, 'It is entirely my fault Ron is leaving, because I couldn't keep my finger out of the pot.' Ron is highly regarded as a merchandiser and retailer. He thought he had an opportunity to run his own show at Ayr-Way and to build a Wal-Mart out of another chain. As it turned out, he missed."

Now, after working hard for twenty or so years, Ron Mayer probably has decided to take it easy, Don

Spindel said, adding: "He came away in good shape, with a lot of Wal-Mart stock. If he held on to it, he's doing okay. There's nothing wrong with that."

After Stephens, Inc., unloaded Ayr-Way, C. Ray Gash joined that company in Little Rock, and Bill Fields eventually returned to Wal-Mart where he became vice-president, merchandise systems, in 1980.

Stock analysts say that immediately after Ron Mayer left Bentonville, Wal-Mart stock began to fall—because Wall Street somehow got the impression that Mayer's departure left the chain leaderless.

"What happened," said Tom Harrison, "I imagine some of these big mutual funds and all that had stock thought the thing would go to pot—without Ron Mayer. They didn't know Sam Walton. Helen said a broker called her and said, 'Listen, you gotta buy some more of this stock. There's no way it can stay down.' And she said, 'I sure was glad he talked me into that.'

"I'd say it wasn't over three months at the max— after Sam took over again—that the stock was back up, and going on up. That was kind of funny. The kind of operation Sam had it didn't cause any kind of permanent ripple. I'm sure he made millionaires out of a lot of people who bought stock."

Jack Stephens told me that Sam Walton asked him to come back on the Wal-Mart board "the day I sold Ayr-Way."

"What did you tell him?"

"That I'd be delighted. Being on their board was an inspiration." (Jack Stephens was reappointed to the board and remained until 1987.)

The 1977 Wal-Mart annual report was the first to be issued after Sam's return to the chairmanship. It revealed the discount chain juggernaut was still rolling on with the old man—one year shy of sixty—again running the show.

"Since our first store was opened in Bentonville," wrote the chairman, "we have experienced twenty-seven consecutive years of sales and earnings growth." He announced a goal—to become a billion-dollar company within four years. Sales for 1977 increased to $478.8 million, an increase of 41 percent; net income was up 44 percent to $16.5 million; and there were now twenty-eight more stores, bringing the total to 153 in nine states.

In the message over his signature, Sam said complimentary things about two retiring directors, Buck Remmel and John Geisse. But nowhere in the twenty-eight-page glossy brochure was there any mention of Ron Mayer or his departure, not a single word. The one-time, short-term ex-chairman was gone—as far as the company was concerned.

But he remains Sam's personal friend; the Arkansawyer stopped in Indianapolis in the late eighties to look over his ex-protégé's new businesses and to play a couple games of tennis with him. On his return he told a Bentonville associate: "Ron has done exactly what he wants to do. He's a millionaire several times over. He's got these glass companies he's done well with. Everybody's got to find the thing they enjoy most. I think they're just as happy as they can be. I would say Ron has been very successful."

—17—

Inside the Family Circle

A huge orchid corsage on her shoulder, Helen Walton smiled and shifted nervously on the dais. In the ballroom of Little Rock's posh Hotel Excelsior 600 $75-a-plate guests looked at her and roared. It was May 3, 1988, and she was being "roasted" for charity.

Reaching this celebrity pinnacle came via endless toil as wife, mother, billionaire's helpmeet, as volunteer in church, colleges, clubs, scholarships, charity, child-care centers, even Girl Scouts, PTA, and bake sales. Tonight's show was for the Florence Crittenton Home for unwed mothers.

Present were her fortyish sons, Rob, John, and Jim. And Sam. Alice couldn't make it. This was what had made sixty-nine years of living worthwhile and exciting—the family.

Everyone whooped when Sam got in a good zinger. "I try to teach Helen to fly," he boomed into the mike, "but her landings are sooooooooooooooooo rough!" The boys didn't say enough to get quoted in the newspapers. "We never were very good at making speeches," explained John.

The Waltons' reputation as fast drivers drew a gibe. Said Wal-Mart President David Glass: "The highway patrol sends self-addressed stamped envelopes to the

Waltons at Christmas. They have preprinted tickets—a book for Sam and a book for Helen."

Helen stood up, laughing. "Would anyone like me to drive you home?"

Hillary Clinton, wife of the governor and a Wal-Mart director, turned roast into toast. "I tried and tried to think of something to tell on Helen, but I couldn't. . . . She is someone I've admired for years. She has courage and commitment to issues she believes in."

Helen sat on the dais smiling, in a Hawaiian print dress, dark hair pulled back in a bun, with her usual silver-copper-turquoise combs and Indian-style jewelry. Sam doesn't buy her diamonds and sable. Her college-girl beauty has departed but she looks happy and is warm, friendly, concerned, and caring. She is sharp of mind and sure of herself, polished and articulate.

In Bentonville—and elsewhere—she is admired, loved, and looked up to. Hers is the ultimate success story. But she has suffered secret pain—more than most people know. Raising four spirited and independent children suddenly showered with dizzying affluence can spell trouble. Trouble came, and although Helen has hidden her heartache, the scars are there. For someone happily married for forty-six years to see all but one of her children go through divorce is painful and sad.

Worse perhaps was the children's rebellion. None really wanted to go into Dad's business. Sam was told, in effect, to take Wal-Mart and shove it. The children defected individually—for varying reasons, at separate stages, and for different lengths of time. Sam, saddened, just rode out the storm. Rob and Jim eventually did accept key executive roles in Bentonville; Alice, living nearby, is involved on the fringes, in finance. Doing his own thing, building ocean sailboats in San Diego, John remains the family maverick.

Becoming rich hasn't changed the older Waltons. Bentonville knows that. Helen is as natural and "old shoe" as ever. "My priorities have not changed," she says. "I am still interested in the same things." Any Sunday morning Helen and Sam are not in their pew in Bentonville's Presbyterian church, it's a safe bet they are out of town.

Always "churchy," Helen was the first woman ever elected vice chair of the board of trustees for the Presbyterian Church (U.S.A.) Foundation, which manages $650 million in church assets. She was long active on the board of University of the Ozarks and is its honorary lifetime chairman.

No designer clothes are in her wardrobe. Looking in a store, she asked a friend, "Is that suede? I can't afford that!" When she goes to the movies in Rogers, she buys senior citizen tickets. In her room at an Oklahoma City hotel—Sam was getting an award that night—she fretted that she didn't have a good enough slip. Her daughter-in-law sat on the floor in faded jeans and a tee-shirt that had a rip in the back. "You would think they were just poor everyday people," said Billy Jo Gourley, an Oklahoma University sorority sister. "If I hadn't grown up in the Depression," Helen confesses, "I probably would be a big spender."

She is smart as a whip in business, friends testify. As his dinner guest in Cincinnati, Helen gave a sales strategy pep talk to John G. Smale, millionaire chairman of Procter & Gamble. "Do more with Oil of Olay—that's a terrific face cream!" she advised. Her own health is excellent; she was overweight when she had her children, but no longer. She is an outdoors type—swimming, tennis, hiking, and camping. She is apt to whip down to the square in her sweatsuit. When plans were drawn to remodel her husband's local bank, Helen took one look, grimaced, and threw them in the wastebasket. The architects erased a lot of glass and chrome in their new blueprints.

Columnist Marilois Bach of the Bella Vista weekly newspaper, noting Helen's "nifty" kitchen, asked: "Do you do any cooking?" Helen grinned. "Well, not as much as Sam thinks I should. But sometimes it is just nice to have a baked potato and a little steak. I brought up four children, so you can bet I have done my share of cooking."

"Her warm personality does not need any enhancing," wrote the columnist. "Her naturalness is perhaps her greatest charm. When she went to move some chairs out on the patio deck, she kicked off her shoes just as any housewife would do, to move faster and safer."

Helen's black cook-maid, Elizabeth Dishman, when she was ninety years old, complained she was getting too old to work. "I'm jest gonna go off an' die," she moaned.

"No, you're not," Helen said. "Not till you get all those quail cleaned!"

After thirty years with the Waltons, Mrs. Dishman finally retired in 1988 and lives alone in her own home in Bentonville. When the ex-maid yearns to visit relatives in California, Helen is known to buy her airline tickets.

Helen supervises a $3.6 million scholarship fund she and Sam started for the purpose of bringing Central American students to three Arkansas schools. "That program was Sam's idea," said Bill Enfield. "Sam feels like competition is the cure for anything. He kept hearing about all these youngsters from Central America that were being taken to Russia for education, and his idea was the way to beat 'em is to compete, and we can get youngsters from those areas down there up here and educate them. Then they, in turn, will compete with the ones that are educated in Russia, and he has no doubt which ones are going to come out on top, you see."

With President Fritz Ehren of University of the Ozarks at Clarksville, one of the three Arkansas schools involved, Helen flew to Costa Rica to interview scholarship candidates personally. The Walton fund also places these students in John Brown University at Siloam Springs and Harding University at Searcy.

"Democracy is better than communism," Sam said. "We want to let these youngsters know what we have in the United States—how many good things are achievable through work and through our democratic system of government under free enterprise."

Sam and Helen in 1987 gave $5 million to the University of Arkansas to erect a performing arts center bearing their name, and put an additional $3 million in an operating costs endowment fund. Helen also gave $500,000 to her alma mater to establish a University of Oklahoma economics professorship.

Sam expresses regret that his labor to achieve success was so costly in time at home. "I think," he said, "anyone can do what we've done. There is, of course, a price that must be paid. It takes an immense amount of solid dedication and determination to excel and to achieve, and a driving desire and an ambition. I wouldn't change because I've enjoyed what I do. But it's long hours and it's a singular dedication, and you have to give up some things with your family that I would like to have had."

From being a frequent overnight guest in the Walton home, Clarence Leis observed the burden of the children fell mainly on their mother: "Sam couldn't give them the time . . . not as much as Helen. She really had to raise them because he wasn't there. Through the years, though, he put in an appearance at their activities, as best he could."

Did the manner of their home life cause the children to develop any distinction in their feelings of loyalty and affection for either parent?

"I'm sure not," says Tom Harrison. "It didn't make a bit of difference to the kids. They now seem as fond of one as the other."*

By coincidence, only a few years after the last child was grown and had left the family nest, a stormy night in April 1972 brought wild excitement, near tragedy, and decided change in the beautiful house down in the Spring Creek hollow as they had known it.

---

*For further discussion of Helen Walton's family/business roles see chapter 23.

Despite rain, the Waltons had gone out to dinner at the Holiday Inn with the Enfields and the Harrisons. When they returned home and retired about 10:00 P.M., thunder and lightning raked the sky.

Tom Harrison was startled out of his bed about 10:30 by a lightning bolt striking nearby. "I thought it might knock out our lights. I got up and heard police cars and sirens going by. The phone rang, and Marian Enfield said, 'Look out your back window!' I looked, and it was like the Fourth of July down at the Walton house!

"Lightning had hit a closet in their bedroom. Fire broke out. Sam ran out and grabbed a hose. It was about twenty feet long, but it wasn't connected. They had two cars in the garage. They got one out—it was the *leased* car! I didn't go down—there was such a crowd, and everything. Ruined about half the house before the firemen got it out."

The Waltons promptly summoned their architect, E. Fay Jones, and got ready to rebuild. "You know," Helen told Harrison, "every family ought to have two homes. One for when the kids are growing up, and one for later." With the children then out of the nest, Helen made a few changes, but largely decided to rebuild the house as it had been before. She had Sam bring in a large double-wide trailer and park it near the gate to serve as their temporary home. Helen wanted to be close at hand so she could personally supervise the rebuilding. The fire didn't faze her; life went on, and the trailer was nice enough to have friends in for bridge or for dinner.

Sam was going away a good bit, and he certainly had no intention of pitching in as a laborer as he had done on the initial house. He had learned his lesson. On that job he climbed a ladder to carry a pretty but heavy rock up to the roof for stone masons to incorporate in the chimney. It was a strain that pulled abdominal muscles, forcing him to have a hernia operation.

"Those big old boys were gone," Harrison remembers, "so Helen used more pastel colors."

* * *

In their school days, "those big old boys" were no laggards in scholastic, athletic, and leadership achievement, even though all held part-time jobs. The same with Alice.

First-born Rob—formally Samuel Robson—more or less emulated his father as a student athlete and leader. He played football four years at Bentonville High School, and was all-state as a senior. He ran track two years, was in several clubs, the junior class play, and competed in the district and state science fairs. He was a delegate to Boys' State.

When he finished high school in 1962, there was a family conference on college. His parents, especially his mother, favored a small campus, preferably with a religious orientation. The choice was Wooster College, a small Presbyterian school near Cleveland. After two years there, he transferred to the University of Arkansas at nearby Fayetteville and graduated with a B.S.B.A. in 1966. Then he went to New York City to attend Columbia University Law School.

When he graduated in 1969, he was recruited—along with a crop of students from other nationally known law schools—by the second largest law firm in Tulsa—Conner, Winters, Ballaine, Barry & McGowen. Rob accepted the offer, with a shot at becoming a partner in the fifty-lawyer office in about seven years. He arrived in Tulsa with his wife Patti and year-old son Sam.

It was natural evolution that the Tulsa firm soon began doing Wal-Mart's legal work. Rob pitched in with Robert L. McGowen and helped take his father's firm public through the regulatory maze of the Securities and Exchange Commission and New York Stock Exchange. Much of Wal-Mart's legal load fell to him. "It was natural to let him work on the family business," senior partner Henry Will told me, "and to continue to develop in that area."

Henry Will said Rob was a high-caliber lawyer and a hard worker. "But he was a character. When he was an associate [later he became one of twenty-one partners] with us, he'd work strange hours. We never knew when we'd see him in the office. He got his work done, but he was quite erratic in his habits. One of my favorite stories . . . Rob wanted to come in early, so he set his alarm clock and planned to be downtown about 6:30 A.M. The alarm went off. He dressed and went jogging and it wasn't until he signed in downstairs at our office building he realized it was only 1:30 in the morning."

Like his father, Rob had an affinity for old, battered automobiles. "He was a fast driver," said Henry Will. "A bunch of our guys were driving in a caravan out for a float [fishing] trip. It was too slow for Rob. He pulled off and took a side road. Every now and then they'd see him ahead, on a bridge crossing the highway or zipping down a side road, and pretty soon he showed up at the destination."

When Rob became considerably overweight, he began playing handball. He had two more children, Carrie and Ben, born in 1971 and 1974, respectively. While remaining in Tulsa, he served as a Wal-Mart corporate officer, secretary, an adjunct to his legal work.

A young secretary in the law firm, Carolyn Funk, was assigned to Rob. "She was a cute little girl, very sophisticated," said Henry Will. "They fell in love. She was divorced and he divorced Patti, and they got married." I believe Patti and the children moved to Boulder, Colorado." (Helen's 1984 Christmas letter said they were living now in Atlanta: Sam, 16, Carrie, 13, and Ben 10.)

About the time of his remarriage, Rob pulled up stakes in Oklahoma and went back to his roots in Bentonville. He became Wal-Mart's in-house legal counsel, and the Tulsa firm was dropped, except for special work such as employee pensions, which they still handle.

In Bob Bogle's view, Sam begged or put pressure on his son. "I guess his dad said, 'Well, Rob, we really need you over here full time.' So he just left the law firm and came over here. And, gosh, he has done a lot of things."

Rob apparently came with much reluctance. Observed Bill Enfield: "Rob is very smart, a CPA and a good lawyer. He just wasn't willing to put in sixteen-hour days, so I would be greatly surprised if he ended up totally in charge."

No longer secretary or company attorney, Rob is now one of three vice-chairmen. "All of the Walton kids are extremely capable," David Glass told me, "extremely capable. Of course, Rob is our vice-chairman and heavily involved."

George Billingsley, as family intimate, has closely followed Rob's career. "Sam's got some very capable people and he has a very, very capable son waiting in the wings. He is not the salesman that his father is, but I always go back and compare Supreme Court justices. The President can select one he feels is just what he wants. They don't always conform to what they were when sitting on a smaller bench. And so, back to your subject, Rob may be twice the cheerleader that Sam is today, when or if Rob chooses to assume that role."

Henry Will, on trips to Bentonville, found Rob slimmed down, and "I think he was the company handball champion. And I can tell you, nobody let him win." An avid handball player, Rob confided to Bentonville friends, "While I am still young enough to do it," he intended to compete in the "Ironman Triathlon," which attracts about 1,000 athletes from forty countries to Kailua-Kona, Hawaii, each October. The three events are a 2.4-mile ocean swim, 112-mile bike race, and 26.2-mile run, all of which must be completed within 17 hours.

After months of grueling training, Rob, at age forty-two, entered the 1986 Ironman. Dave Scott, thirty-five, of Davis, California, won for the sixth time, setting a new record of 8 hours, 28 minutes, and 37 seconds. In the field of 1,039, Rob came in 510, finishing in 12 hours, 29 minutes, and 30 seconds. Though

Walton family doings usually are not chronicled, the hometown newspaper carried a nice story on Rob's feat.

Rob built a handsome brick mansion for himself and Carolyn, at the end of the 500 block of Northeast F Street, on slightly higher ground and barely three hundred feet from his parents' home. He skis and pilots an airplane, and is reported to have purchased a $1.5-million home in Aspen, Colorado. He could easily afford it; the 1989 Wal-Mart proxy statement shows he owns stock worth almost $2 billion—and his three siblings each the same.

Second son John was a star athlete and earnest scholar in Bentonville High. He ran track, played basketball and football. He and both his brothers were tackles, and each made the all-state team and Rob and John in turn played in the annual Arkansas all-star game at Little Rock. John followed Rob to Wooster College and played football, but was too restless to remain there. He craved adventure.

In the sixties when America was deeply involved in the Vietnam War, John became enamored of the U. S. Special Forces, known as the Green Berets. He dropped out of college and joined up. His parents were none too happy about it, but knew he had to have his own way.

"I always swear that book on the Green Berets made him do that," Helen confided recently to a visitor. "It really influenced him." She referred to a realistic novel *The Green Berets* by Robin Moore, who as a civilian endured the parachute drops, etc., of the grueling Green Beret training and wrote it as fiction to avoid breaching military security.

John went through jump school and in his mid-twenties was off to Vietnam as a Green Beret and endured some terrifying years in the thick of the fighting.

"John's my favorite," said Tom Harrison. "Why?

I'll tell you the reason, I guess. . . . Just by his looks you'd never know he was worth anything. He just goes about his business. His personality is wonderful." Clarence Leis takes the same slant: "John is a maverick. I probably like him better than all of 'em. But John is going to do his own thing. He is just as likable as anybody—you like him the first time you see him." Bill Enfield says: "John is pretty much a free spirit. I don't think he would ever end up in Wal-Mart. Even if he was the last Walton, I don't think he would."

"His dad wanted him to try for officers candidate school," said Harrison. "He wouldn't. John didn't want to leave his buddies in the Green Berets."

John went with an American recon patrol sent to spy on enemy use of the Ho Chi Minh trail. "He worked with those Montagnard tribesmen," said Bogle, "and they would monitor food and ammunition shipments to set up targets for U. S. attack bombers. He would either be up in one of those trees in the jungle or they'd dig a hole in the ground along the trail, get in, and cover themselves with leaves and branches.

"They would radio what was going on, and he would stay out there in the jungle three or four months at a time with those tribesmen. It was a pretty hairy job."

John was discharged from the Green Berets and came home in the early seventies, with the Silver Star and Purple Heart. Harrison asked about his battlefield experiences. "Oh, Lord, he wouldn't talk much about it, but he mentioned one story. He liked those Montagnards who fought with him. At one place, the enemy dropped some fire bombs, and one rolled up between his legs.

"As he rolled away there was a Vietcong grinning at him, and I think he shot him, rolled over quick and shot him. . . . I don't think his Montagnard buddy got shot, but a helicopter came in and they ran for it, carrying their radio, and escaped. I'm sure he was in some pretty rough stuff over there."

Tom Harrison got a bright idea. He was program

chairman of the Rotary Club. He asked Helen if John would talk to Rotary. "I don't know," said the mother. "Ask him." Harrison did. John bowled him over by agreeing to talk about his war experiences.

"He made one of the most interesting talks you ever heard," said Harrison. "Lot of stuff you wouldn't expect him to reveal."

The Presbyterian minister later asked John if he would speak at the church.

John shook his head. "No. I've talked."

What career would John seek? Naturally his parents talked to him about a role in the rapidly growing Wal-Mart organization. Retailing didn't seem attractive. Somehow in conversations with his father, he decided to take flying lessons and become the first full-time pilot of what he called "the Wal-Mart Air Force." Until that time it had been up to Sam to roll out the company plane—then a Bonanza—and take the controls whenever his executives needed to make a quick trip.

John was a good pilot and spent nearly a year flying for Wal-Mart. He went in and told his father he'd decided to quit. "Too tame for me," he lamented.

John bought an old biplane, fitted out the wings with spray nozzles, installed hose lines, pumps and tanks to hold insecticide, and went into the crop-dusting business. He flew all over Arkansas and Louisiana. Once his father told a friend: "You can't really do anything more dangerous than that. It's the way he lives. One thing about him, he has tremendous coordination with his hands. He still parachutes—free falls—just for fun."

When John flew in from a crop-dusting trip, Bob Bogle recalls, he would swoop down and buzz the Spring Creek hollow where his parents live so somebody would drive to the Bentonville airport and pick him up.

John married a Bentonville girl he had known in high school, Mary Ann Gunn. Later they were divorced. She resumed her maiden name, became a lawyer, and practices in Fayetteville.

John moved his crop-dusting business to Casa Grande, Arizona, south of Phoenix. In 1984 he went to San Diego and began building oceangoing trimaran sailboats. A manager runs his Arizona crop-dusting company. He also remarried, and has a son, as Helen noted in her 1987 Christmas letter to friends:

We had a wonderful Christmas in Bentonville. Everyone was with us except John and Christie and their son, Luke, who live in San Diego. However, we will see them this week when we go to South Texas to hunt. They are going to join us there with Jim and his family.

There is a tight conspiracy of silence among the Waltons about their private lives. But because of their new national prominence many substantial people in Bentonville will discuss the family freely and candidly, without intending rancor or malice. Nearly everybody has some anecdote about John.

"I was out at the airport here," said Harrison, "and somebody said, 'Whose plane is that?' Well it was John's and the mechanic said, 'If he ever brings the plane in here again like that I won't touch it.' The trouble? Well, the tail was about to fall off. That's the way John ran the plane—like a car. And you know if it has trouble, it's gonna stop.

"A bunch of us were out at Aspen and John flew in to visit us. The plane wasn't set for high altitude or something, and he was coming around this mountain out there and just at the last moment found the opening to the airport. It got kind of hairy. John said, 'If there hadn't been this opening, I don't know what would have happened. . . .' "

Teaming up with Ian Farrier, an Australian yacht designer, John is attempting to make three-hulled sailboats as commercially acceptable as other yachts. On his twenty-seven-foot *Corsair* the two outboard hulls are retractable so the craft can be trailered and also easily dock in a normal sloop berth. In a February 1, 1986, article, the *San Diego Union* quoted John: "We are an underdog. I got into trimaraning because the market was flooded with look-alike white fiberglass sloops. My boat represents a part of the market that has not been explored at all. It combines oceangoing capabilities with the flexibility of easy transport, comfortable quarters, and high performance. . . . Top speed is twenty-five knots, if you want to push it."

In the May 1989 125-mile yacht race to Ensenada, John's *Corsair* won first in the catamaran division, beating Dennis Conner's famous America's Cup champion sixty-two-foot *Stars & Stripes*, which came in eighth, according to the *San Diego Union*.

I reached John at his Corsair Marine factory in Chula Vista, a San Diego suburb, and tried to set up an interview to discuss his attitude toward his parents and the Wal-Mart company. He was pleasant, but said he would first want to get approval from his father. "You know, Vance, I'm not particularly interested in being the subject of anything myself."

Laying out the territory of interest, I mentioned that many family friends felt Helen had largely raised the children because Sam's own heavy work caused him to neglect them.

"We never felt neglected," John responded. "Dad used to run our Boy Scout troop for a while. We used to take off and go on vacations and stuff like that, but we never felt neglected."

Could he explain why the children appeared not too interested in coming into the family business?

"You know as far as the subject of kids working in the company goes, I think we've all been interested in it, to a high degree. At various times all of us have worked for the company. I guess Dad had the misfortune of raising a bunch of kids that didn't want to work at the same thing all the time."

John chuckled.

"We have all worked around at various different

jobs and occupations, but we have all been very close
to the company all our lives. So there is certainly no
alienation, uh, as far as our attitude toward Wal-Mart.
Shoot, we think it's just great, to tell you the truth.

"I think, if anything, we question . . . you know,
the other thing . . . for kids to work in their parents'
companies. If they don't ever get out on their own,
then you never really know whether you're getting a
job because of who you are, or whether you earned it.
So you go out on your own, and you get a lot better
feel for what's really going on."

His father's life is fascinating, I volunteered.

"Well, he's a heck of a guy. . . . Vance, I do appreciate your calling, but before I really . . . go further I
want to check with Dad." That seemed appropriate, I
agreed, and mentioned that everyone has a difficult
time putting their finger on the secret of his father's
success.

"I don't think anyone has managed to do it," John
said, "and the main reason is it just involves so many
different things that he does well. You know techni-
cally he is real strong and I think a lot of people tell
you that his one major asset is his ability to relate to
people and to deal with people . . . and that sort of
thing."

Doesn't the work load burn out top Wal-Mart executives, for instance Jack Shewmaker and Al Johnson?

"The thing is, you know, he gets the very best
people there are . . . and those guys, they . . . they
. . . He doesn't get wallflowers. He gets independent
people, and sooner or later an independent guy is
gonna want to go his own way. . . . I'll check with
Dad. Give me a couple of days to see if I can find him,
and call me back." I did call back; he said he hadn't
been able to catch up with his father. I did not expect
John to be cooperative, and dropped it.

Jim, a 1965 graduate of Bentonville High, underwent
perhaps the most remarkable turnaround of the four

children. He was a popular student, elected class president and "most valuable" as a junior, and named the senior "most likely to succeed." He put in four years at the University of Arkansas at Fayetteville, emerging in 1971 with a B.S.B.A. degree. He was twenty-three years old, and Wal-Mart—then with only forty stores—was a year away from going on the big board. But Jim opted for a different life.

Bentonville looked aghast at this son of the up-and-coming Waltons. Jim let his hair grow long and shaggy, grew a beard, and wore faded clothes. He rode a bicycle around town and often he went out West backpacking. He was, in short, considered a hippie.

Eventually he came back home and bought a house in the rundown section of Bentonville and set up a bachelor life. As had the other siblings, he learned to fly an airplane.

After a year on his own, Jim gravitated to Wal-Mart headquarters. He went in under his uncle Bud's wing, learning the real estate end of the business. Bob Bogle recalled how that went:

"Bud and Sam would decide on the location for a new store and Bud would go to the guy that owned the building or the land and work out the lease or construction. So Bud got Jim trained on all that and Jim operated that for some time, and did a superb job.

"I later ran the maintenance end of it, in charge of keeping up the roofs and parking lots and all that so I got to work with those landlords. Well, they'd tell me how tough Jim was. They'd say, 'My God, we'd a lot rather deal with Bud Walton than Jim!' And here was this kid just out of college and not dry behind the ears, but he was tough as nails—and still is!

"He is sharp, I'll guarantee you! He and Rob could run Wal-Mart—they may not be interested—but they may run it and hire a guy like Glass or Shewmaker or someone as CEO."

Because of his hippie appearance, Jim went into stores where nobody recognized him and was credited with making beneficial intelligence reports to his father.

His parents have told friends about Jim's novel ways. "He had this knock-down bicycle that he'd take in the plane with him," said Sam. "Jim would fly into a town, put the bike together, and pedal in and look over a store location. No fanfare—Wal-Mart coming and all that hoopla! The kid on a bike didn't get ripped off, and managed to make some pretty good deals for us."

Once he played detective—successfully. Rifles were disappearing from the sporting goods section of the Bentonville warehouse. Jim prowled around. In some clever fashion the guns and ammo were being stolen. He watched from outside at odd hours. Finally he knew the pilfering was taking place during the night shift.

From a hiding place, he observed three employees slip out the rear door and quickly throw something over the fence. He investigated and saw a pile of stolen rifles. When the crooks showed up after work to pick up their booty, Jim swooped down. One associate was fired; the other two were given leaves of absence. The thievery stopped. Jim remembers this as chiefly apocryphal.

At age thirty, Jim began courting Lynne McNabb, a year his junior, the daughter of a Pocahontas undertaker. She had come back from New York City where she had spent a few years as a junior editor for a book publisher. On October 19, 1978, they went to the Benton County courthouse and bought a license, and were married two days later far across the state in Randolph County. They now have four children, Annie, born 1979, Steuart, 1981, Tom, born September 25, 1983, and James, August 13, 1987. Lynne opened a bookstore on the square, and is heavily involved in church work.

It didn't make sense for Jim to raise his family in one of the poorest sections of town; his mother kept after him about that. It took until the early eighties for her to get the point across. Then Jim and Lynne picked a hilly site just off C Street NE, a couple of blocks from his parents' home, and put up a substantial four-bedroom white house reached by a bridge over Spring Creek.

Sam came to see that Jim had shown an aptitude and a willingness to shoulder major corporate responsibilities. The youngest son was put in command of Walton Enterprises, Inc., an umbrella under which was placed control of all the family's Wal-Mart stock, as well as banks in Bentonville; Rogers; Pea Ridge; Fayetteville; and Norman, Oklahoma; the old Massey Hotel building that had been restored; the *Daily Democrat*, which Sam had purchased and later renamed *The Daily Record*; interest in a grocery chain; and assorted other businesses.

Jim also headed the Walton Foundation, through which tax-deductible gifts and grants were made for Sam and Helen, mainly to various colleges. Bob Bogle said Jim was the ideal person to control funding. And J. Dickson Black put in: "He was tight when he was younger, and he's still very conservative in business. So I imagine anything Jim deals with is going to make a little money."

A humorous example of Jim's frugality came up when Black visited his office to set up an appointment for an interview on the history of the Bank of Bentonville. Jim started to mark it down in his pocket calendar. Black noticed he was using last year's notebook.

"He asked his secretary for a bottle of White-Out to clear that page. I asked if he didn't know he could buy another of those books. He told me, 'This book isn't worn out. Why should I buy a new one? I can white-out these notes from last year.' That tickled me to death."

Alice, who as a child scared the neighbors with daredevil antics on her bicycle, graduated from Bentonville High in 1967, vice-president of her class. Her mother wanted her to attend a small Presbyterian College, so Alice enrolled at Trinity, in San Antonio. She received her B.S. degree on May 24, 1971, and came home to tackle a job at Wal-Mart headquarters, a move that made her parents happy. Sam gave her a shot at his favorite role in retailing—buyer.

"All the kids were brilliant and likable in high school, and Alice is still just as likable as heck," said J. Dickson Black.

For one reason or another Alice didn't find enough adventure as a buyer. "It's not my bag," she confided to a friend. As a challenge, she learned to fly an airplane but never got a license. She felt she ought to be using her talents in the financial field.

Fred Pickens, the Newport lawyer who has known her from birth and remains a family intimate, agrees. "I think Alice is Sam all over," he told me. "I think she is more of a business person than any of the children."

At the end of 1972 she engineered an escape from Bentonville through her "godfather," James Jones, Wal-Mart director and then president of the National Bank of Commerce in New Orleans. Jones gave her a job in his bank's loan department and soon promoted her to investment research.

Alice fell in love with New Orleans. Tall, pretty, a brunette whose thick hair fell to her shoulders, she took a French Quarter apartment where neighbors gaily chatted across mossy terraces from balconies with wine goblet in hand. She had fun but was serious about her career and began taking classes at Tulane University for her M.B.A.

Alice began traveling in New Orleans's upper crust Mardi Gras circles and met investment banker Laurence Eustis III, whose prominent father served one year as "Rex," the socially powerful king of the Carnival holidays that usher in Lent. After a fast courtship, they were married.

The wedding took place in Bentonville on August 31, 1974, in her parents' home. Only a few friends were invited to attend the ceremony* and the recep-

---

*Walton friends know the reason for the small wedding party was because Alice wanted it limited to only the number who could line the railing of the outside balcony backed by the waterfall.

tion, also held in the Walton residence. The groom's father had entertained the previous evening with a rehearsal dinner at the Bella Vista clubhouse. The local newspaper carried a two-column photograph of Alice in her wedding gown.

By the fall of 1976, at age twenty-seven, she was one of the first female account executives in E. F. Hutton's New Orleans office. At that time Alice managed more than $4 million in portfolios, she said in a *Times-Picayune* interview. She promoted a seminar for women investors, based on the fact that "women in this country own 60 percent of the assets in the public investment area, but control only 20 percent." Even so, she told the reporter, 85 percent of her clients were male.

"I feel I have a slim chance with the sixty-five-and-over male client. Their attitude is that women can actually damage their brains in this business. But younger men have the feeling that women brokers are going to be more honest and not necessarily out for a commission.

"Plus, when you do a super job for a guy, he can't believe it. It's like seeing a kid who found five cookie jars and his mama's out of the room. . . . Besides, having a woman broker makes for great cocktail conversation."

Trouble developed in Alice's marriage. She and Laurence Eustis III legally separated January 11, 1977, and obtained a no-fault divorce one year later. In 1978 he married a girl from Boston, and now has two children. He responded to my inquiry about his marriage to Alice by saying he wouldn't discuss his personal life—"I'm not being inhospitable, but it's a past part of my life." He said Alice was working for James Jones at the time they met, "but we met independently of Jimmy. . . . I have nothing but good things to say about Miss Walton and Mr. Jones; they are both wonderful people."

In the spring of 1977, after her marriage broke up,

Alice met handsome Hall Morehead when his contracting firm built a swimming pool at her New Orleans residence. Later Alice and Morehead were married, but that union did not last long. He remained in Louisiana and now lives in Ringgold, while Alice went home in the late seventies and began handling some family business matters and investments for her father's bank in Rogers. She now uses her maiden name, and refuses to discuss her private or professional life.

In 1983 when Alice was thirty-three, Sam took the entire family to Acapulco for a Thanksgiving reunion and business meeting to study annual reports covering their umbrella stock holding and other commercial interests.

On that trip Helen and Sam were on the street listening to native troubadours. When Helen turned to speak to him Sam was gone. She didn't have to worry long. He had just ducked into a nearby store to check it out.

While several family members swam in the ocean, Alice rented a jeep and whizzed up into the mountains above the resort. These are miserable roads, narrow, steep, studded with treacherous curves. Siren screaming, an ambulance hours later brought Alice into the Acapulco hospital emergency room. Her jeep had sailed off the road into a deep ravine.

"John was there. That was rather a blessing," said Fred Pickens. "John had had all this Green Beret instruction in tropical medicine and first aid. I think it was Helen who told me he went into the operating room, and said, 'Get this girl back to the United States!' And they brought in a hospital plane, and did. They took her to Houston or Little Rock and Sam flew in a specialist from Boston."

Alice suffered a badly broken leg, and was unlucky enough to pick up a Mexican bug that caused a bone infection.

"She had lots of courage, and always bounced back.

But she started having one setback after another. They just couldn't seem to get a handle on that bone infection," Fred Pickens said.

Her father called all around the country for the most skilled surgeons. He consulted with an Oklahoma City bone specialist, Dr. Stephen Tkach, at the suggestion of his Kingfisher friend, Irvin Bollenbach. Alice went through misery, heartbreak, and pain. She endured twenty-two operations on her leg.

During a year of recuperation, she lived on the family's 800-acre farm at Kingston, 75 miles east of Springdale.

Her recovery was complete enough in the fall of 1988 for Alice to launch her own investment firm, Llama Co., in Fayetteville, a twenty-minute drive from her 850-acre horse farm at Lowell. At age thirty-eight, she was undertaking double-barreled entrepreneurship. She opened both a conventional broker-dealer operation and a companion office to manage portfolios of fixed-income securities, including municipals and mortgages, for wealthy individuals and banks running pension and profit-sharing plans in Arkansas and five contiguous states. *Forbes* ran her picture and said:

> She believes she has found a niche with the broker-dealer operation, underwriting debt for small and medium-size businesses, mainly in northwest Arkansas, that are too large for local banks but too small to interest big national firms.

Perhaps almost as much a workaholic as her father, Alice puts in sixty-hour weeks. She hired eleven staffers, several with at least ten years' experience. The odd name of her company was inspired by the hobby of famous J. B. Hunt, the multimillionaire truck line operator who has a cattle farm at Lowell next to Alice's spread and is a longtime family friend. Hunt started collecting the woolly, domesticated South American llama, a creature resembling a small camel without a hump.

Alice asked Hunt to get her one. They are not cheap. Alice's cost about two thousand dollars. She named him Le Roy and told *Forbes*: "He's my buddy. They're intelligent, unique animals with almost 360-degree vision. I like those qualities as they relate to what I'm trying to do in the investment business."

Llama Co. was Alice's idea and she runs it; but it is really just as much a family operation as is Wal-Mart. As Sam explained to associates, Alice has one-third interest in Llama, and the remainder is owned by her brothers and parents.

On numerous occasions the Waltons have demonstrated just how closely and lovingly they are knit as a family, the most recent being Helen's seventieth birthday—Sunday, December 3, 1989.

On that day Helen was scheduled to attend an opera planning committee meeting in Fayetteville.

A few days ahead of time she asked her daughter to accompany her. "Oh, Mother," said Alice. "That would be a lot of fun—but I'm already booked. Can't get out of it."

After church Sunday, Helen started to drive off for Fayetteville. "Don't go," said Sam. "I've developed a great hankering for barbecue. I'm going to take you out to Fred's Hickory Inn."

Helen started and looked at her husband as if he'd lost his mind. "Why, Sam! I've got to go to my opera meeting!"

Sam began arguing, putting on the charm, struggling to get her to change her mind. Finally, she threw up her hands and meekly accompanied him to the barbecue restaurant on the north side of Bentonville.

They arrived about one o'clock, and Helen walked in to confront a cluster of seventy-five people shouting "Happy birthday!" Alice was there. Her two local sons were there. John had come from California. Her closest friends—described as the Who's Who of Northwest Arkansas—were present. And many grandchildren.

Helen was floored. It dawned then that Sam and the kids had arranged the party to be a surprise. It was—totally. And happiness was written all over Helen's face.

— 18 —

New Chiefs and Computers

Someone said Sam Walton used up men the way he threw cordwood into his fireplace. Just like the logs, they blazed up with a fury, generated powerful and beautifully efficient flames, and after a time died down into cold ashes. That is, of course, exaggeration and oversimplification.

It is true that he drove his men as unrelentingly as he drove himself. He expected 110 percent of everyone. Some men did burn out. But he paid handsomely. Sam was not stingy with money for those who helped make it.

Nevertheless, it was necessary for him always to be looking for good men to replenish his stockpile of talent. He was an indefatigable scout of the retail field. For over forty years Sam conducted an almost constant search for promising managers and executives. As Wal-Mart grew, he needed more and more lieutenants, especially right-hand men.

Ron Mayer's abrupt exit in mid-1976 sent Walton scrambling for another high-powered financial officer. He fell back on old habits—he girded up again to go after a whiz kid who had scornfully turned him down before. Thus, swallowing whatever pride he had to, Sam dangled an attractive new job offer before David Dayne Glass.

This was the same David Glass who threw up his hands in disgust when witnessing the donkey-watermelon fiasco at the opening of Wal-Mart No. 2 in Harrison back in 1964. That had been twelve years ago. Sam's operation still appeared pretty much down-home, but a closer look revealed a lot more sophistication.

David Glass was the right age, just turned forty-one, and he had the small-town heritage and hard work ethic that the Wal-Mart chief admired and demanded. Born September 2, 1935 in Mountain View, Missouri, a farming community of about 1,200 ninety miles east of Springfield, David was bright enough to start first grade at five. His father ran a feed mill, and his bright mother spent twenty years as assistant manager and then manager of the Angelica Uniform Company plant in Mountain View.

Though he never brought home books or studied too much, David was a good student. When he was a kid, he and his two brothers played cork ball down by the railroad tracks, and he went on to play high school baseball and basketball.

Graduating from high school at seventeen and facing the draft, David decided to volunteer for the army "and get it over with." Sent to an army post in New Mexico, he met a pretty local girl named Ruth and brought her back to Mountain View as his bride when he was discharged at about age twenty-one.

He decided to go to college and enrolled at Southern Missouri State University at Springfield, studying for a bachelor's in business administration. To support his young family, he took a night job at Campbell's 66, a trucking company. He apparently did prodigious work. Said his mother: "When he left they had to hire two men to do his work."

With his college degree in 1963, David Glass went into the office of Cranks Drug Company in Springfield and made rapid advances. He was transferred to the company's Little Rock office—where Sam Walton first made contact with him. The Cranks company was sold to the Spartan Company of New York, but when it changed owners a second time, going to the Katz Drug chain, David resigned.

He went then to Consumers Markets, Inc., a four-state regional grocery chain with about thirty-five stores, headquartered in Springfield. He was there in 1976 as chief financial and operating vice-president when Sam Walton sought him out again. They had been on friendly terms for years and had occasionally done business together. David now had a much higher opinion of the Wal-Mart chain, which was creating something of a regional splash with 150 stores in Arkansas and 8 contiguous states.

But Consumers did not want David Glass to quit. Every offer Sam made, Consumers topped.

"He had a hard time deciding to leave," said his mother. "Consumers was good to him, and he was vice-president. He liked his job. But finally Mr. Walton just made him an offer that he couldn't turn down."

So in October 1976, David D. Glass moved his family to Bentonville and took over a vice-president's desk at Wal-Mart corporate headquarters.

He was under no misconceptions; with Sam Walton calling the tune he now must dance to, he could expect to work harder and put in more hours than ever before in his life. But there was a rainbow and a promised pot of gold. David Glass would be drawing down the kind of salary and profit-sharing bonus he had never dared dream before.

Already rising in the Wal-Mart hierarchy was another retailer from Missouri whom Sam had tracked down, Jack C. Shewmaker. By the oddity of fate, both he and Glass sprang from the same southwesterly region of the Show Me State, neither more than an hour's drive from the origin of Sam's roots, Webster County.

When the Wal-Mart chief spotted a neat piece of Jack Shewmaker's work in 1970, Sam decided this fellow was a retail genius-in-the-making whom he must add to his Bentonville headquarters. He was a stranger whom Sam had to run down, and he almost didn't get him.

Jack Shewmaker was born March 14, 1938 in Buffalo, a town of 2,000, thirty miles north of Springfield. While going to high school, he worked in his father's Chrysler-Plymouth agency and also bagged groceries at the Maddux Supermarket. Because he wanted to be an architect, he enrolled in one of the best engineering schools in the country, Georgia Tech.

But tragedy cut short his college career. His sweetheart, Melba Prosser, a farm girl from nearby Phillipsburg, was going through rush week at Drury College in Springfield. A chauffeured blue Cadillac returning Melba and four other pledges to campus collided at a Springfield intersection with—ironically—another blue Cadillac sedan. Melba was thrown through a shattered window and smashed a hole in her skull. A physician happened by the scene, found five people dead, and Melba still breathing. In the hospital, she underwent emergency brain surgery, remaining in a coma for days.

Jack Shewmaker rushed from Georgia Tech to her bedside. When she recovered, Jack, shaken, quit college, took a job at Reyco Manufacturing Company in Springfield, and married Melba in 1958 in the First Baptist Church at Buffalo. In 1960 he joined Lawn Boy lawnmower company in Lamar, as sales and service education supervisor. Three years later he managed a Montgomery Ward store in Sikeston. Then he went with Coast-to-Coast in 1964, winding up in the home office at Minneapolis as training and communications director. There he prepared a store manual, which was the item that caught Sam Walton's eye.

Again, in 1966, he switched jobs, joining Kroger in the main office in Cincinnati before managing a Kroger Supercenter at LaPorte, Indiana.

But Jack Shewmaker felt "he was not getting anyplace," and quit this job after nine months, packed their household gear and headed back to Buffalo.

Then ensued another of the dramatic near misses

that often characterized Sam Walton's search for talented new men who were to have major impact on the success of Wal-Mart.

Casting about for a new job, Shewmaker came to Bentonville and was interviewed by Ferold Arend and Don Whittaker. They were willing to take him on as a lowly assistant store manager. He turned them down.

When Sam came back from a day out flying around the stores, he was disappointed. He thought it a mistake to let a man like Shewmaker get away. He picked up the phone and caught him back at his mother's home in Buffalo.

"I wasn't pleased with what we offered you," Sam said. "Can you come back and talk to me?"

"Right now I just don't have the money to come back down there," Shewmaker said.

"I appreciate your honesty. Tell you what I'll do— I'll meet you halfway. How about seeing me in Joplin?"

They met the next day, Sam offered a better job— store opening supervisor. They shook on it, and so in 1970 Jack and Melba and their three small children moved to Bentonville. His first Wal-Mart assignment was to create "the book" for Wal-Mart managers, patterned after the Ben Franklin manual that Sam and Bud had used so successfully to standardize all the buying and selling procedures in their Ben Franklin stores.

Jack Shewmaker, thirty-two years old, hopped right to the task. "It came out very extensive and very complete—just excellent," recalls Clarence Leis. "Jack collected ideas from all our people, from other companies, copied everything of value, just as Sam had always done. I remember going over it for him, and he also had other people proofread it.

"It took him a year and a half, and it was a thick manual, actually two volumes. It is still in use, with revisions made from year to year. It spells out every aspect of the company from the first nut and bolt at the front end to the last ones at the tail end."

Jack Shewmaker was on his way up—rising to district manager, next in 1973 to vice-president for security and loss prevention, and a year later to vice-president, operations. In 1976 when Wal-Mart was growing to 153 stores doing $478 million in sales, with 10,000 employees, Jack Shewmaker was elevated to executive vice-president, operations, personnel, and merchandise. He was running side-by-side with David Glass, who was executive vice-president, finance.

Tall, handsome, and vigorous, Jack Shewmaker was a dynamo, espousing new retailing concepts in a convincing style, winning admiration and loyalty down at the store level. He quail hunted with the boss, and tried his best to out-shoot Sam. It was close enough for them to keep score, but Sam stayed in the lead.

It was his lot, also, to make numerous airplane flights with the chief, and his experiences seem to have been about as dramatic as some of Sam's other passengers. Jack didn't want to alarm his folks, so he seldom talked much about flying, said his sister, Mary Lou Beckner, the speech and drama teacher at Buffalo High School.

"But once he said the cabin door came loose and he had to sit there for a long time and hold it shut or they would have crashed," she said. "I don't know whether Sam was flying, or it was a pilot."

Although the Wal-Mart "air force" saved executives countless travel hours, it also contributed to the loss of one of Sam's right-hand men, Ferold Arend.

On a flight with a company pilot and Bud Walton, Arend spent a day visiting Wal-Marts in Kansas. Heading back to Arkansas their plane got caught, by coincidence, in the same violent thunderstorm which that same night set Sam and Helen's house afire with a bolt of lightning.

Fierce winds suddenly slammed the airplane. The passengers were all jolted. Arend cried out in pain; it felt like a knife had been plunged into his back. He went to the hospital on landing and discovered a vertebra was dislocated or damaged. He had a slow, long recuperation and decided to retire.

Thus in mid-1978 Arend stepped aside for "reasons of health," but remained a director and well-paid consultant. In his place Jack Shewmaker became president and chief operating officer—taking a position just below Sam's chairmanship.

At that time Wal-Mart was on a sensational roll. On January 31, 1979, there were 229 stores spread over ten states doing $900 million in annual sales, with 17,500 associates on the payroll.

Boasting about the 33 percent increase in sales and 39 percent jump in net income to $29.4 million, and a company net worth of $100 million, Sam stated flatly in the 1979 annual report that within less than twelve months Wal-Mart would become a billion-dollar-in-sales company.

Looking pleased and happy, the chairman posed for a photo in that annual report with David Glass standing behind on the left and Jack C. Shewmaker on his right. He also shared the laurels, permitting them to sign the annual report below his signature, the president first, and the money man second.

Sam now had two aggressive, hard-charging, desperately ambitious right-hand men—who were also beginning to rake in big bucks.

It was clear to everyone at the general office in Bentonville, and perhaps elsewhere, that some sort of friendly race was shaping up between Shewmaker and Glass. It looked close; insiders said it was easy to get a bet on either one to emerge the winner.

To a practical, old-time merchant like Sam Walton, the electronic age seemed to offer several fancy ways to waste money. "Sam never did like computers," lamented one top executive. "He thinks of them as overhead." And expense was the one business category that Sam Walton wrestled twenty-four hours a day. The principal elements of success, to his eye, were finding quality merchandise, buying it at a good price, and passing it on with a guaranteed low markup to satisfied customers in clean and bright modern stores run by efficient associates who smiled and tried to call you by name. Computers did not figure into this picture.

His two top men, Jack Shewmaker and David Glass, began arguing with him in the mid-seventies about the advantages electronics offered the company. They were supported by a battery of other controls-oriented executives who recognized that it would be essential to hop aboard the new wave of technology if Wal-Mart was to maintain the explosive growth that already had it closing fast on the leaders in the discount industry.

As a matter of fact it was known that Sears, K mart, J. C. Penney, and Service Merchandise were likewise ready to experiment with bar code scanners not only in the back room—freight receiving—but also at the front-end checkouts.

Finally his lieutenants educated and convinced Sam, and Wal-Mart plunked down $500 million over the course of five years for a modern communications-computer system. Its heart was a 16,000-square-foot air-conditioned building in Bentonville, containing two mainframes, IBM 370s, model 148. Hooked into the system were all Wal-Mart stores, warehouses, and distribution centers, each through its own IBM 3774 store computer terminal.

By 1979 the stores and warehouses could communicate around the clock with headquarters. Over half a million "item reactions" were handled weekly through the general office, this data traveling over telephone lines. Storage capacity was mammoth; each computer contained company-wide payroll for associates (then 17,500 as against 250,000 in 1990), daily sales from the thirty-six departments in each store, bank deposits, estimated sales figures, reports on hot-selling items, personnel records, warehouse inventory, and the capability of cross-referencing all this information.

In the early years computer technology was so rapidly and dramatically jumping ahead that Wal-Mart set up an in-house board of experts to stay up with, or ahead of, practical application of the equipment. The board's aim was to redefine the information avalanche and render it more useful and easier to read. Outdated reports could be immediately discarded and others adjusted.

Before long, Sam Walton's primary apprehension was totally overcome. The 1979 Wal-Mart annual report said: "The financial savings and the number of personnel hours saved daily by using the computer center are incalculable—even by the computer."

In Sam Walton's view, it was well and good to maximize all the new tools provided by the computer, but the true basic engine for building a successful business remained unchanged. It must—first, last, and always—be created from living and breathing organisms —people.

After his disappointment in Ron Mayer, he was skeptical and cautious to a certain extent and kept closer watch on the executive suite, especially Jack Shewmaker and David Glass, though he trusted and admired both. Sam knew both came from small-town families and made it a point to fly up to Missouri and get acquainted with the parents of both. He studied the two men closely, noting that where Shewmaker was a back slapper and heartily gregarious, Glass was retiring and quiet. He often meditated on what effect, if any, their perspectives would have on their Wal-Mart leadership. He saw no peculiarity or shortcoming in either that retarded the discount chain growth.

Even so, Wal-Mart was growing too slowly to suit Sam. He put on his thinking cap and started looking at other discount operators. Maybe he could buy out a competitor. Anyone but Walton might have been satisfied with his company's progress between 1974 and 1977—from 78 to 153 stores, from annual sales of $167,561,000 to $478,807,000.

Sam discovered a chain of 16 Mohr Super Value discount stores, operating in Missouri and Illinois, in trouble. Before the year was out, he bought them and converted them into Wal-Marts, and entered 1978 with 195 stores. Still he wanted to acquire more established stores, at the same time he was starting 2 or 3 new ones of his own every month. So in 1981 he went after the 104-store Big-K chain started from a single five-and-dime in 1913, now run by his friend Jack Kuhn of Nashville. Jack Kuhn was in trouble, having overextended himself in 1977 by spending $8.9 million to acquire the Edwards, Inc., chain of 34 discount and variety stores in South Carolina and Georgia, and by building a 608,700-square-foot corporate headquarters and distribution center in Nashville. Years of Big-K profits turned into million-dollar losses. Sam offered in January 1981 to buy the chain for $17 million. Then Wal-Mart had second thoughts and canceled. In August 1981 a new deal was struck to acquire Big-K for $13 million in Wal-Mart stock. Sam promptly sold off the Nashville building, closed a dozen profitless Big-K stores, and expanded into four or five new Southern states.

About then, as the eighties began, his own runaway retail machine began hitting a few potholes on the road to riches. On his monthly business charts, some disturbing patterns began appearing. Sales didn't reach projections and profit margins slipped. And worse, aggressive competitors were swooping into Wal-Mart's expanding territory. Something had to be done. Sam reacted with a dramatic shift in his marketing strategy. Stores that looked harsh and unappealing were singled out for a face-lift with new earth-tone colors, carpeting in places, and a greater emphasis on attractive merchandise displays. In addition, Sam and his brain trust decided their cheap, private-label brands lacked appeal. They went back to mainly higher quality name-brand goods. And the gamble paid off.

All the while, Sam Walton kept his ears open ready to hear new ideas from his army of frontline associates, who were exploding in numbers in Wal-Marts across the country. "That's a trademark of ours," he told *Financial World*. "We are willing to change. I would just like us to continue to make changes as they need to be made, and every day is a different situation in this retail business. That is one of the blessings that has made us what we are, what we believe in. We have been very flexible and have been looking every day for changes that need to be made, and those ideas come from a lot of different sources. These people out here are smarter and more capable than many of us recognize, and many understand our business and certainly know what the customer wants. But change, and the willingness to change, try anything, try anyone's idea. . . . It might not work, but it won't break the company when it doesn't."

—19—

Guinea Pig—or Death?

Along the crest of the Ozarks, nature's paintbrush already was flecking the majestic red oaks with gold and crimson. An excited woodsman brought into the general store at War Eagle the limp carcass of a wild goose, commenting sourly on the thickness of its breastbone. That meant something. So did his observation that all the coons, squirrels, and rabbits he bagged had extra thick fur. Also walnuts and acorns had fallen heavily. All were harbingers of the severe winter that Arkansas, in October 1982, was expecting.

In his Bentonville office, a fagged-out Sam Walton sat dejectedly at his desk, struggling to escape a climate of gloom and depression that had nothing at all to do with the approaching rigors of winter. His plight was a thousand-fold worse than a six-month blizzard. He groaned inwardly, fretting about the cruel burden that had been mysteriously saddled on him. Never before had he looked this kind of a personal menace squarely in the eye—knowing that he might not succeed in whipping it.

Instinctively, he felt he ought to share his problems with his people—his friends and partners in Wal-Mart. But it was not easy. Usually he would just crank out his regular monthly message on the chairman's page in *Wal-Mart World*. Today he sat down to write, candidly and honestly, what was deep in his heart and soul, but it was proving to be a struggle. The right words would not come. Sam fumbled around, then tried again. Finally, he gave up, got up, and dragged himself home. There was no doubt about it—he was not the same bouncy, energetic, cheerful Sam Walton he had been. Nor was he brimming with good health. He was only sixty-four, but he felt like a man of eighty.

Next day he again slumped at his desk and tried:

My Good Wal-Mart Friends and Partners:
  I've started to write this piece two or three times in the last twenty-four hours, but couldn't quite reconcile myself to do it. I've just been released from the M.D. Anderson Hospital in Houston where I've undergone a series of tests and examination for three days. What a thorough job these people do, and they really care for their patients and customers, which, as we all know, is the real key for any of us doing well in today's climate. Anyway, I've been checked from head to toe, and I'm confident these doctors are right in their diagnosis.
  It seems I have a very rare type of disease—specifically, I think it's called "hairy cell leukemia . . ."

Cancer is a frightening word. Especially to Sam Walton; his mother had died of a malignancy, and in the prime of her life at age fifty-two. The discovery that he had leukemia stunned and frightened him. Not that he didn't have the personal courage to face a potentially fatal illness, but rather fear for what might happen to his company without him in command. Who would take over Wal-Mart leadership if hairy cell leukemia left Sam Walton incapacitated, or killed him?

Two things about his sickness really infuriated him. First, it was so mysterious; doctors didn't know what caused it and hadn't been very successful in treating it. In fact, for years it had been called incurable. Second, it didn't strike many people; only two out of one hundred adult cancer victims suffered from hairy cell leukemia. Why did he have to have the rotten luck to be among this two percent?

Hairy cell leukemia actually crept up secretly on him. Earlier in 1982 he began to feel tired and dragged out. He knew he was working hard, putting in long hours, but that had been his business regimen since the 1950s. So he tried to slack off a little, turn over more chores to his lieutenants, cut down on his hectic travel schedule, relax more with tennis and quail hunting.

But taking life easier didn't seem to be the solution. He still felt tired, and that began to worry him. All his life he had been active, athletic, a goer and doer. He detested the thought that he might be ill, but he finally consulted his local physicians.

Sam was subjected to an extensive physical examination and laboratory workup. When the results of his blood tests came in, the physicians, wearing long faces, gravely summoned him in. The news was bad, very bad. His white cell count was dangerously and critically low. The diagnosis: leukemia, the hairy cell type in which the cancer destroys the white blood cells. Sam's was not an acute condition, but a chronic case that had been slowly developing over the years.

Perhaps his HCL—as hairy cell leukemia is known in medical shorthand—should have been detected earlier. There had been some indicators in blood tests made when Sam had physical examinations in 1975, 1979, and 1980. Looking back, the doctors realized that those exams had all shown a lower than normal white cell count. In his message in the *Wal-Mart World*, Sam commented on this:

As I understand it, this is just the reverse of 90 percent of leukemia patients who usually are low in red blood cells and high in the white cells. Apparently my red blood cell count and hemoglobin are completely within normal limits. The best part of this picture is that my situation is classified as a chronic (not acute) type, which means it's apparently been coming on for years now . . .

The Arkansas physicians were not at all so complacent at discovering Sam Walton's hairy cell leukemia. They knew it was very serious, life-threatening. They promptly sent him to one of the best—perhaps the very best—cancer treatment centers in the United States, M. D. Anderson Hospital at Houston.

Sam went reluctantly, in a skeptical and antagonistic mood. He was deeply worried about his obligation to stay in command of his Wal-Mart empire, considering his illness a distraction he ought not to have to endure.

But when he walked through the glass-doored entrance to M. D. Anderson's admitting office, Lady Luck greeted him with a radiant smile. Sam Walton had come to exactly the right place. Two of the hospital's immunology and biological therapy specialists—Drs. Jordan U. Gutterman and Jorge R. Quesada—were experimenting with a new treatment they thought would help him. To Sam both physicians looked young, but both had devoted their careers to fighting cancer.

They were experimenting with the biological agent interferon, generally called a drug but actually a combination of about fifteen proteins normally present in humans, and which for research purposes could—in minuscule amounts—be extracted from white blood cells.

It was new. It was rare. It was expensive.

Ironically, interferon was discovered by researchers in England in 1957, the same year an American physician described a new and unique blood disorder characterized by malignant white cells with multiple surface projections resembling "hairs," which came to be labeled hairy cell leukemia. It was nearly twenty years before these two disparate findings converged into this new trial therapy at M. D. Anderson Hospital.

In the late 1970s, Dr. Gutterman discovered that Finnish physicians were pioneering interferon research and flew to Helsinki to investigate. He watched them work, dumping blood that had been donated to the Finnish Red Cross into a centrifuge, which spun the red cells to the bottom, the plasma to the top, and the white cells in-between. The white "buffy coats" were siphoned off, and the plasma and hemoglobin returned to the Red Cross to be used in transfusions. The white cells were partially purified, dried, and turned into powder.

This process involved hard work and great expense. Dr. Gutterman was told that by running 90,000 pints of blood through the centrifuge only 400 milligrams of impure interferon could be extracted from the buffy coats. In layman terms, that would be .014 of an ounce. It took about 300 donors to provide less than a quarter teaspoon of powdered interferon needed to treat one patient for three months. That one therapy course would cost $30,000. And the lone supplier was the Finnish Red Cross.

Undaunted, Dr. Gutterman returned to Houston and began trying to raise research funds. Mary Lasker, a New York philanthropist, gave $1 million. Two Houston oilmen, Leon Davis and Roy Huffington, promptly established the private Interferon Foundation and raised $15 million more. With this money, Dr. Gutterman launched the Anderson experiments. A dozen other major United States cancer centers began similar research.

Time magazine spotlighted this medical "breakthrough" on its March 31, 1980, cover, with a big "IF" and question mark. Interferon promptly became an American household word—but, sadly, was misperceived by the lay public as the long-awaited "magic bullet" or miracle drug that could do for cancer what penicillin had done for once-fatal infectious diseases.

In the hustle and bustle of the furiously busy Houston cancer center, Sam Walton felt a little dazed. He had misgivings about this new treatment.

Dr. Gutterman was supervising experimental treatment with patients afflicted with several different malignancies, and Dr. Quesada was the expert in hairy cell leukemia. So Sam Walton became his patient.

They sat down for a serious talk. Dr. Quesada confirmed the diagnosis, described the nature of the disease—how the dangerous hairy cells usually enlarge the spleen and slowly eat up the beneficial killer cells that normally safeguard a person's bloodstream. This diminishment of the white cells thus weakens the body's immune system, which ordinarily fights off invasion of infectious diseases.

Sam Walton listened patiently but with pronounced skepticism and uncertainty. Dr. Quesada has since discussed this case in detail in two interviews for this book. He reports that doctor and patient clashed immediately: "Sam Walton has always been an extremely healthy individual. He does not like the idea of being sick. He likes sports, he likes to fool around, he likes to be a very free man, and, of course, any disease limits your activity."

The physician hit Sam with a sledgehammer blow with his first recommendation—surgery.

Dr. Quesada again pointed out that hairy cell leukemia, most often seen in middle-aged men, progresses slowly and is characterized by pancytopenia (aplastic anemia), splenomegaly (enlargement of the spleen), and opportunistic life-threatening infections.

Traditional therapy, he said bluntly, called for splenectomy—removal of the spleen—followed by single-agent chemotherapy.

Sam Walton shook his head, set his jaw sternly, and squirmed restlessly as if he was about ready to jump out of his chair and bolt.

"He said he wouldn't have surgery," said Dr. Quesada. "He was adamant. He was not going to let us remove his spleen. He said no—absolutely!"

Dr. Quesada did not argue with him. Published reports in medical journals credit splenectomy with success (five-year survival) in 50 percent of hairy cell leukemia cases. "Actually," Dr. Quesada said in our interview, "it's only twenty-five percent."

That left Sam with one option remaining if he was to be treated at M. D. Anderson Hospital. Dr. Quesada explained it. He could become an interferon research patient.

Clearly, no one should become a guinea pig in medical experimentation without understanding both the possible benefits and the risks involved, the potentially dangerous side effects. Dr. Quesada explained how interferon works to reactivate and stimulate the human body's own hormonelike substances that keep its natural killer cells in the blood strong enough to thwart marauding renegades like hairy cells from destroying white cells and possibly triggering malignant growths in the spleen, liver, kidneys, or other organs. The most dangerous complications associated with Sam Walton's disease are infections and hemorrhage.

Dr. Quesada told Sam he might experience side effects from taking interferon. "Different people react in different ways to interferon," he explained. "It's not like chemotherapy, which makes some patients feel just terrible and causes their hair to fall out. You wouldn't experience anything like that. Some people develop flulike symptoms, and have a tendency toward lassitude, loss of energy. But these symptoms don't last long. We still do not know the cause of HCL. We do know that hairy cells are derived from B-lymphocytes [a subset of white blood cells that turned malignant]."

Interferon had been administered at that time— October 1982—to only about ten hairy cell leukemia patients at M. D. Anderson, Dr. Quesada informed Sam. "But I can tell you—it has definitely proven effective."

Sam Walton sat quietly, thinking it over. After a minute or two, he stood up, extending his hand.

"Thank you, Dr. Quesada. That's a pretty hard decision for me. I can't decide today. I appreciate all you have done. I think I'll go home and meditate on this. Maybe later I'll come back and visit with you again."

That was the situation when Sam Walton returned to Bentonville and attempted to explain his illness to his associates through the *Wal-Mart World*. Even though he was still debating with himself whether to submit to any treatment recommended at the Houston hospital, he tried to put the best face on his plight in the letter, which he published in the October 1982 issue. As he continued writing, Sam emphasized the positive aspects of his condition, pointing out that hairy cell leukemia is slow developing and can be treated:

The doctors assured me that in every other respect, except for this deficiency, which is not of serious proportions, my general body condition and various organs are in exceptionally good shape. All this means is that I've got lots of odds going to have successful treatment.

So, my friends, I hope you'll excuse my referring to a personal matter of this type, but we've always believed in communicating with one another for better or for worse, and in being up front and open with most everything that affects our Company and our Wal-Mart family.

If I'm to have a health problem, I'm really so fortunate to have this type of disorder. I'm completely confident, too, that with the right treatment I'll be able to continue doing the things I enjoy most for at least another 20 or 25 years. I'll be coming around— maybe more infrequently—but I'll be trying and wanting to see you. You know how much I love to visit with you all on how you're doing and how we can further improve our Wal-Mart Company, so I'll be stopping by. Let's put this subject to rest.

I am, and have been, so blessed to have enjoyed the support, affection and loyalty of you wonderful Wal-Mart associates through the years. Together, we can be more than a little proud of our accomplishments. You know we are, and will continue to be, partners. I've just been lucky in so many ways, and feel that this is certainly the case now. The last thing I need or want would be undue sympathy or undue conversation concerning my health. I just wanted to clear the air and not let there be a lot of untrue rumors floating around as many of you knew of the recent tests I have been undergoing.

To add levity to the grim medical report, Sam wound up his letter on a lighter note, vowing to "continue doing the things I enjoy most" and promising to take off for more vacations. He added parenthetically: "Helen will want this in writing and signed." He said he would still play all the tennis "I can work in. And even more bird hunting than I've been able to do previously. I've got two new setter pups named John and Buck, and hopefully, one or both will take the place of Ol' Roy. So with that kind of a schedule, I guess we will have to come up with a nine-day week. Do you think we can?"

Hairy cell leukemia can't be laughed off. Sam Walton knew that; he knew he had something wrong that had to be fixed. Physically he didn't feel any worse off— but no better, either. Sam couldn't get this dire malady off his mind. He was still thinking about the company; what would happen to his dream of becoming the biggest discount retailer in America if he were laid low?

He agonized, silently debating with himself. Should he give in and become a guinea pig for Dr. Quesada? Would interferon cure his hairy cell leukemia, or at the very least control it?

After struggling for about a month, he decided to get another appointment at M. D. Anderson to discuss interferon. Upon his arrival at the hospital, he found everyone excited about new advances in interferon research. Dr. Gutterman had a lot of irons in the fire. The biggest gain in the drug's short history occurred when the chemical was cloned through genetic engineering techniques. This achievement had quickly led to the first doses of synthetic interferon being given to patients at the hospital.

Sam was told that pure synthetic interferon was

proving effective against about a dozen malignant diseases, including hairy cell leukemia. He had another long talk with Dr. Quesada.

"The truth is, he doesn't like going to doctors," said Dr. Quesada. "He had objections about interferon, the same objections that any patient will, you know, raise when you are talking about an experimental agent. In those days the drug was experimental; nobody had really treated hairy cell leukemia with it. I had some preliminary notion that it was working and that's the reason I offered it, but you have to make clear to the patient when you interview him that the drug is in investigation, it may or may not work, some side effects are not known. And that every patient also reacts differently to a new drug. So you know a person that is inquisitive has to think more than once before engaging in a treatment like that."

Inquisitiveness was part of Sam Walton's nature. He still was not certain. He got up, thanked the physician, and again went back home. He meditated back in his Bentonville haunts, mulling over this seeming last-chance option, while on the tennis court or out in the fields with his new bird dogs and shotgun.

After another month of mental debate, Sam set up another appointment at M. D. Anderson, climbed into his airplane, and flew to Houston. He walked into Dr. Quesada's office, and with a weak smile, said: "Okay. I'll try interferon. Let's go."

There was more than a touch of bitter irony in the experiments with interferon at M. D. Anderson. Dr. Gutterman's mother had died of pancreatic cancer. Likewise cancer had killed the mother of oilman Leon Davis, the co-founder of Houston's Interferon Foundation. Davis and Roy Huffington from the outset personally picked up the overhead for their foundation, so all donations could be used 100 percent to purchase interferon, which would cost as much as $25,000 to $50,000 a year for each patient.

"Sam Walton is our prize patient," said Leon Davis. "This thing worked beautifully for him. Because you see, he had it. There was no cure for it. He was bound to die. No question about it. You know, you see him on TV and never guess that he had a problem or that he ever had a problem.

"The fact is, it saved his life. I'm sure he would have died by now if he hadn't been able to get on the natural interferon."

Dr. Quesada's appraisal is less dramatic. "I've heard Leon Davis's statements, but I wouldn't go to that extreme. His disease was active, but he never was close to being a terminal case, or anything like that. HCL can sometimes behave in a very benign fashion, and it can go for years without giving you any trouble. And that could have been the case with Mr. Walton had we not treated him. However, there was indication that the disease was progressing and his counts [white cell] were coming down and one didn't want to wait too long before starting treatment. But to say that he would have died if we hadn't treated him—no, I don't think it's necessarily accurate. Because he still would have had the option of the splenectomy—even though he had initially rejected that course."

The administering of Sam Walton's interferon treatment was no more dramatic than someone getting insulin shots for diabetes. It was quite simple. The interferon powder—just a tiny dab—was mixed with sterile water and injected into a muscle (usually arm or hip) with a hypodermic needle. The dose of 3 million units was administered daily for almost six months, then switched to three times a week.

It was not an ordeal. Dr. Quesada demonstrated to Sam how to mix his solution and give himself the shots, or let someone in the family administer the hypo. "We didn't keep him in the hospital. It was all on an outpatient basis. The patient learns how to do it."

Within a few months, Sam Walton's cancer went into remission—not cured, of course, but stopped cold and no longer active. (According to Leon Davis, Sam Walton later made a $200,000 contribution to the Interferon Foundation.)

Helen Walton hailed this success in her Christmas 1984 letter to friends and family:

> Sam opened quail season November 1, in Missouri. His hairy cell leukemia is in remission, but he will stay on interferon for a year to assist in the research program. This year Sam has received many honors for his work in the retailing industry. Sam manages to keep track of trends and looks for new opportunities through his extensive traveling to check the Wal-Mart stores. For him it is still tennis in warm weather, and quail hunting in cold.

Helen added a P.S.: The family took advantage of Sam's visit to M. D. Anderson at Thanksgiving time that year to hold a family reunion in Houston. Said Helen: "We've had a great three days in Houston with the family—all children and most grandchildren."

Sam behaved splendidly as a patient, according to his physician. "He has always been very precise in following his indications, taking his blood examinations, coming to see me. He hasn't actually missed an appointment; he frequently postpones them for a week or two, but always comes on a schedule. The statement is, yes, he's an excellent patient."

When hairy cell leukemia goes into remission, does the patient have to remain in treatment? Said Dr. Quesada: "It varies. There are patients I have treated for one year, then we stop and they are basically cured. Four years, five years down the road they are still in remission, and they don't need any more interferon. Then there are others who have to be on interferon all the time, because if we stop the disease comes back. In a way like diabetics need insulin, some of these patients just need constant administration of interferon, but very small doses. Really, you know, I don't think of interferon as a drug because it's part of all of us."

Sam Walton has an excellent tolerance to interferon, and never experienced any side effects. As to what he might now face should his disease become active and threatening, Dr. Quesada explained:

"What I'm trying to tell all my patients is the following: Regardless of whether interferon stops working, your chances of controlling or perhaps even curing your disease are excellent. I tell all my patients, 'You are not going to die from hairy cell leukemia. All of us are going to die one day or another, but it's not because of hairy cell leukemia. We now have a variety of different treatments we can offer.'

"Even in the event interferon stops working on a given patient, they have one, two, or three choices. We can go ahead and remove the spleen or we can use two totally new drugs. The prognosis for a patient with HCL is excellent today. Considerably better than five or six years ago when we hadn't these new drugs available."

Dr. Quesada left the M. D. Anderson staff to establish private practice as an oncologist, continuing his work with interferon. Sam Walton has remained his patient, receiving periodic checkups through the years. They talked about whether there was any chance HCL would interfere with Sam's other great love—flying. "I told him never to worry about that. The disease itself would cause no physical limitation, he has never had any physical limitation. The treatment can make you a little tired, yes. But he never lost any hair; he tolerated it exceedingly well."

When asked how often Sam Walton came for a checkup, Dr. Quesada clearly indicated he now knows quite a bit about Sam's peripatetic life-style. With a chuckle, he said: "Usually twice a year. You know he has business in Houston, so he always uses his checkups as a chance to come by and visit some of his stores."

—20—

Wholesale and Hometown

On a sunny January morning in 1983 Sam Walton flew into San Diego to investigate a new wrinkle in the discount business—a membership wholesale club. The idea was originated five years earlier by a savvy California entrepreneur named Sol Price. Reports in the trade said Sol Price was making an astounding success by selling merchandise at only 10 percent above manufacturers' prices—and getting rich.

If Sol Price could do that, Sam Walton figured he could do it, too. But first he needed to look over Price's clubs, talk to the owner, and find out all about the nuts and bolts. If it really worked, Sam intended to crib from Sol Price just as he had copied schemes originated by J. C. Penney, Herb Gibson, and many other good merchants.

The wholesale club idea was good, extraordinarily good!

Sam, fortunately now suffering no ill effects from his in-remission hairy cell leukemia, returned to Bentonville and called together his top strategists. Walton hopped on this new scheme with enthusiasm. He had already taken a long look at his hole card at the start of the eighties and decided that the time had come to gamble on getting out of his long-time rut of operating exclusively in small towns with traditional

Wal-Mart discount stores, fairly large in size with a stock of 30,000 to 70,000 items of general merchandise.

Brashly copying from Sol Price, Walton began creating a division of Sam's Wholesale Clubs. This concept called for a warehouse-looking building where he sold auto tires, office equipment and furniture, microwaves, TVs, and computers, canned goods and frozen steaks—at least 3,500 different items. Most of the merchandise, in cartons and on shipping pallets, would be brought in by forklift and stacked up to the fifteen-foot ceiling. The no-frills club was designed to actually be a plain warehouse with concrete floors and bare steel girders holding up the roof. Sam's would operate on a very low markup and offer merchandise primarily to small businesses for resale or personal use. While Sam's Wholesale Club could be utilized by a small merchant as his own warehouse, individuals also were eligible for membership.

"Our prices will be only 9 to 11 or 12 percent above what the manufacturers charge us," Sam said. "We'll need a high volume. Each warehouse club must do $25 million a year in sales to be profitable."

Moving fast, Wal-Mart opened the first Sam's Wholesale Club in Midwest City, a suburb of Oklahoma City, in April 1983.

Sam's took off like a NASA rocket.

For years Walton has been seeking some effective way to get his everyday low-price methods and concepts into the rich and sophisticated metropolitan markets, and now he had finally found it.

The top men from the general offices in Bentonville hopped in their planes and flew all over the country looking for sites for more Sam's clubs. They found many, and at Bentonville the lights burned late at night in the design section of the Wholesale Club division.

New Sam's were opened rapidly. By the end of 1983 3 clubs were running, with sales of $37 million. Eight more opened in 1984, increasing total annual sales to $221 million. In 1985 12 more clubs were opened, bringing the total to 23 and sales to $776 million. The billion-dollar mark was passed—$1.67 billion—in 1986 with the addition of 26 more stores. By early 1990 Wal-Mart had 105 of these wholesale clubs in operation, with annual sales in excess of $5 billion.

Each wholesale club, containing 100,000 to 135,000 square feet, was about one-and-a-half times the size of an ordinary Wal-Mart discount store. The key factor in the success of a Sam's Wholesale Club would be inventory turnover at a high rate; while regular Wal-Marts counted on four "turns" a year, the wholesale outlet would have to achieve a remarkable sixteen to eighteen total changes in inventory each twelve months. Not content to sit still, Sam permitted his wholesale club managers to do their own tinkering. Some of the clubs added fresh meat, produce, telefax, and express service.

"Sam's doesn't carry everything you want to buy," said Walton. "We concentrate on items wholesalers need most."

These stores offer two levels of memberships. A business firm can buy a primary card for an annual fee of $25. Up to four of the owner's associates can have cards for $10 a year. Individuals also may purchase a $25 card. These members are photographed and issued an I.D. laminated with their postage-stamp-size photo.

But others are eligible to be Sam's members with no fee—such as employees of government entities, school systems, financial institutions, hospitals, airlines and railways, as well as Wal-Mart stockholders and senior citizens with AARP cards. However, these members are required to pay a 5 percent surcharge on top of the regular price. Sam's accepts no credit cards but will take personal checks and cash. In the same year the wholesale clubs were born, it dawned on Silk Stocking Row and the other leaders in Bentonville that the Waltons' adopted town ought to stir itself and show them a little appreciation. So the folks decided, as they say in Arkansas, to "put the big pot in the little pot" and have a party.

There was the traditional parade—which included the Wal-Mart eighteen-wheeler rear-ended by Sam's car—plus a reviewing stand on the square opposite Sam's old five-and-dime location. Because Bentonville is a "Saturday town" that's when they staged the all-day celebration—October 8, 1983.

Sam and Helen, in the reviewing stand, were genuinely delighted—smiling, talking, signing autographs. Helen, holding an armful of long-stemmed roses, wore a navy suit with matching pumps, her straight black hair pulled back in a bun, decorated with silver and copper combs. She also wore wide Indian bracelets. In a tweed jacket, white shirt, dark tie, and navy slacks, Sam stood and waved and called a lot of people in the parade by name. The columnist for the Bella Vista weekly newspaper observed that Sam was wearing the same kind of thick-soled Airfoam walking shoes she had on. "I don't know where he got his," she wrote. "I got mine at Wal-Mart."

At the high school stadium in the afternoon there was a show with Grand Old Opry stars, bluegrass music, and college choirs and singers from the local schools. Kids from the third and fourth grades stole the show, with two original songs, "Hi, Mr. Sam, we think you are grand you're a super man," and "It's great to be a kid in Bentonville." One six-year-old marching out on stage stuck out his hand and said soberly, "Mr. Walton, I've wanted to meet you all my life!"

Bentonville renamed the junior high school for Sam, the day-care center for Helen, and designated one street "Walton Boulevard." The climax came at a "toast and roast" banquet attended by 1,200.

So many awards and plaques were presented that at one point Sam called out, "That's enough." But they kept coming. Speakers ranged from Vice President George Bush via videotape to Governor Bill Clinton, Jack Stephens, University of Arkansas football coach Lou Holtz, and U.S. Senator Dale Bumpers.

Then came a telephone call from President Reagan,

amplified over the PA system. "I want to pay a special
tribute to the both of you for being an outstanding
example of those principles of dedication, hard work,
free enterprise, and the spirit that has made this nation great and strong," the President said.

"Because you had a dream and because you committed yourselves to that dream and to each other,
you have achieved the success for which your friends
and all of us honor you tonight."

Sam Walton told the President his call was "the
icing on the cake" for the day of appreciation. He told
Reagan "to keep up the good work." The President
replied he would "do my darndest."

At the end, when it came time to respond to all the
adulation and speeches, Sam Walton tried to turn the
tables. "You people," he said, "should not be thanking us. We should be thanking you for all the support
you have given us through these thirty years. You
know, our family excelled in two areas. We owed the
most money at the banks, and we had the most broken
bones. With four lively children who climbed trees and
played football, we had a lot of fractures.

"But we always managed to get the youngsters
patched up and our loans paid. We could not have
done it without your patronage and support."

He choked up a little, says a close friend, and he sat
down with tears brightly glistening in his eyes.

On as many occasions as possible, Sam stopped by
Columbia, to see his aging father. Tom Walton had
converted his six-room bungalow behind Stephens College into a duplex, renting one side to a couple of
students. He still puttered around with minor real
estate, and often dropped by one of the three Columbia Wal-Mart stores to kibitz with the managers and
associates. He was on friendly terms with Frederick
Tim Allen, one of Sam's high school classmates, who
worked part-time at one store.

When Sam scheduled a "grand reopening" in the

fall of 1982 for his store in his hometown of Kingfisher, he asked Frederick Tim Allen to drive his father, who refused to fly, out to participate in the
ribbon cutting with the mayor, and to visit the haunts
of his earlier years. It turned out to be quite a trip—
both going and coming.

Tom Walton was then ninety. "He wanted to drive,"
Frederick Tim Allen recalled. "He drove my car from
Springfield to Joplin. After we got over into Oklahoma, he wanted to drive again, and I said okay. I
knew he could drive. He always has. Just to show you
how his reflexes were, we were going through the
middle of some town, about thirty-five miles an hour.
Some kid pulled right out in front of us on a bicycle.
Tom stopped on a dime. Stopped just as quick as I
could of. It scared him a little bit. But his reflexes
were perfect."

Seemingly like most Waltons, Tom had a heavy
foot. "We were going along out there in Oklahoma,
and I happened to notice he was doing eighty-five. I
said, 'Hey!' He looked at me and said, 'This car picks
up speed awfully fast.' It was a more powerful car than
he was used to. I said, 'They'll probably pick up your
driver's license if they catch you.' He said, 'Well, I've
had it a long, long time.' He just laughed, but he
slowed down. He just hadn't noticed he was going so
fast."

During the ribbon cutting, Tom Walton made a few
remarks, telling the modest crowd of store employees
and local dignitaries that he'd come 600 miles for the
occasion. "I wouldn't have missed it. I love Kingfisher." Tom wanted to stay for Mayor George Brown-
lee's luncheon, but that presented a problem. To make
it back to Columbia in time for a doctor's appointment
the following day, he and Allen would have to head
out by car at once.

"Oh, stay," Allen urged him. "Sam will have his
plane fly you home."

"No, I'm afraid to fly. You know that. Never have."

"That doesn't make sense. You've driven jillions of

miles. You're the same as flying there, sitting just a few feet above the ground. In a plane you're just a couple thousand feet higher. Your car could crash same as a plane. So why be afraid of an airplane?"

Tom Walton stayed for the luncheon and was flown back in one of the Wal-Mart planes. He alighted in Columbia with stuffed up ears and a splitting headache. It was his one and only airplane trip.

"Sam was good to his dad," said Frederick Tim Allen. "He would come up to Columbia at least once a month and visit him, and they'd go over there to the cafeteria. That's where Tom liked to eat. Sam would go wherever Tom wanted to go."

On August 15, 1984, Sam got a call from Columbia. His father was dead, at age ninety-two. It was a hard blow. Friends said Sam went into a mild depression for a few weeks. He selected a familiar token from his father's life—Tom's favorite walking stick—and hung it on the wall of his office in Bentonville with his prized plaques. He wanted the people of Columbia to remember his father, too. Sam gave him a memorial by donating $150,000, along with Bud, for construction of a new Columbia Chamber of Commerce Convention and Visitors Bureau headquarters to be named the Thomas G. Walton Building. It was dedicated October 3, 1986, with both Sam and Bud taking part in the ceremony.

Over the years Sam Walton has maintained keen and lively interest in the Bentonville community other than just as its richest resident, banker, discount magnate, and the town's largest employer. He put his personal brand on Bentonville's only newspaper and also the historic Massey Hotel, which he had resurrected from fire damage.

Wesley Hunnicutt, the owner-publisher of the weekly *Benton County Democrat*, was quite aware that once Sam Walton set his mind on a goal he was mighty hard to budge. He also knew that Sam gave patient as well as deadly pursuit. In the end, he aways got his man—or, in this case, his newspaper.

Sam decided he wanted to buy Wes Hunnicutt's newspaper. They had been warm friends since their days around the courthouse square, beginning in 1951 when Wes came in from Oklahoma at age thirty-seven and acquired the small weekly. Together they had commiserated and marveled at the class barriers "Silk Stocking Row" raised to make certain that newcomers exhibited the proper socioeconomic etiquette before joining the Bentonville inner circle.

The *Benton County Democrat* was not for sale. But this obstacle didn't faze Sam. He wanted the newspaper.

"Of course I've known Sam for years," Wes Hunnicutt said. "We worked together in the chamber of commerce, belonged to the same church. Had a lot of connections with Sam when he was just getting started.

"What happened was he was going to print his own circulars. He tries to be an integrated company—does it all. And he bought all this equipment to do it with, and he approached me about buying the newspaper.

"He said, 'I've been told I've got enough equipment I could put out a newspaper.' He didn't know a damn thing about the newspaper business, or that type of equipment. I told him, 'Sam, that's right. You have.' I guess it was 1971 when he first mentioned it to me.

"A veiled threat? No. I don't think Sam was going to start something he didn't know a damn thing about. So I put him off for quite a while. About a year. Ever so often he would call and want to talk about it. I never did set a price. I told him I wasn't ready to retire—maybe two or three years, not now. [Wes Hunnicutt was then 57 years old.]

"Finally, he just came out of the sky and gave me a price that was about twice what the paper was worth on the open market. I told him, 'Sam, that's a very attractive offer. I guess I ought to consider it. But my wife's in Europe, she's on a trip and I'll have to wait until she gets back, and talk to her.'

"When she came back, we talked about it and I

decided to sell to him. It was such an appealing offer, I just couldn't turn it down."

The purchase price apparently was around $200,000. Wes Hunnicutt had estimated that on the 1972 market, when the deal was made, his paper was worth $90,000. "I'm not going to say what I sold it for; it was part of my deal with Sam that I wouldn't. He paid about twice what it was worth, but it was growing quite rapidly."

The newspaper had evolved from several weeklies, the first started in 1886. Under Sam Walton's ownership, the newspaper's course was not smooth. Although the town was not growing much, Sam converted the paper to a daily in 1978, the *Benton County Daily Democrat*.

"Billy Moore went in as Sam's publisher, and he started the daily," said Wes Hunnicutt. "Billy was there five or ten years. Then one day they just came in and fired him. I don't know why, never heard. He went into real estate and printing in Rogers. I guess they did him a favor. They tell me Billy has made a lot of money since he left there."

Sam turned the newspaper over to his son Jim. In turn, Jim for the family holding company sold a working interest to New Jersey and Florida newspaperman Steve Trollinger, who is listed as publisher. In August 1988, the newspaper shifted with the growing tide of Republicanism in Benton County and changed its name to the *Benton County Daily Record*.

It was actually not part of Sam's original master plan to branch out into other business endeavors, but his purchase of the Bank of Bentonville and the newspaper sort of steered his left hand in that direction. These subsidiary operations were stuffed under the umbrella of Walton Enterprises, Inc., which son Jim was running. He was doing a good job, and father wanted to help him develop his executive skills. His hands-on experience certainly would make him more aware of Wal-Mart opportunities and problems.

Into his busy schedule, Jim Walton shoehorned a

dramatic historic restoration—the three-story Massey Hotel, built in 1910 and gutted by fire in 1975, located a block west of the square. Walton Enterprises' expenditure of $700,000 gave Bentonville a new public library and a few shops on the ground floor, and offices on upper floors—including Jim's—retaining the charm of the horse-and-buggy-era exterior. Said Jim: "It was the first time I'd done something like this, and maybe my last. I do not have the time."

Sam acquired so many banks he had to create another holding company called Northwest Arkansas Bankshares, Inc., with Jim as chairman. In December 1985 the Waltons bought control of the McIlroy Bank of Fayetteville, founded in 1871, with assets in excess of $140 million, about $5 million less than the Bank of Bentonville. Already owned by Northwest Arkansas Bankshares were the First National Bank of Siloam Springs, the Bank of Pea Ridge, and the First National Bank of Rogers.

At a Federal Deposit Insurance Corporation "fire sale" in early 1987, Sam bought one-half interest in the failed Security National Bank in the college town of Norman, Oklahoma. His equal partner was Little Rock's First Commercial Bank. With $150 million in assets, it was the largest bank in town, and one of the three "originals" chartered in the 1920s. It was a victim of the petroleum "bust" and a variety of other deficiencies, which also closed four other Norman banks. Jim was elected chairman of the board of Security National, and by 1989 the bank was again sailing on smooth seas.

Throughout the late seventies and early eighties, Sam was doing some hard thinking on various ways to increase his sales volume and revenue. His genius went to work on more new ideas, as well as remodeling some of his earlier concepts.

Rightfully considering himself a master merchandiser, Walton looked askance at various departments in his own stores he had leased out to other retail merchants. He began negotiating to get these in his own hands. He bought the Hutcheson Shoe Company and the Cohen-Hatfield Jewelry Company, both of which were leasing considerable store space in the Wal-Mart chain.

To keep pace with the rapid expansion of the Wal-Mart stores across the South and into the Midwest, Sam built new warehouse-distribution centers, large and automated. He took a plunge into the deep-discount pharmacy field, opening a store he called dot (with a lower-case *d*) Discount Drug store in Des Moines. Also he launched in Springfield "Helen's Arts and Crafts." These last two ventures were profitable but did not show great promise of expansion. Sam's time could have been better spent quail hunting.*

When Walton got over his initial prejudice toward modern electronics, he embraced the technology, as his Bentonville associates say, "whole hog."

His biggest venture was installation of a six-channel satellite system that gave the remote and rustic Wal-Mart headquarters, according to *Fortune*, "a computer-communications complex worthy of the Defense Department."

Started piecemeal in 1985, it was expanded to link up every location in the entire Wal-Mart chain by voice and video, making possible store-to-store or store-to-general-office communication. The satellite system also gathers store data for the master computers, and at a reduced expense flashes back a credit card response in four to five seconds. This quick response was in line with Sam's constant drive to get shoppers through his checkout counters as rapidly as possible.†

For a start-up price of $16 million, Hughes Network Systems provided the equipment, a Ku-band "hub sta-

---

*Only three "Helen's" were opened Fourteen dot Discount Drugs were opened, and all were sold by Wal-Mart to another operator on February 1, 1990.

†One office visitor heard Sam speaking over his satellite phone and complain: "You hear these pauses between words. I don't like that a bit."

tion" at headquarters consisting of a 9-meter antenna dish and "personal earth stations" (PES) with smaller 1.8-meter dishes at the stores and warehouses. The lease on satellite time would run $50,000 a month.

One aspect of the satellite system strongly appealed to Sam. He could appear before the video camera in Bentonville headquarters, deliver one of his inspirational pep talks, and have it instantly beamed live to associates huddled around television screens in the hundreds of stores and facilities scattered across twenty-seven states.

Wal-Mart was so big now that going on the air like this was the best substitute Sam had for those personal visits he loved to make, but no longer had time enough to do satisfactorily.

Via the satellite, David Glass told *Fortune*, "We can talk to every store at the same time as many times a day as we want, and we've dramatically reduced our phone costs. We train by satellite. But the biggest advantage is sharing of merchandise information. A buyer can get on and say, 'These are the new items in Department sixteen. Here's how you should display them.' "

Use of the bar code, the UPC, and hand-held pistol scanners are by now familiar sights to the average shopper. For Wal-Mart these devices speeded up merchandise handling not only in the warehouses and distribution centers but also at the checkout counters. Explained David Glass: "Our distribution facilities are one of the keys to our success. If we do anything better than the other folks, that's it."

Wal-Mart distribution centers rely on laser scanners to route goods coming off company trailers along conveyor belts, some eleven miles long. At the Cullman, Alabama, distribution center, where 1,000 employees work under one 28-acre roof, the general manager boasted: "The technology we use is standard—mechanized conveyors, bar coding, computer inventory. A lot of companies use it. But no one runs it as hard as we do."

The average Wal-Mart distribution center ships and receives about 240,000 cases of merchandise each day. It stocks about 9,000 basic everyday items that can be ordered any day in the year. In addition, the shelves hold 2,000 seasonal items on a predetermined basis. The Douglas, Georgia, distribution center, whose floor covers 705,000 square feet, has 6 miles of rack storage space, with 12 shipping lanes and 86 doors onto the truck dock. It is fairly typical of a large Wal-Mart warehouse that can service about 150 to 200 stores.

An even greater utilization of technology called "QR" is coming on rapidly for the nineties. Explained in simple terms, it permits manufacturers to hook up their computers to retailers' checkout registers and keep track of inventory; they can then dispatch "Quick Response" shipments to keep the store's shelves stocked. To a limited degree, Wal-Mart has already experimented with such a device with several vendors, including Procter & Gamble. Bob Martin, Wal-Mart vice-president for information systems, says questions about the technology "are behind us" and ability to adapt to new rules of the game "may well determine who will be successful in the future."

Without the computer, Sam Walton's retailing dream would not have exploded as it did in the midseventies to the late eighties. The drama of Wal-Mart growth can be quickly grasped in this table:

Year	Number of stores	Annual sales (billions)	Net profit (millions)
1970	38	$ .030	$1 .1
1980	330	1.2	41.1
1985	1,114	6.4	270.7
1989	1,364	20.6	837.2
1990	1,528	25.8	1,080.0

— 21 —

Corporate Shake-up

In the summer of 1984 Sam Walton abruptly announced a change in top personnel at Bentonville corporate headquarters that shook up and puzzled practically everyone else in the company, and definitely mystified Wall Street and other outsiders.

To this day, it has not been officially explained.

As the business grew, Sam had kept careful and diligent watch on his two chief lieutenants. They were the best men he had, and they had worked side by side for six years. Yet he began to wonder whether they had the appropriate assignments. When he finally came to the conclusion that they did not, in a remarkable move, he switched their jobs!

Jack Shewmaker was moved sideways to become chief financial officer and vice-chairman. David Glass was lifted out of that position and became the new president and chief operating officer.

Sam refused to consider this highly unusual corporate maneuver as cause for concern. But discreet whispers buzzed around the general office; the "switch" was Topic A for weeks, and gossip filtered to the outer reaches of the Wal-Mart grapevine. Many of the associates said they couldn't quite understand the reason for the change in jobs.

Walton would not talk about it—then or now. Jack

Shewmaker and David Glass have also refused to comment on the switch.

Despite the switch in top command, the general headquarters didn't miss a single beat. New stores were opened; sales and profits set new records. The one job that seemed to count the most was chairman. And Sam Walton appeared to have settled back in for life. However, as his hair grew grayer, the business media occasionally speculated about whether he was grooming a successor. *Business Week*, in October 1985, spotlighted Sam, saying in part:

> Walton is showing his usual quirkiness in designating an heir apparent. The choice: Shewmaker, 47, or President David D. Glass, 49. But the wily chairman is not tipping his hand as to which. To keep things confused, Walton had them switch jobs last year. Shewmaker, now chief financial officer, is reporting to Glass, the chief operating officer. Walton described it at the time as cross-pollination. But [former President Ferold] Arend isn't buying. "He is throwing them at each other," Arend says. "He did the same thing to me."

Despite raised eyebrows in the inner circle, the team of Glass and Shewmaker forged ahead in harmony, and with perhaps even more acceleration. It was generally agreed Sam had made the switch to try to get 110 percent out of each man. There seemed to be no resentment or conflict. Tom Harrison could jest with his good friend Jack Shewmaker: "First time I ever heard of a president stepping down to controller!"

Even though corporate lips were sealed on the subject, the families of both executives expressed their views to me in interviews in 1989. David Glass's mother, Myrtle, said from her home in Mountain View that there was a wide belief among Wal-Mart underlings that a dangerous rivalry had developed between her son and Jack Shewmaker.

"I don't think Dayne [she called him by his middle

name] ever felt competitive," she said. "Shewmaker may have thought Dayne was threatening him. But Shewmaker is a good man. Walton could see that."

There was, however, a marked difference, she said, Shewmaker being the type who wanted to hold on to everything, and not delegate authority, while her son was quieter, did not appear to be visibly aggressive, and was not identified as a "people" man.

"Dayne sends people and tells them what to do," she said. "and if they don't do it . . . Well, this one guy says if you don't do what he tells you, when you come back he talks to you. And believe me, you know you've been talked to!' That's the difference."

The Shewmaker family knows the switch did not lessen Jack's standing with the boss. When Shewmaker's mother died in December 1984, Sam flew to Buffalo to attend her funeral, and he telephoned condolences a year later when his father died. Said Jack's sister, Mary Lou, "Mr. Sam is really a caring person."

But also demanding. As Jack's sister discovered firsthand.

"My husband and I and our children went down to Bentonville to visit Jack and Melba," she said. "That's when I found out just how hard he had to work. We were going to stay just the weekend. Mr. Sam called and there was something he wanted Jack to do and he wanted Melba to go along. Jack said, 'Well, we're going to have to go.' I said, 'Well, great! Here we are, and we won't get to visit much.'

"So we stayed there, with our kids and their kids. I don't remember where Jack and Melba went, but that was our weekend with them. That gives you an idea—if there was something that needed doing, Jack did it. I never heard him complain about the long hours."

Nor did David Glass complain. But the strain took its toll, and he paid a price. Never very athletic, Glass had been mainly a bear for work. When I asked him in our 1989 interview whether Wal-Mart executives actually put in sixteen-hour days, he said: "No. I think all of us work pretty much as required. Not a question of how many hours you can work and physically survive. It is a question of what's required."

"How do you relax?"

"I go home and relax. I don't have to do anything. I go home and visit with my wife. I can walk away from the business and relax."

After a strenuous annual top-level meeting, David Glass went home one evening in February 1985 and sat down to help his daughter Dayna with her homework. After a few minutes he began to feel decidedly uncomfortable and short of breath. He left Dayna and went in and flopped down on his bed. His wife, Ruth, and his daughter, suddenly frightened, loaded him into a car and drove to the Bentonville hospital.

"He didn't want to go," recalled his mother. "It's a good thing they took him. He was having a heart attack. They said if he hadn't gone to the hospital he probably would have died."

Sam Walton, on being alerted, rushed to the hospital and talked extensively with attending physicians. They agreed it was a serious heart attack. Sam made arrangements and flew David Glass to a hospital in Tulsa for evaluation by cardiologists. He moved into a motel near the hospital and waited. The Tulsa doctors recommended bypass surgery. David Glass, who had never before been in a hospital, balked. He refused to undergo any heart operation. Sam promptly got on the telephone, searching for the best heart specialists in the country.

They turned out to be at the University of Texas Medical Center in Houston. That did not surprise Sam, who was very familiar with that huge hospital complex, as it includes M. D. Anderson where he was receiving his hairy cell leukemia treatment.

When David Glass's condition was stabilized, Sam flew him to Houston. The heart specialists there concluded he was—at fifty—too young for bypass surgery and prescribed medication, diet, etc., and sent him home. After a brief rest, he plunged back into his Wal-Mart presidential chores.

* * *

Now functioning as vice-chairman and chief financial honcho, Jack Shewmaker accepted with outward equanimity his sideways shift, and went resolutely about the business of helping Wal-Mart forge ahead. He and David Glass enjoyed each other's confidence and respect.

But Jack Shewmaker was doing some serious thinking. From the first he had set his sights on being able to retire at age fifty. He wanted to be free to travel, to see the world. His mother had hoped, too, to do that. Her death shook him. Now she never could, his sister Mary Lou reminded him. Jack's wife also was pressuring him to quit working "before its too late." In addition, he had such a strong urge to get into the cattle business that in 1983 he bought a large tract of woods and pasture, fed by a pretty crystal stream on the edge of Bentonville, and put up a sign: "Jac's Ranch." He collected a herd of registered Angus and Polled Hereford breeding stock, and quickly began winning national stock show championships.

In no way, however, did this divert his attention from Wal-Mart. He was still a loyal lieutenant to Sam Walton, and a close personal friend, so much so that he felt called on to defend the boss from swipes aimed at him in the national trade press about being a skinflint. The media was off-base, Jack felt, to depict him as greedy and uncaring, because no tycoon in America accepted his wealth with more humility—genuine humbleness—than did the chairman of Wal-Mart.

So Jack Shewmaker got a few things off his chest to the whole Wal-Mart family by addressing them directly in the company magazine *Wal-Mart World* for April 1987.

His essay took the place of Sam's usual "Message from Our Chairman" on page two—because Sam was off on a trip to look over retailing in Australia with Wal-Mart director Bob Kahn, a California consultant.

"I have a different point of view on his personal wealth than the trade publications," Shewmaker asserted, after explaining about Sam's six-week absence and why he was a preempting the boss's magazine spot for a column of his own. He continued:

> It is true that, on paper at least, he and his family are very wealthy because of their ownership of Wal-Mart common stock, which is nearly 40 percent of the total stock outstanding. But, frankly, a lot of us could own more stock than we do if we had invested everything we own into Wal-Mart stock when it first went public in October of 1970.
>
> Since that time we have split the stock two shares for one seven times, and a share of stock converted for splits could have been bought for just over 12 cents a share in October 1970, whereas today it is selling for $56, $57, or $58. Or, putting it another way, $10,000 invested in Wal-Mart stock back then would be worth over $4.7 million today.
>
> Since the stock was traded publicly, any one of us who could have raised or borrowed that amount of capital could have made a similar investment just as Sam and his family did. Now the fact of the matter is that Sam could have sold his stock at any given time for considerable profit and bought a house on an island, or several houses in different parts of the world. Certainly he didn't have to visit Wal-Mart stores or warehouses. Nor would he have had to put up with the sometimes obnoxious articles printed in trade journals about his personal wealth and greediness.

Shewmaker then raised the question of why, under the circumstances, Sam retained the controlling ownership and his "personal commitment" to Wal-Mart and advanced what he termed the correct answer:

> Perhaps you don't read financial publications as much as I do, but you probably have heard about the unfriendly takeover and acquisition of companies by so-called corporate raiders. The corporate raiders often zero in on companies where dominant ownership is not maintained, borrowing large sums of money to

make the acquisition. By grabbing controlling stock ownership and restructuring the corporation, the raider often attains immediate and substantial profit.

Frequently this is done through liquidating undervalued assets (stores, warehouses, etc.) or other things, or by breaking the company into smaller pieces. Sometimes the raider may keep one or more of the remaining pieces after having sold the majority of the company to pay back the money borrowed to buy the target company in the first place.

By Sam and his family maintaining a large percentage ownership in the company, they have helped to safeguard Wal-Mart Stores from being an unfriendly takeover target. So, quite contrary to the magazines' articles on his reported greediness, Sam's unselfishness has led to a protected situation that has allowed us to grow and prosper. Once again we are back to Sam's commitment to you and the customer.

At this point, Shewmaker interrupted his panegyric to urge his readers throughout the company to join in wishing the chairman a happy sixty-ninth birthday—which occurred on March 29, 1987. "His health, energy level and schedule portrays a much, much younger man. I hope you are as fascinated as I am about Sam Walton's lifetime commitment to the Wal-Mart Company." He went on:

Most of us in Wal-Mart understand this better than outsiders. Like me, many of you have seen Sam in action in a support division, store or warehouse quite early in the morning or late at night, asking questions about you, your family and the role you play in this partnership. His interest was direct, sincere and, seemingly, exclusive to you alone at that time.

In recent years a lot has been written about Sam and his personal accomplishments—especially the personal fortune attributed to him by major publications throughout the United States. I am perplexed by the suggestions, or, at least, insinuations made by these articles that Sam is obsessed with making money and with personal wealth achievements.

Nothing could be further from the truth!

I think I can speak with some degree of authority since I have known Sam for over seventeen years and since our offices have been side by side for the last ten years. Except for his brother, Bud, I have probably quail hunted with him more than anyone who has worked for Wal-Mart and have gotten to know him both as a friend and as a boss.

Now before you think I am about to put Sam on a pedestal, let me clearly state that he is a human being just like me and you. He has been right an awful lot insofar as Wal-Mart is concerned, but he will be the first to admit he has made some pretty good mistakes and that he hasn't made his last mistake on any given day that you talk to him.

Shewmaker said Sam had no idea he was writing the article, and "as in times past, he may or may not approve of what I have said." Even so, Sam would know he was speaking the truth as he saw it—"and I think my view on this position is correct."

Sam is not a greedy person, but, on the other hand, he doesn't believe in squandering money, nor would I recommend that to any of you. He does drive a very old Chevrolet and has little interest in new or replacement automobiles, so long as the old one still works. His pickup truck is a shambles next to my '85 model.

I probably have bought his lunch as many times as he has bought mine, although he has gotten better about that in recent years. A lot of his clothes are bought in Wal-Mart stores. Is that a front or a facade? No, I don't think so.

It is just Sam. He is more interested in people than things! So, what's so bad about that?

Jack Shewmaker turned the tail end of his accolade to the boss into the typical kind of cheer-leading he had so often seen the associates respond to with wild enthusiasm. Under Sam's leadership the Wal-Mart family had "rewritten the history book on retailing. I know you are proud to be part of this accomplishment." But had any of the readers made a commitment to the company that even came close to Sam's? Why should the associates strive even harder?

> Not because we want to be bigger than our competition, but simply because the opportunity is there and in the process of reaching our potential, we can make a good thing better for a lot of people . . . and better than any of us have dared to imagine!
> The new Associate Incentive Bonus program is a fantastic opportunity to get involved in the real issues and challenges facing your store, warehouse or operating unit! I wonder how much we could learn? . . . how much each of us could improve? . . . how much each of you could earn in bonuses? . . . and how far Wal-Mart could go? . . . If (or perhaps I should say when) we all make a commitment to involvement in reaching our goals—not just for ourselves, but for others.

Before another year was out, Jack Shewmaker had finally resolved that it was time for him to step out of his demanding Wal-Mart office. He talked it over confidentially with his family. Said his sister Mary Lou: "He asked me how I felt about it, and I told him it was his decision, and whatever he did, I would be proud of him. It was okay, if that was what he was asking. Why did he call? He said he just didn't want us to read about it in the newspapers. That business about there being a race between Jack and David was. . . . I suppose that looked good in print. That was not the actual truth. Jack was not running away. It was not true that Mr. Sam wanted him to quit. I do know that Mr. Sam didn't want him to step down at that time. But there were no hard feelings. Jack still goes hunting with Mr. Sam, and they are good friends."

Jack's resignation was announced after a February 20, 1988, Wal-Mart board meeting. He was to remain on the board for five years and serve as a consultant at

$100,000 a year. At the same meeting Sam surrendered his position as chief executive officer to David Glass but retained his chairmanship. Sam issued this statement:

"David has exhibited excellent leadership and management skills during the last four years as president and chief operating officer, and prior to that as chief financial officer for seven years. I am certain he will do an outstanding job as Wal-Mart's chief executive officer in the future."

Sam said that Jack Shewmaker "is leaving the company to be with his family and oversee his growing cattle business." Other lieutenants moved up: Don Soderquist to vice-chairman and chief operating officer; Al Johnson to vice-chairman and vice-president for Sam's Wholesale division; and Paul Carter to chief financial officer.

Reporters asked whether Sam Walton had any retirement plans. Wal-Mart's press spokesman responded: "I don't know what his plans are, but if you're prudent, you're all the time planning . . . so business carries on. There are 200,000 [employees] out there, so it's important to have management in place. The thing Mr. Walton would hate worst would be if something happened to him that would impact on people's jobs."

Typically, Chairman Sam was playing his cards close to his vest. Everybody would just have to wait to see how the game went.

Shewmaker left Wal-Mart after eighteen years—and a week or two before his fiftieth birthday—with a stock nestegg worth close to $20 million, based on SEC records. He promptly made a gift of $1 million to Drury College at Springfield to erect a new communications building, named in honor of his parents.

He was honored at a roast in Springfield. His ex-boss Sam came and joshed him about quail shooting, and handed him a 20-gauge shotgun with a bent barrel. Jack Shewmaker held it up, and sighted down the crooked barrel.

"Sam," he said, with a quiet laugh, "you're never going to let anybody get an edge on you in anything, are you!"

—22—

Labor Unions Not Welcome

In Arkansas, when money and politics are exhausted as topics of conversation, the talk turns next to labor relations. And tongues have wagged for years about Sam Walton's anti-union attitude. He has fought efforts of organized labor to lure his associates out of what he considers his "family" environment. On several occasions when union representatives tried to sign up employees, Walton jumped up and made strong personal arguments that the associates already had better wages, benefits, and bonus incentives than any union could possibly gain for them. So far, he has convinced the majority of his people.

However, in the late 1950s Sam lost the first confrontation of his career over labor law—to no less an adversary than Uncle Sam. But there was an ironic flip side—that very defeat spurred him on to expand his discount store chain dramatically. At least, that's the way his former lawyer Bill Enfield sees it.

When Sam back in his early days began consolidating merchandise purchases for all his stores, the U.S. Department of Labor ruled that because of his size he was required to pay his employees minimum wage. Sam wanted to fight the decree, and Enfield went into federal court and argued that the stores "were not all one coordinated bunch," but the judge ruled otherwise.

As Bill Enfield told Mara Leveritt of the *Arkansas Times* magazine: "Walton wasted no time fighting the inevitable. Sam was never one to drag his feet. Once he knew where he stood, he started moving. If the courts considered his operation big, Walton saw his advantage in getting even larger. The decision was the catalyst to his development of a giant chain."

It was Sam's custom in the early days in opening a new store to call in all his experienced managers to help set up fixtures, uncrate the merchandise and place it on the shelves and in the aisle displays, and stick around for a few days to help get the new place off to an efficient start.

Several of these old-timers recall that during the opening of the Clinton, Missouri store, union agents showed up demanding the right to set up the fixtures. Sam got rid of them, indicating he would talk to them later. Then he covered the store's windows with brown paper, and he and his crew worked furiously through the night to get the store ready for opening.

Next day, the union men discovered they had been outfoxed and set pickets parading in front of the store carrying UNFAIR signs. Sam consulted someone who suggested a successful ploy. That was to erect huge signs that said STRIKE SALE. The old-timer said bargain hunters literally ran over the pickets in their rush to get inside the discount store.

Later a union attempted to organize two Wal-Marts in Missouri. Sam sought help from a respected labor lawyer named John E. Tate and found him a down-to-earth realist. As Tate described the episode to *Fortune*: "I told him: 'You can approach this one of two ways. Hold people down, and pay me or some other lawyer to make it work. Or devote time and attention to proving to people that you care.' "

Sam listened and decided to take the latter approach. Within a short time, Sam was undertaking such management seminars as "We Care," and concocting attractive and meaningful profit-sharing schemes, as well as a variety of incentive bonuses, all stressing his sincerity in selling his "family" concept. Sam was impressed by the lawyer and in 1988 added Tate to his corporate staff as executive vice-president for professional services.

The most vigorous labor union onslaught against Wal-Mart was launched in the early eighties by the Teamsters against the giant distribution center in Searcy, just fifty miles north of Little Rock. In and out every day went 100 to 200 eighteen-wheelers. The drivers and dockworkers presented an attractive target for the Teamsters union. Recounting this battle, the *Arkansas Times* said:

> According to Alfred H. Pickering, president of the union's Local 878 in Little Rock, the Searcy employees contacted the Teamsters complaining of low wages, unsafe working conditions, and failure to recognize seniority and provide compensation for work-related injuries. Pickering said Walton told employees in a special meeting that if they voted in favor of the union, he would take away their profit-sharing program. According to Pickering, Walton also reminded the workers that he had 500 job applications on file.
>
> "This threat from management resulted in the union losing the election for representation," Pickering said. He also said that when asked at the meeting why distribution center workers in Texas were making $1.50 more per hour than workers at the Searcy plant, Walton straightforwardly told the employees the reason was that he could get workers in Arkansas for the lower wage, while he could not in Texas.

The subject is a sore one in the Wal-Mart home offices, where the notion of a union mixes with the Walton "family" approach to management not at all. As [Don] Soderquist explained it, "Some companies are afraid to level with their employees, afraid to tell them things like how much money is coming in and where it's going. We take the opposite view, which is this: If we say we are partners, if we say we are family, we've got to talk with each other. Sometimes we show them a pie chart so that they *know* where the profits are going. We share that with them openly."

After the Searcy vote, Walton wrote in the February 1982 edition of *Wal-Mart World:* "Wal-Mart and the Teamsters Union . . . another chapter has just been written when, last Friday, our good associates at our Searcy distribution center rejected the union by an overwhelming margin of over three to one. Bless them all . . . We will never need a union in Wal-Mart if we work with and for one another and keep listening to each other."

Melva Harmon, a Little Rock labor lawyer who represents the Teamsters, was able to view the union failure philosophically even seven years later. "They are not organizing or trying to organize Wal-Mart right now," she told me. "Wal-Mart has too many benefits to make inroads. Searcy is sort of conservative, and there is not a lot of pro-union sentiment there. I think that has a lot to do with it, plus the fact it's a small town and that's a good job for that town. It's just that there aren't that many good jobs up there. It was a good industry [Wal-Mart] and I think the people were thankful for it to be there, and they don't want to rock the boat."

The Food and Commercial Workers and the Retail Clerks unions have not tackled Wal-Mart, according to Lawyer Harmon. "They primarily have organized Kroger and Safeway, and also have a few shoe manufacturers," she said. "The poultry plants are about half unionized. Only one or two of Don Tyson's plants [the industry giant], but it is mostly not organized. None of the department stores are organized."

The Carpenters Union sent an agent from Washington, D. C., Tom Holman, to the 1986 Wal-Mart shareholders meeting in Bentonville to complain directly to Sam. Robert McCord, opinion page editor of the *Arkansas Gazette*, watched Holman get up and ask why union carpenters didn't get to bid on Wal-Mart's stores.

"Walton thanked him for his question (although

urging him to make it short) and answered that there were no restrictions in bidding and that a lot of Wal-Mart's 913 stores had been built by union carpenters," McCord wrote.

Generally credited with being one of the most knowledgeable observers of the labor scene in Arkansas is Ernie Dumas, who has been a state capitol correspondent and editorial writer for thirty years on the *Arkansas Gazette*. He said in our interview: "Arkansas is the weakest labor state in the country. We are a right-to-work-law state, and labor is just weak here. Everybody's scared of Sam Walton." For whatever reasons, Dumas characterized the Wal-Mart "operation" as "kind of scandalous."* Totally ignoring profit-sharing, incentives, and bonuses, the Little Rock newspaperman said: "They have hardly any fringe benefits, and wages are low. They ought to be ripe for unions."

On one of his observations, Dumas was right on target: "You almost never see any union activity with Walton operations."

J. Bill Becker of Little Rock, president of the Arkansas AFL-CIO, and the main mouthpiece for labor in that state since 1964, seemed a trifle blase. Asked what organized labor was doing about Wal-Mart workers, he said genially, "Not a hell of a lot."

Becker has never seen or talked to Sam.

"At one time I did get a call from the AFL-CIO union labor department in Washington wanting to say some nice things about him in regard to his 'Buy American' program, and I told them it was a bad idea."

Why?

"Because of his labor relations with his people," said Bill Becker. "We're told that once a week, or periodically, he sends down on the computer some anti-union bullshit." Becker said frankly he did not personally know about Sam Walton's labor relations

---

*When Sam Walton read that statement he bristled and said: "I can't see why he would say such a thing."

policies. But he volunteered the standard pro-organized labor hostile line: "He pays minimum wages, or slightly above minimum wages, and I guess you can testify he's the richest guy in the world. That's how he makes his bucks—by exploiting his workers."

The labor chief wanted to talk about Sam's role in the current "bitter battle" in Arkansas over workman's compensation benefits. "Sam has the ear of [Governor] Bill Clinton, and Bill believes everything Sam says about how high workers' comp costs were in Arkansas compared to his other states. Sold him a bill of goods. Arkansas compensation costs were too much."

Hillary Clinton, he observed, is on several boards of directors of "large corporations with bad labor policies." But Bill Becker said the Governor and his wife are neither anti-labor nor antiunion. "They are not pro-union, either. They are not union haters. They don't do a hell of a lot to help working people. Story in the *Gazette* about some injured workers picketing a meeting of the Workman's Compensation Board. One of the lines in the story said, 'You communicate to Governor Clinton your grievance?' And the answer: 'Yes, we have and we hear nothing.' "

Bill Becker said Arkansas has had worse governors on labor issues—and better. "I think Dale Bumpers [(D) 1971–1975] was better." Worse? "Frank White [(R) 1981–1983] was worse. Winthrop Rockefeller [(R) 1967–1971] was better on labor issues than Bill Clinton. Is that ironic? Well, Win Rockefeller was sort of a liberal; he probably did more for race relations in this state than any governor before or since."

The only direct dealings between the AFL-CIO and Sam were on the workman's compensation battle. "We had a really bitter fight. We had a hell of a time. Clinton got bad information [from Sam]. It was not only bad, it was inaccurate."

Contrasted with the militant stance of organized labor, there is a quite different aspect of being an on-the-floor associate in a Wal-Mart store.

Consider Shirley Cox, forty-two years old, married

with two stepchildren and a twenty-four-year veteran
of that donkey-and-watermelon fiasco store, Wal-Mart
No. 2 in Harrison. I met her strictly by happenstance
in Harrison in April 1989, while doing research for this
book. Her story is interesting and revealing:

"I went to work in November 1965 when I was
eighteen. I had been bowling on the Wal-Mart team,
and they asked me if I wanted to go to work there. I
did. I started at $1.25 an hour. Don Whittaker hired
me and I started out working in the candy department
and with jewelry. I'd sell popcorn and cotton candy
and get it all over my hands, and then I'd run and try
to sell jewelry.

"When I started 5 men made up the company. Now
we have 300 associates in our store alone. Now the
company is so big it's not as interesting to me as it
was. Last time I went to the stockholders meeting, it
was standing-room only. We all went down to Mr.
Walton's house for lunch. I wanted to say hello to
him. But I didn't get to see him. I couldn't find him
there were so many people standing around. I saw
David Glass. I said, 'I want to see Mr. Walton.' 'Well,
you'll find him right over there in that bunch.' So he
parted the way, and we went over. I like the 'Buy
America' program. I admire him for coming out with
that."

We were in Shirley Cox's living room, and I casually
mentioned I had come from listening to a Sam Walton
talk in Little Rock where he had mentioned that Wal-
Mart had just issued $17 million in 1988 profit-sharing.

"Oh yes, I got mine today," Shirley Cox said. "I'll
show it to you."

She returned with a letter. "We don't get the money
until we retire. Look, last year my profit-sharing was
$37,662.65. The whole account, what I've got coming
is—look here—$220,127.10. I'm proud of that, real
proud. Pretty good for a cashier in the office, huh?"

It struck me that a woman equipped with only a
high school education, although intelligent and articulate, probably felt quite lucky to have had a job for

nearly twenty-five years that would present her with approximately a quarter-million dollar nestegg if she retired today.

I then understood why the Teamsters and other unions found Wal-Mart to be an organizers' Mount Everest. In addition to profit-sharing the associates get numerous fringe benefits, including high-caliber medical protection.

A few months later Shirley Cox told me that she had decided to retire from Wal-Mart around the end of 1989, "while the tax law is still favorable. They estimate that my benefits will wind up around $262,000."

In 1989 Shirley Cox's wage was $7.10 an hour. So there had to be a secret or gimmick behind the phenomenal growth of her account. It was simply that these profit-sharing funds were invested in Wal-Mart stock, which has been running away with itself. There are a lot of Shirleys throughout the chain, since the same formula applies to all other long-term associates.

This profit-sharing program was begun in January 1972. The first year the company contributed a total of $172,237 to the Wal-Mart profit-sharing trust, in which 128 associates participated.

In ten years the trust totalled $47 million, having been accelerated by growth in both company earnings and in the price of the stock on Wall Street. In 1985 the trust held $218 million, in 1986 $303 million, 1987 $453 million, 1988 $525 million, 1989 $649 million, and on January 31, 1990, after a $90 million contribution from the company, the Wal-Mart employees' retirement nestegg stood at $810 million.

The retirees in 1989 included ninety-three associates, each of whom left with a trust fund check of at least $100,000. The April 1990 *Wal-Mart World*, in reporting this, pointed out these were hourly workers as well as management associates.

One of them, Violet Collins of St. Robert, Missouri, after nineteen years as clerk and manager in ladies wear, retired at forty-eight with $154,000 after taxes. The April house organ showed her enjoying the sun in

San Diego. At Newport, Arkansas, Virginia Arnett received $175,000 in profit-sharing at sixty after nineteen years. Betty McCullough, fifty-two, worked in the Sikeston, Missouri, store twenty-one years, and is now traveling. She has no trouble buying tickets; her profit-sharing was $167,000. After fourteen years as assistant manager of Wal-Marts in the Tulsa area, Thomas Cole quit with $149,000 in profit-sharing. Wilma Rader started in the Bentonville warehouse and moved around: Searcy, Arkansas, Claremore and Tulsa, Oklahoma. Her check at age fifty-seven was $153,000.

Don Rolle gave the *Wal-Mart World* a colorful story, recalling that starting in 1970 as a warehouse inventory man he had only a folding chair, a card table, and a pencil. He quit at sixty-three and did not reveal the size of his retirement check, but was asked if he thought profit-sharing was important. He replied: "I sure do! I was with Kresge for twelve years and left with $520 —that's not like Wal-Mart. At Wal-Mart you are expected to work, but you are well rewarded for it."

On the record, it would seem there are enough incentives for a whole army of Shirley Coxes.

Fully aware of Sam's ardent desire to maintain the "family" atmosphere, David Glass as president and CEO stepped in with a warning against unionism aimed especially at new employees.

In his travels he had encountered informational pickets established at various retail operations. "They picket the Hypermart in Topeka, Wal-Mart in Terre Haute, Sam's in Ferguson, the Supercenter in Washington, and on and on," he wrote in the July 1989 edition of *Wal-Mart World*, continuing:

> Sometimes it's the construction unions complaining they are not *exclusively* doing *all* the work. Sometimes it's the meat cutters complaining we are selling meat and not employing them. Other times, it's different reasons or other unions but with similar motives . . . I was reminded that many of you are new enough in our company that you may not have

had the same exposure to union organizational attempts, pickets designated to hurt our business, etc. Therefore it is probably an opportune time to recount our recent experience to date since this will help you to understand our approach and why.

From the beginning, we have all agreed that Wal-Mart did not need unions. We are all partners in our business and work together with a common goal. We absolutely do not need a third party to speak for any of us. A third party would only get in the way of the relationship we have with each other. The "grass roots" philosophy our company has, which says most of the best ideas surface from the bottom up, our programs of sharing profits with everyone and our commitment to take care of each other simply wouldn't work under any other circumstances.

Consequently even though we have exceeded 200,000 associates, none of our partners have ever been represented by a labor union while working with us. I know of no other company that communicates as effectively as we do in Wal-Mart, and it would be a tragedy if anything would disrupt the trust we have established with each other.

Glass recounted previous attempts unions had made to organize the chain, citing the Searcy episode. Ten years ago, he said, unions blitzed the retail stores in an organizational attempt, but gave up when the employees showed no interest. The most recent efforts were designed to protest the way Wal-Mart buildings were constructed.

Interestingly, 25 years ago almost 80 percent of all commercial construction was performed by union contractors. Today, the union work rules and featherbedding make union construction much more costly, and as a result, 80 percent of all commercial construction is now open shop or nonunion. When we decide to build a new store, we take bids on the construction from qualified general contractors—union and nonunion alike. We award the contract to the lowest

bidder. Noncompetitive unions tend to picket the
store site if the construction is done by nonunion
members.

Glass warned his readers to expect new union organizational efforts and asserted that as the company
has grown, "We have added a large number of associates who have no experience with unions and have not
been exposed to the Wal-Mart philosophy." He said
flatly that unions make money by having members pay
dues, and that is their incentive.

Unions have relatively few legal restraints on what
they say or promise. They often promise raises and
numerous benefits that they have no way of delivering. They do not pay anything. Unions do not provide wages, profit-sharing, hospitalization, holidays,
vacation, etc. They can only take money from their
members and ask companies to provide them.
    We, here at Wal-Mart, believe that we do not
need a union or any other third party involved in
our business! We have a great relationship with each
other and unbelievable opportunities for everyone.
By working so well together, we are building security for ourselves and our families. If you, as an
associate, encounter any situation involving attempts
to unionize fellow associates, remember the facts. If
you have questions, discuss it with your manager,
supervisor, or call one of us in the general office.
Let's protect this great thing we have going—our
partnership in Wal-Mart. We do our best by working together—*always!*

—23—

The Nine-Billion-Dollar Man

Who is really the richest man in America?

No longer does Sam Walton head the pack, according to *Forbes* magazine, which knocked him off the pinnacle in 1989—and down to twentieth place.

Metromedia tycoon John Werner Kluge took number one, with $5.2 billion earned in businesses ranging from TV and radio stations to the Harlem Globetrotters.

It was ironic that Sam had created a much greater fortune—$9 billion—made with his own head and hands, steadily parlaying it from the nickels and dimes that went into the meager till of his first country-town variety store.

Sam got knocked down the list when *Forbes* changed the rules of their 400 Richest in America game. The editors decided not to credit Sam with his own pile but to belatedly acknowledge that he and Helen had already split it up to include Rob, John, Jim, and Alice.

The magazine seemed to become aware only in 1989 that this was not an individual fortune but actually the combined wealth of the family. What tipped them off was a petition filed by Walton Enterprises, Inc., in federal tax court seeking a ruling that would avoid double taxation on dividends paid the children.

But if Sam was not individually the richest man in 1989, he never had been. For when and how and why he and Helen shared their business resources with the four children is one of the more fascinating untold Walton episodes.

The children have each owned one-fifth of their parents' stock and property since 1954! Sam and Helen created the trust that set this up when Ron was ten and Alice only five.

Doing this kind of estate planning so early in the game was urged on Sam by his father-in-law, L. S. Robson, who had earlier done precisely the same thing in giving Helen and her siblings equal shares in the vast ranch he had assembled in Oklahoma.

"Mr. Robson was a banker and a lawyer and pretty smart," Sam once explained to a friend. "I could see it was the thing to do. And this all took place four decades ago. I came home and had Bill Enfield draw up the papers."

Rob Walton, sitting with Sam on that occasion, observed: "At that time all Dad and Mother had was a variety store or two. Our shares then couldn't have been worth more than five thousand dollars each."

It has been Sam's imagination, genius, and drive— with extraordinary good luck—that has exploded these shares to a value of almost $2 billion each. And he has not been a mere titular head of the family business but the actual number one chieftain. So *Forbes* in ranking him previously the richest man in the country was on solid ground, but the 1989 issue said:

Fans of Sam Walton have grown accustomed to seeing him at the head of our list for the past four years. This year, though, they will find John Kluge heading The Forbes Four Hundred instead, at $5.2 billion. Don't worry, Sam is fine, and the Walton shares in Wal-Mart Stores and other assets are worth more than ever, some $9 billion, up from $6.7 billion last year. But this year, for the first time, the Walton fortune becomes a family affair, so Sam and his children appear together on page 162, with the Wal-Mart money allocated among them, at $1.8 billion each.

One of our major headaches in compiling our list is making this sort of decision: At what point does actual control of the family fortune pass from parent to child, and therefore at what point should the family's wealth be realigned? In Sam's case, he has made it relatively easy for us. At age 71 this year, he clearly is becoming less active. He has given up the job of chief executive officer at the company he founded and built, retaining only the chairmanship. The children— who are all active adults in their 40s with professional interests and families of their own— are taking an increasing role in investment decisions for the family holding company. Even the holding company itself is being reorganized this year from the family corporation Sam initially set up into a straightforward partnership, with Sam and each of his children full and equal partners. To us, this means that the mantle has begun to pass in Bentonville, Ark.

Sam could care less about no longer occupying the number-one position. In fact, as he tooled around the streets of Bentonville in his pickup, he was mighty glad to be off the top. He seethed anyway at the *Forbes* editors for publishing their infernal list. They had blown his cover as a hideaway Croesus back in 1982 when they printed their first list. There was Sam ranked number nineteen of America's wealthiest four hundred, with a fortune then of $619 million.

Until that day only a handful of people in Arkansas, and probably only a couple dozen elsewhere in the United States, realized he had a vast fortune stashed out in the Ozark mountains. Sam sent a succinct message to *Forbes*, which the magazine printed: "I could kick your butt for ever running that list!"

But the Forbes Four Hundred, capturing the curiosity of a celebrity-and-money-mad populace, rolled merrily on—the special October issue was eagerly awaited every fall, generally considered *The* authority on which billionaires and millionaires were holding the biggest fortunes.

On the 1983 list, Sam jumped to number two, credited with $2.15 billion. In the top spot, with $2.2 billion, was Gordon Peter Getty, then forty-nine, amateur composer-pianist son of oil tycoon Jean Paul Getty.

In 1984 Sam again was number two, at $2.3 billion. Number one that year was again "Gordo" Getty, with $4.1 billion.

Sam Walton jumped to number one on the 1985 list, with $2.8 billion. In the number two place was Dallas electronics whiz H. Ross Perot, with a mere $1.8 billion.

For the next three years, Sam was number one—with $4.5 billion in 1986, $8 billion in 1987, and—after the October 1987 stock market crash—only $6.7 billion in 1988.

The day the market dropped 500 points and knocked $1 billion-plus off the value of his stock holdings in Wal-Mart, Sam was on his way to Little Rock for a press conference on higher education. When he walked into Governor Bill Clinton's office, reporters asked his reaction to the disaster on Wall Street. He hadn't heard about it. When they told him, the Associated Press reports that Sam didn't change expression (which is usually sober, anyhow).

"It's paper anyway. It was paper when we started, and it's paper afterward," Sam said. "I fret, and I'm concerned for our investors, our stockholders, who might not be able to stay with us for the long term. Some may have to sell, and that's tragic."

Sam told the AP that he did not worry about his personal situation. "As far as I'm concerned, we're focusing totally on the company doing well and taking care of our customers. I think that eventually the market will correct, and I think that eventually we will be rewarded. And in a way that's in line with our performance."

Typical Sam Walton optimism—and, as subsequent events clearly demonstrated, eminently justified.

When *Forbes* in the 1989 list credited Sam and his kids with a combined fortune of $9 billion they were illuminating the modern trend of American wealth.

Simply put, the rich were getting richer. The 1989 list contained no fewer than sixty-six billionaires. Even those holding fortunes of $250 million—quarter billionaires—didn't have enough money to qualify for the exclusive Four Hundred.

Forbes listed Sam number twenty, Rob number twenty-one, John twenty-two, Jim twenty-three, and Alice twenty-four—each with $1.8 billion.

A further irony of dividing Sam's pile in this fashion is that neither John nor Alice is directly involved in Wal-Mart, and certainly do not control or direct their $1.8 billion shares in any meaningful way.

Brother Bud Walton remained on the *Forbes* list for 1989, but is listed far down among the just-plain millionaires, number 172, with $415 million in Wal-Mart stock. The magazine had him pegged accurately, saying: "James (Bud), low profile, quiet, ran real estate. Now senior VP gone fishin'; prefers solitude of fisherman's boat in Venezuela, Alaska, etc., to Bentonville headquarters. His 10.3 million shares Wal-Mart worth about $415 million."

Sam's younger brother has always taken a secondary role in the affairs of Wal-Mart, but his considerable contributions to the company's success are recognizable. And Sam, while admitting that Bud is extremely laid back, has never in the slightest demeaned him as a businessman.

Talking about their relationship, Sam not long ago told a friend: "Bud has been real important to this company. He has common sense and superior judgment, and I have listened to him more times than folks realize. On balance, he is a little more conservative than I am. But that's good. He took off a lot more than I do, but he has really made contributions. I wish more of the credit could have passed around to him and to some of the others."

It was no surprise that on the *Forbes* 1989 hit parade eighty of the richest lived in New York, sixty-four in California, and thirty-one in Texas. What startled the magazine editors was to find that Arkansas had a

disproportionately large number of megamillionaires.
The magazine said: "Though Arkansas is one of the
poorest states, there are no fewer than twelve razorbacks among The Forbes Four Hundred."

Though relatively "poor" compared to his brother
and niece and nephews, Bud was wealthier than all the
other Arkansawyers on the list except one, Winthrop
Paul Rockefeller, great-grandson of John D., who in-
herited his late father's fabulous mountaintop farm
and $850 million.

Those on the 1989 *Forbes* list after Kluge and before
reaching the five Waltons, were the following:

Number two, Warren Edward Buffett, Omaha, investments and textile, $4.2 billion; number three, Sum-
ner Murray Redstone, Newton Center, Massachusetts,
movies and video, $2.88 billion; number four, Ted
Arison, Miami Beach, Carnival Cruise Lines, $2.86
billion; Ronald O. Perelman, New York City, lever-
aged buyouts—Revlon to entertainment, $2.75 billion;
numbers six and seven, Samuel I. Newhouse Jr., and
Donald E. Newhouse, brothers, both New York City,
newspaper, magazine, book publishing, $2.6 billion
each; numbers eight and nine, Barbara Cox Anthony,
Honolulu, and Anne Cox Chambers, Atlanta, sisters,
newspapers, TV-radio, and cable, $2.5 billion each;
number ten, H. Ross Perot, Dallas, electronics, $2.5
billion; numbers eleven and twelve, Jay Arthur Pritzker,
and Robert Alan Pritzker, brothers, both Chicago,
finances and manufacturing, $2.35 billion each; num-
ber thirteen, A. Alfred Taubman, Bloomfield Hills,
Michigan, real estate, $2.15 billion; number fourteen,
Lester Crown, Wilmette, Illinois, inheritance and in-
dustrialist, $2.15 billion; number fifteen, Edgar M.
Bronfman, New York City, Seagram liquors, $2 bil-
lion; number sixteen, Leslie H. Wexner, Columbus,
The Limited women's clothing chain, $2 billion; num-
ber seventeen, David Packard, Los Altos, California,
computers-electronics, $1.9 billion; number eighteen,
Harold Clark Simmons, Dallas and Santa Barbara,
California, investments and real estate, $1.9 billion;

number nineteen, Donald Leroy Bren, Newport Beach, California, real estate, $1.85 billion.

The two right behind the Walton five are interesting: number twenty-five, Robert E. (Ted) Turner, Roswell, Georgia, broadcasting, $1.76 billion; and number twenty-six, Donald John Trump, New York City, real estate, $1.7 billion.

Where he ranked on anybody's list and how many billions of dollars he actually had—well, neither item seemed to matter at all to Sam Walton. He was just the same ole Sam—about as unassuming and ordinary as when he had his Walton five-and-ten-cent variety store on the square.

"Sam is a pretty common man," Richard W. Hoback, said in an interview as mayor of Bentonville. "He's been very generous to the city. He doesn't think he's better than anybody else. He's one of the truly great people. You go into a room where Sam is, you visit with him a little, and you simply feel better. He dresses very casual, but when the occasion arises, he looks like a million dollars in a suit. He's just one of these people that when the occasion arises, he fits the occasion."

Perhaps several times a day the Walton cars whip up and down Northeast Second Street in front of neighbor Tom Harrison's house. Talking about how "they haven't changed," Tom Harrison told me:

"Sam gets busier and Helen is busy. She stops in real often, and Sam . . . Well, not long ago Helen came down the street on the far side and stopped and talked . . . my wife and I and my brother-in-law were out in the yard. Sam comes down this side and stops. I finally told him, 'You're going to have to move. Here comes some traffic.' Sam hasn't changed. And that's the amazing thing about it. Instead of having a house in Delaware or New York or Boston, they've got it here!"

Similar sentiment came from eighty-year-old Buster Latham of Gainesville, Texas, who worked all his life in retailing, the last twelve years with Wal-Mart, as clerk and "people greeter." In the *Wal-Mart World* he described flying one morning with Sam to take part in two store openings in Abilene.

"Mr. Walton, here I am, an employee, dressed in my best. You're a wealthy man, dressed casually."

"Buster," Sam replied, "the clothes I have on, with the exception of the sport coat, came from Wal-Mart, and don't refer to yourself as an employee. You are my associate. We all are associates."

That comment struck a chord in Buster Latham. He wrote: "This impressed me and I shall never forget that day with Mr. Sam."

Because of his emergence as America's richest man, Sam was expectably hounded for gifts to "worthy causes." To deal with these requests, he established the Walton Foundation, which would receive and pass on all applications for money. Heading up the foundation was another job saddled on Jim. Sam chose wisely, said Bentonville wiseacres, who considered the steely-eyed son more tightfisted with a dollar than Dad ever was.

And even though he shoveled something like $150 million to $200 million into bonuses, incentives, profit-sharing nesteggs, and the like, distributed directly to his vast army of associates in the stores, Sam Walton had a less than favorable reputation nationally for charitable giving.

With critical overtones, *Town and Country* magazine in a 1986 article on gifts from the rich, listed Sam Walton as having handed out something "over $5 million," which it calculated as "barely one-one-thousandth of his net worth."

Sam and Helen had given a few million, as already related, to colleges and universities in Arkansas and Oklahoma, to Columbia, Missouri, for the Thomas Walton Building, and financed day-care and health facilities in Bentonville and a few other places.

His old town of Newport knew how to put the touch on him. P. K. Holmes Jr., the "villain" in his lost-lease drama, hauled out an old Newport chamber of commerce letterhead that carried Sam's name as president, and wrote asking $250,000 to remodel the public library. Sam sent a check.

Author Vance Packard was denied an interview for his book *The Ultra Rich*. Robin Leach chased him at a charity golf event and got only three minutes of innocuous chit-chat and had to flesh out his "Lifestyles of the Rich and Famous" TV segment with old footage. "The hell with Perrier, I want to know what kind of water Sam Walton drinks," said Leach. "They should nominate him for president and let him run the country like he runs Wal-Mart." More persistent was James Kindall of the *Kansas City Star* magazine. He fruitlessly dogged Sam Walton around Bentonville for a week, and, just as he was about to give up, spied him at dawn getting out of a dusty Chevy to go into the general offices. Sam took pity and invited the writer inside for a twenty-minute interview. No such cave-in, however, for a TV crew that came all the way from Sweden. Sam rebuffed the *Washington Post*, and Bentonville locals felt that the *Post*'s subsequent feature story was unfair, based heavily on the comments of an unreliable source found lounging on the square.

Probably about a thousand people in the media— reporters magazine writers, television anchors, producers, and cameramen, etc. —can readily testify that the chairman of Wal-Mart has given them a pretty consistent cold shoulder since he became rich and famous.

He has held press conferences on numerous occasions, especially at stockholders meetings, new store openings, and promotions celebrating Wal-Mart's new ventures. Newspaper and magazine libraries have hundreds of clippings bristling with his quotes. Action and portrait photos abound in wire service morgues, and TV station canisters hold miles of video footage shot on public occasions.

Even so, Sam is a very private person, almost totally

unwilling to sit down one-on-one with interviewers. He has granted some rare personal interviews to publications such as *Time*, *Fortune*, *Forbes*, and other prestigious journals. But even when *Financial World* selected him CEO of the Decade in 1989 he proved a difficult interview for the writer assigned to do the cover story, Sharon Reier.

"He's an unpredictable man," she said. "I was supposed to meet him at a store at noon. I just had a feeling . . . and went an hour early. Sure enough, he came thirty minutes early, and told me he really didn't have time to talk. Could I meet him later? But he didn't know when. I told him, 'Let's just sit down now and get as much done as we can.' He acceded to that, but I couldn't keep the man sitting still."

Sam doesn't get angry with the press. He fields hard questions with aplomb, and perhaps some grace. He respects interviewers and nearly always first-names new acquaintances. Even the writers who found it impossible to pierce his shell seem in the main to appreciate his obvious integrity and fairness. "I liked him, no matter what," said Reier. "I think his place in American corporate history is assured."

My pursuit was fairly typical. I listened to him speak in Little Rock, caught him coming off the dais, and asked to set up an interview later in Bentonville. People were milling around and it was noisy. But he agreed—tentatively. When I arrived in Bentonville it was off, but David Glass talked to me for an hour. Later I wrote Sam protesting the iron curtain that had been drawn against me by Wal-Mart minions. Out of the blue, he telephoned me, heard my complaint, looked into it, and invited me to come to Bentonville for a visit. We set a date. A week later he called and said he had to cancel, because such an interview might in some way diminish the value of the autobiography he wanted to do. I could understand that.

Even so, we talked a few other times on the phone and he mailed me some Wal-Mart material he thought would be helpful. But like Sharon Reier—and apparently hundreds of other frustrated interviewers—I was left with a pleasant feeling about the man. I liked him. I am amazed at what he has made out of the very ordinary financial resources he had to start with.

There are valid reasons for Sam's "no comment" posture. He's busy. He's already told his story—or a good deal of it—thousands of times. He'd really rather scatter around credit for his amazing success; he thinks, and with some reason, that the dedication, loyalty (and long hours), and ideas generated by his associates have helped him tremendously. Bentonville is protective, and most everybody there wants to help Sam keep a low profile. He doesn't travel with a bodyguard, and he's perhaps too visible for a $9 billion man. As his director-friend George Billingsley observes: "There are a lot of crazies out there!"

The not-too-surprising upshot of all this—which the expert Robin Leach was quick to observe—is that Sam Walton is not the least uptight about his life-style—or anything else. He knows who he is. He is at peace with himself. If he gets to fretting about something, he can find a respite by going quail hunting or hopping in his Cessna 414 and proving that he can still handle it. Now he does not often get out on the tennis court; his gimpy knees are beginning to creak a bit, and his health is poor.

The accolades of a stupendously fruitful career are showering in on him. To list them all would eat up a ream of paper. They don't actually mean a lot to him, but he is polite and shows up and graciously accepts the plaque or whatever it is they're inscribing with his name.

Shedding some of his rustic mystique, Sam began emerging as a national business leader in the early eighties. *Forbes* ranked Wal-Mart as number one in the retail industry. *Dun's Business Review* dubbed it one of the five best managed companies in America. It made the list of the "hundred best companies to work for" in the best-selling book of the same name. And author Tom Peters praised Sam and his company as examples of good management in his book *In Search of Excellence*.

In the fall of 1987, Sam was happy to step into the spotlight in Oklahoma City to receive homage from his native state. It was a black-tie affair, and he was a distinguished figure, although he obviously is more comfortable in a $45 Wal-Mart polyester jacket, $16 slacks, and blue-and-white mesh Wal-Mart baseball cap.

Governor Henry Bellmon presented him with the first Libertas Award in honor of his free-enterprise achievements. "This is really a tremendous honor, but you didn't have to put me into a tuxedo tonight," Sam joked before the presentation. "We don't sell tuxedos at Wal-Mart." Created by an organization called Enterprise Square, the award is designed to be the annual business equivalent of the Nobel prize or the Pulitzer prize.

In 1986, when *Financial World* elevated Sam to the gold medal "CEO of the Year," he swept past nine other high rollers in big business. In addition to tabulating ballots from several hundred securities analysts, the magazine also sent ballots to 2,300 CEOs who were asked to vote for their competitors. Four independent judges made the final selection. Said Roger B. Harris, editor of *Financial World*:

What qualities were the judges looking for? To facilitate their search, the judges relied on certain criteria that this magazine has traditionally set. The top CEO was expected to embody the managerial touch that put his company among the leaders in its industry, as measured by such standards as return on capital, net income and management of debt. The judges were also looking for a CEO whose sense of innovation inspired and motivated his work force.

While considering Walton, the judges were tremendously impressed with the almost compulsive passion he has for his stores, for the people who run them and for his customers. . . . Walton has clearly shown that it is possible to combine the folksiness of a small company with the managerial sophistication of a large one. One judge used words like "alchemist," "wizard," and "magician" in characterizing Walton's managerial ability.

It is no secret that all great CEOs share certain traits. More than just exhibiting self-confidence and a winner's mentality, they have an almost mystical ability to inspire confidence and trust in those around them. The judges found those qualities outstanding in Sam M. Walton.

When Sam was awarded the prestigious Gold Medal of the National Retail Merchants Association in 1988, he demonstrated that he could poke fun at himself. In a fifteen-minute off-the-cuff talk, he recalled his early struggles, saying that he used to tell college students Wal-Mart would zoom, especially after it hit "big" cities such as Fort Smith, Arkansas. "The professors just shook their heads," he said. On retaining his celebrated common touch, he said: "I'm worried about my carefully cultivated humility. Just recently, you may be interested to know, I bought a new pickup truck, as well as a new shotgun."

Two signal honors were bestowed on him in 1989. He was among ten business leaders selected by the editors of the *Wall Street Journal* "who have made a difference." Dubbed "Ten for the Textbooks," the group included Lee Iacocca of Chrysler, Frederick Smith of Federal Express, Ted Turner the broadcaster, P. Roy Vagelos of Merck & Company, and Wall Street tycoons Henry Kravis and Michael Milken, though the latter ironically became a junk bond pariah.

"Beyond their superficial similarities," said the newspaper, "these men share something profound: the energy, vision and arrogance to have burst industry boundaries and to have reshaped the possibilities of business at large."

Likewise Sam and Wal-Mart stood tall with Dr. Vagelos and Merck among *Fortune* magazine's enviable list of "America's Most Admired Corporations." For the third year in a row Merck was number one. Wal-Mart never made the list at all until 1988, when it came in at number nine. But in 1989 it jumped to fifth place, behind Rubbermaid, 3M, and Philip Morris. *Fortune* pointed out that. Wal-Mart's 46 percent average annual return to stockholders (dividends plus appreciation in the stock) over the past ten years led all 305 companies surveyed. Nearest rival was Herman Miller at 27.4 percent.

Discount Store News, the industry's leading trade paper, in mid-1989 designated Sam's company "Retailer of the Decade" and raved:

> Can you imagine one company which operates in a territory with less than 50 percent of the U.S. population . . . going from $1 billion in *sales* to $1 billion in *profits* in just ten years?
>
> Can you envision one company adding as much in sales over the next five years (1989 to 1993) as K mart and Sears each had last year? Or, that this company's growth in profits will be greater than its sales growth over the next couple of years?
>
> The company, of course, is Wal-Mart. And the above observations point out just a few of its many amazing accomplishments.

After asking and answering these questions, *Discount Store News* unveiled another stunning statement: By conservative estimates, Wal-Mart's sales volume would exceed $32 billion in 1990, $50 billion by 1993, and $70 billion by 1995!

—24—

The War over Main Street

In late 1988 when Professor Kenneth Stone walked into the new Wal-Mart in Ottumwa, Iowa, the store manager gave him a dirty look and said, "Say, I called Mr. Walton about you." And, indeed, the manager had. Within a few days the professor was catching a rain of heavy flak from down in Arkansas. It did not come directly from Sam but was fired out of Bentonville headquarters by Vice-Chairman Rob Walton, Corporate Affairs Vice-President Don Shinkle, and even Don Shinkle's secretary.

"I got calls from Wal-Mart," the professor said. "They were really upset. It was all kind of intimidating, like they were going to sue me."

All Dr. Stone, professor of economics at Iowa State University, Ames, had done was to make a survey in November 1988, showing that Wal-Mart's invasion of Iowa's county seats was putting some mom-and-pop stores out of business and generally ruining the traditional appearance and character of Iowa's Main streets.

The Wal-Mart invasion of Iowa had started in 1982, when the Arkansas company already had reached the 550-store level and was operating in 13 other states. By the time Dr. Stone stirred up his hornet's nest, Walton had 19 stores in the Hawkeye State, and hoped to grow even more. Controversy also dogged Wal-

Mart's expansion plans elsewhere in the West. The discount "plague" met with resistance in Steamboat Springs, Colorado, and caused an uproar in Arizona that left Sam's men searching in vain for new store sites. Trouble flared in the Oklahoma legislature to such an extent that Sam wrote strong letters to stockholders, consumers, officials, and newspapers, but to no avail.

All these snags developed while Sam Walton was whipping up the horses to try to reach the 1,000-store level (which he achieved in 1987), and Bentonville lieutenants actually did swarm in on little communities unaware that they were about to be blindsided by Big Business. According to *The New York Times*, many of the assaults were covert operations. Indeed, there were normal business reasons for secrecy in acquiring land, leasing buildings, etc.—to prevent prices from being jacked up. But Wal-Mart was also finding that when news leaked out that they were putting in a store, many communities in several states tried to block them with all manner of official obstructions, involving zoning, permits, and so forth, under pressure from local merchants who figured they would be hurt by the discounter.

One can only wonder how Sam Walton himself would have reacted to a similar threat from the outside in the days when he was one of those classic mom-and-pop-store owners, with his little five-and-dimes in Newport and later in Bentonville.

He assuredly would have howled bloody murder, just as Main Street merchants in Iowa—at Shenandoah, Waverly, Red Oak, Creston, as well as Ottumwa, and the fourteen other Hawkeye small towns were doing when confronted with the Bentonville-based bulldozer.

But now that he was a discount merchant and the second or third biggest retailer in the country, Sam Walton had to weigh his loyalties—and make a decision. Should he relent and hold back progress so as not to smash the mom-and-pops and cause For Sale and For Rent signs to plaster dusty plate glass storefronts in scores of small-town business districts? Or should he continue his crusade for the consumer—the equally important John Q. Public to whom he was bringing quality merchandise at "everyday low prices"? In Sam's mind, it was not even a contest.

The Iowa State University professor was not taking sides. Ken Stone had just put together a routine survey, but in doing so he put himself in the unexpected position of being a visible and handy lightning rod for all sides in this Little-versus-Big business feud.

"I try to lay out the facts and help existing business people understand what the changes are likely to be, and help them see they must change if they want to cope with that kind of environment," said Dr. Stone. "Before Wal-Mart I could tell people, you need to improve your customer relations or you need to improve your pricing, or you need to do this, that, or the other. And they yawned and disregarded what I said.

"Now I can point out that this is the way that Wal-Mart has got to where they are, and their eyes light up and it means something to them. It's interesting that it takes something like this to get people's attention."

The principal criticism of Dr. Stone's survey came in the form of phone calls from Rob Walton. "They thought I was being a little bit too negative," Dr. Stone told me. "Basically all I'm trying to do is document what has happened in this state with the idea that if businesspeople in a town Wal-Mart is coming into know what to expect, and know some of the adjustments that need to be made, then the adverse impact on some of those merchants is not going to be nearly as bad, and I think it is possible actually to benefit from them coming into town. And the non-competing merchants do, but those that are competing directly against them usually do suffer somewhat."

After Dr. Stone mailed a copy of his study to Bentonville, Wal-Mart got off his case a little bit. "We do live in a free enterprise or capitalistic system, and if somebody has the wherewithal to do what they're doing, you can't stop it. All these people who claimed they believed in freedom are about to change their minds now. But that's the name of the game. I will say, Wal-Mart called me back and they said they didn't agree with everything in my study. They basically respected my right to do it, but they didn't think they had hurt anybody."

However, some notion of the harmful impact on one small Iowa town was documented in March 1989 by *U.S. News & World Report*, which pointed out that few local merchants can compete against 50,000-square-foot stores whose notions counters alone dwarf many rural mom-and-pop concerns, adding:

Nor can many match Wal-Mart's direct-from-factory prices, which are often cheaper than the wholesale prices local shopkeepers pay for their merchandise. As a result, downtown business districts begin to empty, leaving fewer sponsors for Little League teams and a smaller pool of advertisers for the high school yearbook. "When Wal-Mart comes in, something has to go out," observes Rex Campbell, professor of rural sociology at the University of Missouri.

That certainly has proved true in Waverly, a northeast Iowa prairie town of 8,500 that welcomed Wal-Mart three years ago. With its healthy economic mix of agriculture, industry and services, plus a liberal arts college, the community made an attractive target for the discount chain, despite lack of a nearby interstate. But local businesses were wary. "Just the word that Wal-Mart was coming made some stores close up," says Don Huston, editor of the biweekly *Waverly Democrat and Independent*.

Among the first to bail out were Coast-to-Coast and Pamida, two discount chains that would have found Wal-Mart's prices and merchandise hard to match, let alone beat. Other establishments along Waverly's Bremer Avenue quickly joined them. Tradehome Shoes locked its doors after Christmas. Patricia's Fashion Fabrics and Sports Shop athletic goods are holding going-out-of-business sales. Down the road the Willow Lawn shopping center is virtually deserted after Schultz's Family Department Store went out of business, while Hy-Vee grocery has moved next door to Wal-Mart, hoping to cash in on the traffic generated by the discount center. "Unbelievable," says Patricia's Fabrics owner B. E. Mick. "If we didn't have a good industrial base, Wal-Mart would have killed us."

Another of the Iowa towns Dr. Stone examined is Independence, population 6,100, on four-lane Highway 20, sixty miles due west of Dubuque. First came the farm crisis, bankrupting 200 farms in Buchanan County. Then the John Deere factory in the next county laid off 10,000 hands. Next the new bypass on Highway 20 hurt Main Street merchants. A final blow to downtown stores was the arrival of Wal-Mart on the west edge of town.

"Wal-Mart threatened us," Mayor Frank R. Brimmer told *The New York Times Magazine.* "They told us if they didn't build here, they'd build in a nearby town and that would have been equally hard on Main Street. Our people were going to shop there whether it was in Independence or twenty-five miles away. You simply cannot beat Wal-Mart, so we joined them."

But not without a furious, divisive community battle that spawned raucous town meetings, hurt feelings, threat of legal action, and in the end, after three or four years, the death of a number of small businesses. "Small towns used to be a last bastion of loyalty," said the former publisher of the Independence newspaper, Geoffery Mosher. "People would support the local businessmen all their lives. But people aren't motivated by that kind of sentiment anymore. Wal-Mart has replaced the need for Main Street."

Of Sam Walton's glowing success, *The New York Times Magazine* piece on April 2, 1989, observed:

He has incurred the enmity of thousands of Main
Street retailers in hundreds of towns. While local
chambers of commerce may hail the arrival of Wal-
Mart because of the jobs and tax revenues it gener-
ates, local retailers fear that few of them will be able
to compete against the monolith.

"Wal-Mart just cannibalized Main Street," says
Jack D. Seibald, a retail analyst at Salomon Brothers. "They move into town and in the first year
they're doing $10 million. That money has to come
from somewhere, and generally it's out of the small
businessman's cash register."

Fourteen months after Wal-Mart opened, a fixture
for thirty years on Independence's Main Street, Anthony's, part of an Oklahoma department store chain,
closed. In the next four years a 100-year-old men's
store, a variety store, an auto supply, a furniture store,
two shoe stores, and about a dozen other businesses
all shut down. Duane H. Gray, who closed his two
shoe stores, told the *Times*: "They buy shoes by the
sea container and semi-truckload, 5,200 pairs of a
single style and color. The end result is they're selling
shoes at my cost."

From Wal-Mart's Don Shinkle, the magazine got
this rebuttal: "The small businesses might have to
make some minor adjustments, but there's usually room
for everyone to survive. The smart businesspeople react
and make out pretty well. Too often people with failing businesses use Wal-Mart as a scapegoat for their
own inefficiencies."

I was curious why Dr. Stone had not made a study
of the impact of K mart in Iowa. "They were pretty
well entrenched by the time I came here thirteen years
ago," he said. "They didn't go into small towns as
Wal-Mart did. K mart, Sears, and Target and the
others basically went into the major markets and worked
their way down to the midsized markets and never
really went into the smaller markets as Wal-Mart has."
The Iowa State professor observed that Wal-Mart

tends to serve as a magnet to draw millions of dollars in new business to a host community and says that can help on-the-ball businessmen, such as druggists, hardware dealers, dress shops, and the like to prosper instead of suffer. He suggests that small merchants actually have a competitive advantage if they offer individualized services. "A lot of people are willing to pay for that," Stone said. He cites an Iowa druggist who lowered prices and added 24-hour prescription service and free delivery—and survived. A hardware dealer did repair, expanded tool rental, and gave helpful advice. A dress shop took on high-fashion lines that Wal-Mart did not carry.

By observing the Wal-Mart phenomenon from its first foray into Iowa, Dr. Stone came to this conclusion: "They are pretty masterful at what they do. I drive all over the state. Many times I've seen a Wal-Mart on one side of the street and a K mart opposite. The Wal-Mart parking lot will be three-quarters full, and the K mart one-quarter full. These are just casual observations, but it is easy to see that Wal-Mart is really appealing to the mass public."

Part of the professor's tactics call for comparison shopping. "The other day I went over to Wal-Mart and bought just nonfood items like toilet paper, paper towels, cleaning supplies, and so on that I could have bought at the grocery store. About 40 bucks worth. I kept the receipt and went over to my grocery store and compared the prices, and they were about 26 percent higher at my grocery store. People aren't stupid. That is a bad omen for grocery stores because traditionally they have made a lot of money on their nonfood items."

Dr. Stone feels he is on better terms now with Wal-Mart. He has never met Sam Walton. "It would be interesting if I could, but I think he has bigger fish to fry. He's not too worried about me. . . . I don't want to beat this thing to death, but as long as people are interested I'll keep updating my study as long as I get new information."

* * *

Colorado newspapers called it "The Shootout at Steamboat Springs" when Wal-Mart encountered major problems in trying to invade the ski region 160 miles northwest of Denver. The city council refused Wal-Mart permission to build a store on 9 acres of commercial land on U.S. 40 between the century-old downtown and the 20-year-old ski resort. Part of the opposition came from small downtown merchants, but Wal-Mart also encountered opposition from the glitzy shops and condominiums farther up the mountain. These owners felt that Wal-Mart's cut-price image was not in keeping with the rest of this first-class resort.

The battle raged for two years. It got so hot that Wal-Mart filed a damage suit against the city. Countersuits were filed. A petition demanding a town referendum on the question was finally upheld by a Steamboat Springs judge. But at the last moment, in April 1989, just before the election, Wal-Mart blinked. Don Shinkle announced Wal-Mart would abandon its store plans. "A vote would not be good for Steamboat Springs, and it would not be good for Wal-Mart," he said. "I truly believe Wal-Mart is a kinder, gentler company, and, while we would have the votes to win, an election would only split the town more."

Although this was the end of the battle, some people, pinched by resort prices, formed "Advocates for Affordable Shopping," and vowed to pursue efforts to get Wal-Mart to change its mind and come into Steamboat Springs after all, but to no avail.

Sam Walton rarely, if ever, got directly involved in any of these battles with small downtown merchants. He wisely let local hired guns such as real estate agents and developers, who stood to pocket handsome commissions, take the heat, and quietly and from afar advised and directed by his Bentonville executives.

But in 1987 Sam plunged into the middle of a Wal-Mart effort to erase an Oklahoma law that dictated minimum profit margins for all merchants. Enacted in 1941, the legislation required all merchants to mark up the price on their products by a minimum of 6.75 percent, described as "an obvious attempt to outlaw cutthroat competition that would favor the larger chain stores."

The *Tulsa World* said Sam and others put up $100,000, hired lobbyists, and persuaded powerful House Majority Leader Guy Davis to write the proposed repeal law. Oklahoma's Wal-Mart stores began collecting petition signatures and running prorepeal ads in rural newspapers.

Sam got into it by writing personally to newspapers, officials, and his own stockholders, asking them to push for repeal. "The issue is free enterprise," said his letter, adding that the present law mandates minimum prices to consumers. He told shareholders passage of the bill could "have a direct impact on the value of your stock." He said his company could be forced to reprice Oklahoma merchandise "at a cost to stockholders as well as Oklahoma consumers."

Representative Davis's bill was dubbed "the Wal-Mart bill." The leading opponent, Representative Rick Littlefield, used harsher terms. "I call it the plywood bill," he told the *Tulsa World*. "Should this piece of legislation pass, we'll be putting plywood on the windows and doors of businesses up and down Main Street, Oklahoma."

The issue was hotly debated in the legislature at Oklahoma City, but in the end Sam was rebuffed. The Wal-Mart bill never got off the ground. And when a group of Oklahoma merchants filed suit alleging Wal-Mart was luring customers with "loss leaders," the *Tulsa Tribune* spoke up with a sharp editorial—with the ironic title "Sam Walton's Menace"—pointing out that small towns had been suffering retail decay for half a century.

The Model-T Ford made America mobile. . . . Unfortunately, the automobile had to be parked. Patrons of downtown merchants soon ran out of curb space. Municipal parking areas came years too late.

In too many towns and cities, long-time competitors, unused to cooperation, let the chains establish themselves at the city limits and then boarded up their old stores and joined them.

But all is not lost, even now. . . . Instead of cussing Sam Walton and other major chains for their successes, it might be wiser to consider why. "Why" is the availability of a wide selection of goods close to the family automobile, attractively displayed in climate-controlled comfort and requiring few steps.

Saving the value of downtown retail property is not always possible. . .But in many smaller towns, bold, cooperative planning could still work wonders.

The conventional wisdom in the discount industry is that Sam Walton is a sure-fire genius who is totally shot with luck. But that legend falls short of 100-percent accuracy. Walton has come up with his share of promising brainstorms that did not pan out. In fact, over the years he has pulled some prize business boo-boos.

Perhaps one of his most foolish ventures was to try to sell new automobiles at discount. He cooked up a scheme to enhance his Sam's Wholesale Clubs by arranging for members to buy new cars at $100 over dealer's invoice. To the chairman of Wal-Mart that idea was totally in keeping with his concept of quality merchandise at everyday low prices.

Scouting around northwest Arkansas and Little Rock for dealers to go in with him, Sam got a mixed reaction. Several dealers turned him down cold. Springdale Ford owner Andy Lewis told the *Springdale News* that personally and as a Wal-Mart stockholder he opposed the scheme and thought it might not be legal. Fayetteville's Olds-GMC-Buick dealer and Springdale's Chevrolet-Olds company protested, asserting "there's a lot more to this business than just selling a car, there's warranty, backup, and service. We're trying to get it stopped."

The Arkansas Automobile Dealers Association sent out a newsletter condemning Sam's "experiment," saying, "What if Sears, Penney's or K mart decided to do the same thing? Next thing you know Piggly-Wiggly [a grocery chain] would be selling 4x4s."

But Bill Schwyhart, owner of Hart Motor Company of Rogers, went along with Sam Walton. "It will be a sad day for free enterprise if Sam's can't sell new cars cut rate," he said. To him it was merely a referral service. "All it does is take the negotiating out of buying a new car. The dealer is guaranteed a $100 profit. That doesn't go to Sam's—that goes to the dealer."

Hart Motor Company sold ten cars—and then the scheme went up in smoke.

Auto dealers filed a complaint with the Arkansas Motor Vehicle Commission, which immediately ruled that Sam's Wholesale Club was acting as a broker, "which is illegal under state law." Sam's officials said they didn't want to violate the law and volunteered to forego the $100 fee if that would bring the scheme into compliance. That wouldn't, the Motor Vehicle Commission ruled.

So Sam's Wholesale Clubs promptly went out of the car business but continued to sell parts—tires, batteries, shocks, mufflers, radios, etc. New cars at discount was a Walton brainstorm that never really got rolling.

Nor did Sam's first idea of expanding his Texas Wal-Marts across the Rio Grande. He got interested in a Mexican discount operator and apparently took a financial stake in one of his stores. Just when friends thought Sam was ready in the late 1980s to take the plunge into Mexico with a string of Wal-Marts, the peso was devalued. That created panic and a monetary crisis south of the border. Sam immediately discontinued plans to expand into Mexico. But he was still interested in having Mexican outlets and patiently bided his time. In March 1990 the idea apparently was revived when Wal-Mart executives, headed by Rob Walton, made what they called a "fact-finding" excursion. The *Times* in Laredo carried a report that Wal-Mart was considering Monterrey, Chihuahua, and Guadalajara as possible store sites.*

Though Walton rarely was personally visible in any controversy involving his stores, on another battleground an unflattering portrait of the Wal-Mart chairman emerged in the late eighties; he was cast in the role of villain when the Bentonville general office undertook to eliminate the manufacturers' agents who dealt with Wal-Mart buyers. Sam's buyers were reputed to be the toughest in the industry, forcing sales reps to cough up the lowest possible price—absolutely the lowest. Yet at the same time *Wal-Mart World* occasionally claimed it wanted closer relations with its suppliers.

In secret, or at least quietly, Wal-Mart in 1987 began pressuring manufacturers to eliminate their sales representatives and deal only through their corporate sales director. *Sales & Marketing Management* magazine, in researching an article on the feud, found very few, on either side, willing to talk. Value Line analyst Ray Cowen pointed out that "in the Southwest Wal-Mart's the only show in town." Not only the sales reps, but also their companies were fearful of getting hurt by losing the account.

The *S&MM* magazine's conclusion was that Wal-Mart was seeking to squeeze out the 2 to 6 percent middleman commissions manufacturers paid their independent reps (who might also sell for other firms) and then pass on the savings to customers to win greater market share and shopper loyalty. About ten big companies were reported to have caved in to the Wal-Mart demand that sales reps be prohibited from calling on the Bentonville general office. However, these companies were said to have paid the regular

---

*Later in 1990 the idea was "off" again. Rob Walton told associates that his father remained very interested in trying to establish Wal-Marts across the border run by Mexicans if he could figure some way to circumvent the greed of entrepreneurs so that low prices would actually be passed on to the poorer citizens.

commissions to their sales reps. Ten other large firms refused to bow to pressure from Walton.

It was not the first antirep assault. Wal-Mart tried the same thing earlier, in 1981; J. C. Penney and K mart did likewise. All flopped. The newest antirep war teetered back and forth for a while, and eventually Wal-Mart again backed off, and the trade press dropped the story.

But in almost the same breath Sam Walton suddenly played hero and leaped into the national spotlight with a serious attempt to curb the loss of American jobs to cheap-labor foreign competition.

By buying foreign-made merchandise—simply because the price was lower, which he felt was part of his obligation to serve his customers—Sam Walton realized that indirectly he was helping get thousands of American workers thrown off the payroll. He began fretting about this in the early eighties and tried to think of some way the economic teeter-totter could be tilted back toward U.S. factories, instead of so grossly and unfairly benefiting the Orient.

Sam was meditating on this nationwide problem when he got a phone call in 1984 from Governor Clinton in Little Rock that provided an example of this American dilemma right in his home state of Arkansas. This phone call was the inspiration for Sam's "Buy American" idea.

Governor Clinton was calling to see if he could get help for Farris Burroughs, a clothing manufacturer in trouble in Brinkley (population 5,000). Burroughs's plant employing ninety people had been making flannel shirts for Van Heusen that were distributed through J. C. Penney and Sears. Now the work was being moved to China, and Burroughs feared he would have to close his factory.

"I'd hate to see an Arkansas plant shut down," said Sam. "I'll call you back."

At that moment, like the majority of merchants, Wal-Mart was buying nearly all of its dress shirts from overseas. Sam decided he would "Buy American," and give Farris Burroughs an order, if they could agree on a fair price.

But there were obstacles. The Brinkley shirtmaker had financing problems, and he couldn't locate any American-made flannel. Sam had big textile manufacturers come into Bentonville to discuss this problem. "They flew here in their big corporate jets," Sam lamented to a friend, "and complained they couldn't afford to make flannel in this country."

The "Made in the USA" bug had bitten Sam hard. He refused to give up. He worked things out with Farris Burroughs. They would have to compromise and get the material from overseas, but all the other manufacturing would be done in Arkansas. Sam agreed to give a guaranteed order, help with scheduling, and pay faster for shipments.

With a lot of fanfare, Sam gave Burroughs's factory a $612,000 contract for 240,000 flannel shirts. The factory immediately hired 100 extra workers, with the assurance that their sewing machines would be kept whirring for about six months.* Governor Clinton went on record saying: "I think this is an act of patriotism. Wal-Mart is the only company of its size in this country that I am aware of that is making a major effort to do this."

In the same stroke, Sam took his idea nationwide with an open letter asking 3,000 American manufacturers and wholesalers to join him in the "Buy American" plan to help save jobs at home and reduce the trade deficit. Between 1981 and 1983, 1.6 million American jobs were lost, he declared, due to the rise in imports, which jumped 78 percent in two years. "Some-

---

*Sam Walton not only rescued Farris Fashions, but set the company on Prosperity Avenue. In March 1990, Farris Burroughs said his factory employed about 350 with an annual payroll of $4 million, turning out more than 2 million flannel shirts, jogging shorts, and other sports togs annually, most of which went to Wal-Mart stores. It was his understanding that all Wal-Mart's flannel shirts in 1990 would be manufactured in the United States. "Oh, boy," he said, "I'd like to nominate Sam Walton for president!"

thing must be done. . . . We cannot continue to be a solvent nation as long as we pursue this current, accelerating direction. Our company is firmly committed to the philosophy of buying everything possible from suppliers who manufacture their products in the United States."

Sam put his money where his mouth was. He actively sought other manufacturers who could sell him items Wal-Mart was currently buying in Hong Kong, Taiwan, and other foreign trade centers. Before long he had written checks and issued a number of other contracts for goods that he had previously been buying abroad to be manufactured in the United States.

Wal-Mart's competitors did not meet the "Buy America" challenge. K mart public relations executive A. Robert Stevenson told *The New York Times*, "If you can buy domestically, we had rather do that, but we're looking for the best deal for the customer." Third-ranked Target discount stores also had a lukewarm response. "We're for free trade," said President Robert Ulrich. "We're the customer's representative, and we try to get the best deal for that customer."

But some Wall Street analysts were impressed. Walter Loeb, retail industry analyst at Morgan Stanley & Company, said: "He's somebody coming out and saying, 'Hey, we don't have to buy everything from the Far East!' I think this is the beginning of a major drive of American retailers to buy American products."

A. Gary Shilling, an economic consultant, told *The New York Times* that Sam was following Henry Ford's footsteps. "Ford said that if you don't pay your workers enough, they are not going to be able to buy Fords. Wal-Mart is saying if you don't buy the worker's goods, they are not going to be able to buy your goods."

In some quarters Sam Walton's "Made in the USA" was characterized as a public relations gimmick at best or at worst a hoax, but in February 1986, he staged a sort of "show-and-tell" in Little Rock's huge convention center to demonstrate its effectiveness.

Wearing $29.84 shoes made in Wynne, Arkansas
(and sold at Wal-Mart), Sam led reporters and businessmen through a mock-up of one of his stores. Off a
wall rack he grabbed a child's size two tee-shirt manufactured by Pixie Playmates of Florida. "They say we
can't do it in the United States, but we're going to
have these in our stores for two for five dollars," he
said, beaming.

Sam slung a $4.93 wire chair over his shoulder—
missing Governor Clinton by inches—and sat in it to
prove it was superior to one made overseas that Wal-
Mart sold last year for $6.99. "This year we'll do three
million dollars worth of business with them, and they
did us a favor," he said. "Folks, that can be done time
and time again."

To demonstrate similar success stories, Sam led reporters through a display of American-made goods,
extolling microwaves, candles, shirts, boots, shoes—and
caps for toy cowboy guns. Enthusiastically he waved
cooking utensils and tossed washcloths to a reporter so
she could feel the difference. He called for impromptu
comments from representatives of thirty "USA-made"
companies. Whitney Stevens of J. P. Stevens Company said he worried about Wal-Mart buying so many
two-for-$7 beach towels. "If he doesn't sell some of
these by summer, he's going to be up to his ass in
beach towels," said Stevens.

Sam snatched up one of the beach towels and
wrapped it around his waist, twisting to show it off.
"How many did we order?" Stevens gave him a smile.
"At retail, eight million dollars worth." Sam smiled
back. "Don't worry. We'll sell 'em all."

The press conference lasted ninety minutes. Sam
estimated that in the previous twelve months, his "Buy
America" program had restored jobs to 4,538 people.
He also admitted that the company had somewhat
shaved its own profit margins to make the idea succeed. Wal-Mart now was purchasing only 5 percent of
its merchandise directly from overseas companies. Another 25 percent was manufactured overseas by Ameri-

can-owned companies. That portion, said Sam, would be his next target, by making contracts that will permit some of these companies to bring jobs back home.

The *Arkansas Democrat* described the event as having "a circuslike atmosphere" and said, "In many ways, Walton resembled a preacher extolling the virtues of good versus evil, with company representatives giving testimonials on how much better off they were because of Wal-Mart."

Whether it ever took hold in a major way among other big corporations—which were, ironically, at that moment trying to get Congress to lower trade barriers to permit even more foreign imports—Sam's Americanization campaign met with applause in the heartland of the country.

If politics is the rich man's sport in Arkansas, why doesn't Sam Walton, with a stupendous power base in money, men, and influence, as well as proven leadership qualities, leap into the game?

"He just doesn't care much about it," says John Brummett, the *Arkansas Gazette* political columnist.

For many years Walton has contributed advice to his state's political leaders but little money. He has no desire, says Brummett, to be a political powerbroker or kingmaker. When Sam does contribute, his check usually goes to a Republican, but he is on friendly terms with and usually supportive of Governor Bill Clinton, a Democrat.

Was there any political overtone in Walton putting the governor's wife, Hillary, on the Wal-Mart board? Columnist Brummett, who has covered the state capitol and Arkansas politics for twelve years, said: "I doubt if it was because she's Clinton's wife. She's a pretty smart, capable woman who has made a lot of money as senior partner in the Rose law firm in Little Rock. I don't know; maybe he wanted a woman on the board and she was the best available."

Capitol insiders adopt a wry attitude about Sam

Walton's low political profile. Said one veteran campaigner: "He could wield plenty of clout if he wanted to. I know this much, I'd rather have Sam for me than agin' me!"

A few years ago Sam Walton did open up his purse for a behind-the-scenes socioeconomic enterprise with vaguely political overtones that came to be known as "The Good Suit Club."

Nineteen "fat cat" Arkansawyers pooled a total of $700,000 in 1986 to fund a study of state issues "and make recommendations for good things—especially education." Sam was not only one of the nineteen, he was chairman of "The Good Suit Club," more formally known as the Arkansas Business Council.

Meetings are secret, but Brummett got a tip and broke the story, and because all the members were well-dressed millionaires, gave the council its jocular nickname. The name stuck. Even Chairman Sam joked about the tag.

It has been difficult for the business group to influence public policy without getting snared in politics. "At times," said Brummett, "they haven't been real comfortable." "The Good Suit Club" supported Governor Clinton in 1989 when he asked the legislature to assess $210 million in new taxes for education. But one of its own members, Jack Stephens, hired lobbyists to scuttle the tax. "It went down in flames," said Brummett.

Because of his insight on "The Good Suit Club," Columnist Brummett was invited in October 1989 to review its history before the national advisory board of Little Rock's First Commercial Bank.

Sam Walton, one of the thirty members of the bank's panel, arrived late. He slipped into a chair in the board room and remained quiet until the newspaperman concluded. Then he turned to Brummett. "I'm sorry I missed most of what you had to say, but I appreciate your observations. When I got up this morning I realized I was supposed to be down here and I'd be listening to you, so I dressed especially for you."

Sam stood up with a big smile and opened his dark green sports jacket to show the label. "This is off the rack at Wal-Mart. Forty-six dollars." He fingered his maroon trousers. "Sixteen dollars. Also Wal-Mart."

The other tycoons at the table laughed. They were chairmen, CEOs, or retired heads of big corporations ranging from McKesson Corporation and Ralston Purina to Pan Am Airways, Prime Computer, Inc., and Montgomery Ward.

"How much discount did you get, Sam?" someone called.

Another round of laughter.

Sam grinned at John Brummett. "This is all in your honor, so I wanted to wear my best clothes."

—25—

Clerks and Customers

Feeling somewhat squeamish, Sam Walton lifted onto his plate a steaming Louisiana crawdad and eyed it with doubt and hesitation. He turned, quizzically, to his dinner companion, the mayor of New Iberia.

"The way we Cajuns eat 'em," Mayor Bob Bodin quickly volunteered, "is to snap off the tail. And then go after that slimy green stuff in the head. Lots of folks just suck it out."

Sam had flown down to the Evangeline country of Louisiana to visit store associates. It was mid-March 1989. This was business—and pleasure. He loved visiting Wal-Marts. In three decades, he had made several thousand such visits.

In celebration, the New Iberia associates were throwing a crayfish "boil." Six hundred chairs held Wal-Mart employees and their kinfolk at tables on the parking lot, next to an impromptu stage. Seven hundred fifty pounds of sizable crayfish simmered in boiling vats. Tables were heaped with rice, potatoes, hot sauce, and jambalaya ("dirty rice"). Jana Jae and her Hot Wire Band from Tulsa waited to give a show. Everyone, including the mayor, came to eat and sing and cheer—and have a Cajun fine time.

Store manager Brent Drum and district manager Bob Erickson watched the big boss from Bentonville with sly smiles. Would he go all the way with this Cajun delicacy? Sam, trying not to make a face, toyed with the succulent crustacean from the Bayou Teche.

"If it's all right with you, Mayor Bodin, I'll just eat the tail."

There was laughter, and the Cajun mayor shrugged, and snapped open a crawfish. He peeled and ate the tail, and then poked his index finger into the chest cavity. He brought out a greenish glob. "Fat," he explained to Sam. "Don't know what it does to your cholesterol—but we find it tasty!"

When pretty brunette Jana Jae mounted the stage, took out her violin, and raced into "Joli Blond" and "Jambalaya," the crowd exploded. "She's the greatest fiddle player you ever heard," Mayor Bodin said, recalling the event.

Sam agreed, in his comments in *Wal-Mart World:*

Our associates and our New Iberia customers experienced one of the finest Jana Jae concerts I've ever attended. Jana and team really came on with that wild Cajun music. We had those sensational New Iberia Shrinkettes in their cheerleading uniforms leading the action. That crowd didn't need much encouragement either. Soon, there was general foot stomping, dancing and singing "Louisiana Saturday Night," "Jambalaya," and even a local talent who jumped up on the stage and did a couple of great numbers with Jana.

No slouch as a performer, Sam himself loudly joined in the singing, said Mayor Bodin, "and he's got a good voice and is just as down to earth as anybody, even if he is the wealthiest man in the world."

The frivolity did not in the least diminish the serious purpose of Sam getting in his Cessna 414 and flying all the way to Louisiana. In two days he had already visited his stores in Baton Rouge, Gonzales, Port Allen, Morgan City, Houma, and Franklin to see with his own eyes how his associates were treating the customers, and to hear any ideas they—or the customers —had for doing it better.

More than anything else, the headman's insistence that everyone in his stores—both employees and shoppers—get first-class treatment is the premier hall-mark of Sam Walton's success formula.

If Sam had wanted to take the pulse of his New Iberia store and get the typical customer's reaction in a nutshell, he could have asked the mayor. The 80,000-square foot Wal-Mart store, opened in 1983 in a former Wool-co site, sits opposite New Iberia's K mart.

"Which store is the best?" I asked Mayor Bodin.

"Oh, Wal-Mart! It out-sells K mart ten to one!"

"Why?"

"That's a good question," said Mayor Bodin. "I think a combination of things. Let me tell you an ironic thing. They are opposite one another. I think it's the good merchandise and a reasonable price along with, you know, people who wait on you are very friendly and courteous.

"I'm not saying that K mart doesn't furnish the same thing, but I've been to both stores. To be hon-est, I don't really see a big price difference. And I tell you, Wal-Mart is doing something right. . . . The only problem we have here—there aren't enough checkout lines. We probably have twenty-four or twenty-five of 'em. You get in that store particularly on weekends, it's wild!"

Did the mayor ever return anything to Wal-Mart?

"I bought a rod from Wal-Mart. I fished with it twice. I actually broke it; I don't think it was a defi-ciency in the quality, but it broke. I brought it back to them and they didn't ask me two questions—gave me a brand-new rod! I've never really had a problem with anything I bought.

"That has a lot to do with it—that attitude that Sam Walton prefers to have a satisfied customer than an unsatisfied customer is what causes his business to succeed."

What the New Iberia mayor had to say was the kind of nonscientific market research Sam banked on at the inception of his discount retailing. Instead of having a professional survey made, Sam would count the cars passing an intersection he thought might make a good location for a Wal-Mart. He is noted for his MBWA technique, which is exactly what he was doing in Cajun country.

But the industry itself measures discount retailers as meticulously as a tailor would George Bush, to critique and define every little thing in obtaining a perfect fit. And in the race between leader K mart and Sam Walton's outfit, the edge does seem to come down to "little things."

Consumer perceptions of the two chains are vastly different. Shoppers polled by Chicago, San Francisco, and Philadelphia researchers said they spent more money in Wal-Mart, were better satisfied, and were more impressed with what the survey takers termed Wal-Mart's "esteem."

Probing "the oft-ignored side" of discounting, the *Wall Street Journal* in the fall of 1989 reported:

> Some retailing specialists . . . say that unlike manufacturers, whose success depends more on the quality of their products, retailers can rise or fall on the tiny signals they send consumers in everything from the stores' logos to the width of their aisles.
>
> It might not seem significant that Wal-Mart employees wear vests, while K mart employees don't, or that Wal-Mart bags its merchandise in brown paper bags, while K mart uses plastic. But these little things can make a big difference in consumer perceptions of what a retailer stands for and the vibes shoppers get in its stores, the specialists say.

"Everything a company does sends a signal about who they are, what they believe, and what they want to be," Carol Farmer, a retail consultant in Boca Raton told the *Wall Street Journal*. "One little bad thing can wipe out lots of good things."

In recent years, K mart has struck back, renovating older stores, upgrading customer service, and cutting prices. But many retailing executives and consultants say Sam Walton's outfit is still the leader in attention to details that motivate consumers. Observed the *Wall Street Journal*:

> They say the [Wal-Mart] chain is particularly adept at striking the delicate balance needed to convince customers that its prices are low without making people feel that its stores are too cheap. These same consultants say K mart, on the other hand, sometimes risks cheapening its image with tactics that generate quick sales—such as offering to double manufacturers' coupons or running its "blue-light specials," the spur-of-the-moment sales that K mart stores announce over their public-address systems and mark with flashing blue lights.
>
> Consultants also contrast Wal-Mart's simple logo, in white block letters on a brown background, with K mart's bright red-and-blue store signs. The brown in Wal-Mart's logo conveys "a warmer invitation" to shoppers, says Clive Chajet, chairman and chief executive of Lippincott & Margulies, Inc., an image consultant in New York. "It's friendlier and less blatantly commercial."

To evaluate how the two chains compete, the *Wall Street Journal* went to Madison, Wisconsin, and checked two representative competing outlets. At Wal-Mart on the west side of town, the aisles were wider than those at the nearby K mart. Fluorescent lighting was recessed in the ceiling, creating a softer impression than the glare from the exposed strips at K mart. And the apparel departments were carpeted in a warm, autumnal orange, while K mart's were tiled in off-white. There was also a contrast in customer service:

> At the Wal-Mart store, an aggressively friendly grandfather guards the entrance, smiling at babies and striking up conversations with shoppers, while

another employee follows customers to their cars to pick up shopping carts and even stops to pet a puppy. At the nearby K mart, a young woman working as a greeter stands stoically and waits for people to ask her questions.

The Wal-Mart employees also wear blue vests that make them easier to pick out from a distance than K mart employees, identified only by small nameplates. And the vests' subdued blue color reinforces Wal-Mart's image as a friendly, nonthreatening place to shop.

The friendliness exhibited in Madison, and everywhere else in the chain, is a habit the chairman consistently stresses. He hopped up on the stage in Cincinnati in mid-February 1989, wearing a Procter & Gamble baseball cap and a blue nylon jacket, to open a new Sam's Wholesale Club. As he has done hundreds of times in several hundred places, he raised his right hand and led his associates in the "Sam Pledge":

From this day forward, every customer that comes within ten feet of me, regardless of what I'm doing, in this house, I'm going to look him in the eye, I'm going to smile, I'm going to greet him with a 'Good morning,' or a 'Good afternoon,' or a 'What can I do for you?'—so help me Sam!

Sam Walton harps constantly that customers must feel "it is their store" and know they will be "treated fairly, honestly, and with respect." Borrowing, and remanufacturing, some maxims from Bob Kahn, a Wal-Mart director, he said no retailer makes a profit on a transaction, but only on a customer. "A dissatisfied customer is generally lost forever to us and probably with a host of their friends as well. It is a proven fact—it costs five times more to gain a new customer than to retain a current one."

Also: "The nicest sounding word to any person is his own name, especially in this day when computers are making numbers out of all of us. You know this; I know this. Are we doing all we can . . . in calling our customers by their names? Let's do it . . . every opportunity, whether it be a check, credit card, membership card, or simply by introducing yourself and saying, 'Your name is what?' 'Thanks for trading with us,' or 'Please come back.' I'm sure we can do this much better than we have."*

Tom Harrison knows firsthand about Wal-Mart's customer satisfaction policy. "You get something, you don't want it, you're dissatisfied—no questions asked. I was out at the store here in Bentonville and fellow came in with a weed eater he'd had over a year. They took it back. They buy in such volume no manufacturer is going to turn them down on taking something back."

Tom Harrison was in the store to return a television. "They asked for a sales slip, and I happened to have it. The clerk said it wouldn't have made any difference. It had a broken chip in it or something. They do that on anything.

"My daughter lives in Rogers and she had gone to the store there to buy a pair of shorts for her father-in-law. She bought them, found they weren't the right size, and they didn't have the right size. She wanted her money back and the manager wouldn't give it. She argued awhile, and then she called me.

"We were at a bridge party with the Waltons, and she wanted to speak to Sam. He got on the phone, listened, and told her, 'Well, Sarah Belle, let me talk to the manager.' And he talked to the manager a little bit and hung up. And the manager got awfully nice and gave the money right back.

"Not long after that Sam and I were talking and I said I wanted to apologize for Sarah Belle calling while we were at the bridge party. 'Oh,' he said, 'I'm glad Sarah Belle called. Boy, that's been worth its

---

*Associates are now wearing a CHANT button to remind themselves that "Customers Have a Name, Too."

weight in gold! I told that manager that I wanted him to bring that pair of shorts to our Saturday morning meeting. I made him stand up and hold up those shorts. Then I asked him, what is our motto? And he said, "Satisfaction guaranteed." You know, every once in a while you have to refresh their memory.' "

Time after time, with something of an evangelical fervor, Sam has stressed both daring and discipline, often describing the Wal-Mart family as a melting pot made up of former retailers, housewives, college trainees, people from all walks of life.

"Our people want to win so badly, they just go out there and do it," he said in the July 1986 *Wal-Mart World.*

They have known instinctively that determination and perseverance are far more important than many of the technical and theoretical approaches often advocated by the "experts." Our folks don't expect something for nothing, and they don't expect things to come easy. Our method of success as I see it, is ACTION with a capital *A*, and a lot of hard work mixed in.

We've said it through the years: Do it. Try it. Fix it. Not a bad approach, and it works. There are a lot of people out there who have some great ideas, but nothing in the world is cheaper than a good idea without any action behind it. We must be . . . action-oriented doers. A whole lot more fun, and accomplishes so much more.

For all of his easygoing "aw, shucks" mannerisms, the Wal-Mart boss has stepped forth on occasion with a straight-from-the-shoulder stern talk, not for the clerks and little people in his vast organization, but for the executives and store managers. In the same article, he explained:

In so many businesses, most managers lead by fear and intimidation. They think that being tough is being a leader. Nothing is further from the truth. Good leaders will treat people "good" and add the human factor to all aspects of their business. I like this, "If you manage through fear, your people will be nervous around you after a while. They won't approach you with a problem, so the problem gets worse. They will be afraid to be creative or express a new idea. They don't feel like they can take a chance because they won't want to risk your disapproval. When this happens, the people suffer, and the business suffers, too."

In Wal-Mart we must treat our people with real genuine respect and courtesy. Your people aren't numbers on your own success chart. They're real people and deserve to be treated that way.

So in summary, management by intimidation is easy management. It's "chicken management." It is so easy to just fire somebody with a problem. It's easy to reprimand people. Let's make our "Positive Discipline" philosophy in dealing with our associates work. If done right, it will.

Build strong personal relationships with your people. Let's think for a moment about this seemingly controversial subject. To help your associates grow and be all they can be, you must show that you really care. You must become a master at communicating with them all aspects of your business and their place in it. The only way you can let them know how much you value their contributions is to show them and tell them. And the best possible time and way in Wal-Mart is to do it one-on-one as we walk around the house, "MBWA."

We've got to get to know our people, their families, their problems, their hopes and ambitions, if we are to help them grow and develop. We must appreciate and praise them as individuals. Show your concern daily.

Another very important principle for us is to live and stay with our people through the good times and the bad times. . . . Life is a business of momentum; sometimes you are up, sometimes you are down. In "down times" your associates need your love and support more than at any other time. Unfortunately, many managers ignore people when there is trouble. They run from people rather than deal with their problems.

We are all just people with our varying strengths and weaknesses. So true commitment, plus a generous portion of understanding and communication, will certainly help us win. Remember, leaders must always put their people before themselves. If you are able to do that, your business will take care of itself.

To stress the value of taking care of customers, Sam cited the lawn and garden manager of his New Smyrna Beach, Florida, store, who learned that a lady had purchased at a nearby Wal-Mart a picnic table that lacked its nuts and bolts. She couldn't drive back twenty miles to pick up the hardware. "Our department manager drove his pickup to the other Wal-Mart, picked up the hardware, took it to our customer in the country, and helped her put the table together. You talk about expectations over and above—we have a customer there for life!"

Similar praise went to Dana Syata, a salesclerk in electronics in the Hope, Arkansas, Wal-Mart. "She always has time for customers, even off the clock, to go to their homes to hook up VCRs, adjust televisions, or whatever the need may be," the manager reported. By return mail came a letter commending her outstanding performance, signed Sam M. Walton.

Whenever Sam visits a store the major portion of his time is spent wandering the aisles, looking over merchandise and talking to and listening to his associates. He likes occasionally to make a surprise visit. Such as in February 1986, when he dropped in on the grand opening of a Sand Springs, Oklahoma, shopping center that his store anchored. "I was absolutely flabbergasted," said developer Bob Kucharski. "No one knew he was going to show up—not even the Wal-Mart store manager."

It was much the same way at the mammoth Sam's Wholesale Club in Houston across the highway from the Astrodome. He drove up in a rented car, found an ordinary customer parking spot, alighted wearing a tan blazer, nondescript brown tweed trousers, and brogues, and walked in unannounced and without an entourage or security detail.

Arriving by surprise to help celebrate the store's first anniversary, Sam got on the PA near the front door and announced his presence, with his Arkansas twang. Employees wearing red, white, and blue Sam's Wholesale Club sweatshirts shrieked. It was the kind of commotion, said *Financial World*, you'd expect if Elvis Presley had risen from the dead.

"It doesn't seem to take much to set this crowd loose," Walton joshed. They shrieked again. Sam Walton laughed and exhorted his troops, praising them for a job well done. Cheers broke out, again and again. As long as he remained, the store was electrified.

It is pretty much that way everywhere Mr. Sam mingles with his folks on the floor—even at the annual stockholders meetings, which are now too large to hold in the Bentonville headquarters. In 1986 2,000 jammed the general office auditorium, 450 of them store associates selected by their fellows for the honor of attending. They drew their regular pay, meal and motel money, and rode chartered buses to Bentonville.

Sam called several to the stage to recognize them for their achievements. Many brought him gifts— handmade shirts, an Irish cap, etc. He invited them out to his house for a picnic lunch in the front yard. For two hours without stopping he cheerfully posed with these clerks and cashiers who wanted to have their pictures taken with him.

Robert McCord, a Little Rock editor, saw Sam put his arm around a short chubby woman from Louisiana and pose while her friend shot their picture. "Greta," Sam said, "we are really proud of what you have been able to do with that snack bar." McCord remembers being impressed by the sincerity of Sam's comment.

As the Wal-Mart empire has grown, the sheer size of the shareholders' meeting has meant moving it again, to the University of Arkansas's Barnhill Arena, where on June 2, 1989, 9,000 came for this unusual annual combination of old-time camp meeting and high school pep rally. In that throng were 1,147 associates, brought in from as far away as Arizona, West Virginia, Minnesota, and Wisconsin aboard 21 chartered buses and private cars. Some were called up and given performance prizes—and a hug—by Sam. For the sixth year in a row, Linda Richardson from Corinth, Mississippi, was hailed as the champion in health and beauty aids department sales.

The traditional employees' picnic in the Waltons' front yard at Bentonville attracted 2,500. They were handed box lunches, and the headman, in blue-and-white Wal-Mart baseball cap and shirtsleeves, wandered around listening intently to ideas and suggestions, greeting old friends, posing for pictures.

The 1989 meeting, said *Wal-Mart World*, was "the largest of its kind in the world."

Letters from employees and customers pour into Wal-Mart headquarters, sometimes as many as 4,000 a month. CEO David Glass says most contain praise, some are critical, and a few offer new ideas. All are answered.

A retired banker wrote to tell about seeing Margaret Chambers in Little Rock's Asher Avenue Wal-Mart help an obviously illiterate person by reading Valentine cards so he could make a choice. When the shopper left, the banker complimented her on her kindness. "Oh, I don't mind," she said. "He's been here before—he's a customer."

Another letter, signed by a Wildwood, Georgia, customer: "Dear Wal-Mart: Upon visiting your store in Kimball, Tennessee, I was very impressed with your 'greeter' David Rollins. David was smiling and offered me a buggy. What could be so special about this, you must be wondering. David was confined to a wheelchair. I applaud you for the willingness to employ disabled Americans."

From the days of his orange crate shelves and plywood desk in his 1950 Bentonville five-and-dime, Sam has disdained even normal executive opulence. His corporate offices, tied in to his original Bentonville warehouse within earshot of busy loading docks, attest to his antipathy for lavish business surroundings. To Sam's way of thinking, a corporation ought to be able to limit its administrative expense—which would include salary, bonus, perks as well as headquarters staff and their offices—to 2 percent of annual sales. Wal-Mart has generally fallen below that target.

Walton has been equally vigorous in waging war on what the trade calls shrinkage. That simply means loss from inventory. If a store orders 144 nail clippers, for instance, and can account for having received money at the checkout for only 100, it raises the question of what happened to the missing 44. As explained by COO Don Soderquist: "That merchandise which is unaccounted for may have been stolen internally, stolen externally, or may be improper paper handling or the combination of these three primary elements."

Whether the shrinkage was the result of shoplifters, associates who were stealing, or shipping clerks who were balling up paperwork, Sam Walton wanted to crack down, and hard. He recognized it was an industry-wide cancer, which in most retail chains eats up 2 percent of annual sales volume. He talked it over with his top people and did a lot of private "meditating" about it.

Out of the brainstorming came the Wal-Mart scheme, which was simply to distribute bonuses to all employees in stores that managed to reduce their shrinkage levels. This bonus represented substantial money— enough, in fact, to make alert detectives out of most associates. They not only watched for shoplifting by customers, they also watched each other. If a fellow associate slipped out with a few flashlight batteries, a pair of gold earrings, or just anything at all—that inventory loss would cost the other clerks. So the thief was apt to be privately warned or reported as dishonest to the management.

"The one area of our performance that has not been satisfactory," COO Soderquist informed the associates, "is in the area of shrinkage." For 1988, the Wal-Mart shrinkage goal was 1.5 percent, and for 1989 Sam and his officers set it even lower, 1.2 percent.

In a deliberate effort to stir up salespeople on the floor, tips and ideas were solicited from every store and published regularly in the company house organ. Apparently many fitting rooms were vulnerable to shoplifters. The Halletsville, Texas, store suggested nailing chicken wire across the top of these booths: "Shoplifters would not be able to throw [color-coded] hangers into the next room, or dispose of anything in the fitting rooms." In the Tullahoma, Tennessee, store, women were handed just one bra at a time to try on: "This keeps people from leaving with two stuffed in one box or even wearing one in exchange for their own." The flip-top Tide boxes were a worry in Baton Rouge, an associate warned: "It would be very easy to drop jewelry or any other small, easy theft item into the box without anybody knowing." Wind chimes were hung outside rest room doors in the Jerseyville, Illinois, Wal-Mart, alerting the nearby layaway clerks to remind customers they must leave packages outside, "thus preventing a lot of shoplifting." Other ideas for reducing store expense were not overlooked; if everybody leaves one light on or the adding machine running, said a warning from Wynne, Arkansas, "thousands of dollars are lost each year that could be put back in your incentive bonus. So please, turn out that light!"

In Mustang, Oklahoma, several customers rooked the store by switching caps on spray paint cans. The cure: sticking the price tag on the can, instead of the cap. Shoplifters at the Zachary, Louisiana, perfume counter were outwitted in this way: a motion sensor light was installed and theft dropped because shoppers thought it was a surveillance camera. In Longview, Texas, shoppers peeled off clearance sale tags and stuck them on higher priced items—until a new kind of sticker was developed. And in DuQuoin, Illinois, the music department clerk decided to unbox replacements she handed out for defective tapes or records, so the customer couldn't return the box for a cash refund.

A remarkable turnaround in inventory control occurred in fiscal year 1989 at the Edinburg, Texas, Wal-Mart. The previous year shrinkage ran 4.58 percent. Manager Jose Garcia took drastic measures, probing for the "whys," and holding store meetings to discuss the problem, with 100 percent attendance required. Shrinkage amazingly dropped to .97 percent—and profit jumped in only four months to 75 percent higher than the previous year's total!

Manager Garcia proudly reported to Sam Walton: "We are headed toward a net profit that will qualify our associates for the $1,000 stretch incentive check."

For savvy professional businessmen the summons to a Wal-Mart job usually required only the decision to grab fast for the fat paycheck, plus the promise of stupendous stock and profit-sharing bonuses. Not too many men hesitated. Such million-dollar opportunities come up maybe once in a lifetime, if at all.

But what of their wives, who are often confronted with the necessity of yanking up comfortable roots, packing up the furniture, pulling kids out of school, and heading down into the Ozark Mountain country to a little backwater town nobody ever heard of? The tears and the anguish could be monumental, and in many cases were.

Sam Walton was usually oblivious of the trauma. Or, at the least he didn't openly talk about it. He was, and is, the ultimate pragmatist. He not only accepted life in Bentonville—he absolutely loved it! He and Helen were small-town folks.

When Donald Soderquist, quit his job as president of Ben Franklin Variety Stores in Chicago to come to Bentonville in 1980 as Wal-Mart executive vice-president, his wife was very apprehensive.

"Sam and Helen didn't talk to us about it before we moved down here," said JoAnn Soderquist. "I don't think they really know what it is like. It was very hard for me. It took me two years to adjust. This is a whole different style of life."

The Soderquists took a house in Rogers, looking for the best school for their ten-year-old son and because it is closer to Beaver Lake where they keep a 27-foot speedboat. "We first looked at homes near the lake, but Don didn't want to be that far from the office," she said. "Except for the board of directors meetings, there is not much social activity, and you kind of pick your own friends."

Many of the young wives, especially those with children, and those from the East—even one from Little Rock—are torn by moving to the Bentonville area, said Jo Soderquist, even those whose husbands are high-salaried vice-presidents. "On the other hand some come and love it right away!"

Jo Soderquist and several other wives have taken active roles in Rogers's junior auxiliary, and in a welfare group that helps pregnant teenagers. These wives are also active in the new 600-member interdenominational Fellowship Bible Church, which meets in the junior high school. Jo has taken up golf and plays tennis. "I'm not good enough to play Sam. I play with Helen. She is a lovely lady."

The Soderquists have been married thirty-four years, and even though her husband rose rapidly to become, in 1987, Wal-Mart's $500,000-a-year chief operating officer—with a stock nestegg worth $20 million—Jo says candidly:

"If Don came home tomorrow and said we had to move, it really wouldn't bother me. This is a nice place to live, but once I cut that tie back in Chicago, I said I'd never put my roots down like that again. I have made some lovely friends here, but I could move tomorrow and it wouldn't really bother me."

When Ron Mayer served briefly as chairman, his wife had a hard time getting used to Bentonville.

"Sam told us in confidence," said Tom Harrison, "we ought to do anything we could to make them feel at home. The same with Burt's wife." He was referring to Shirley Stacy, wife of the bank president who was uprooted from her lifelong home in Virginia. Burton Stacy said: "My wife was very unhappy about coming here. It took her about two years to start feeling the qualities of the community. She got elected to the school board. Now you couldn't drag her away from here. We don't have opera or theater, but we can go to Kansas City. We really don't miss much, and we have a lot of clean air. My children were able to get on a bicycle and ride across town to the Little League park, and I never feared for their safety. The education system is very good here."

Jack Shewmaker's wife, Melba, fell in love with Bentonville. They built a pleasant house on the edge of town and bought enough land to start running a herd of cattle with an eye toward his retirement.

David Glass sat at his CEO desk in the general offices in the spring of 1989 and tried to minimize the family-life problems of Wal-Mart headquartering in such a remote spot.

"I came from Springfield, Missouri, and for my wife it was no big deal," he told me.* "I think that gets blown out of proportion. If you were moving from New York to Bentonville, it would probably build a little character for you.

"Somebody said one time that being headquartered in Bentonville makes it difficult to attract people, and easy to keep them. Once people are here for a while, they fall in love with this area."

*Ruth Glass, who says she underwent a "dramatic experience" a few years ago while watching Jim and Tammy Bakker's PTL broadcast, travels a great deal as an inspirational religious speaker. She told me: "I was born again. I am writing a book about my life. I believe it will be inspirational to others."

—26—

"Oh, It's a Big Sky"

Without wings, Sam Walton readily admits, the Wal-Mart juggernaut could never have taken off.

Having corporate headquarters located back in the hills, not on any superhighway or scheduled airroute, Sam realized thirty years ago that private company planes were absolutely essential for Wal-Mart. In many speeches over the years, Walton has identified as a principal "success" ingredient his lieutenants' ability to hop in a plane to make quick visits to stores and find out what was right—and what was wrong—with the way customers, merchandise, and employees were being handled.

Based at Rogers's municipal airport, barely six miles from Wal-Mart headquarters in Bentonville, the company now has a fleet of nine turboprop Commanders and two Piper Navajos, each carrying about half a dozen passengers, as well as Sam's twin-engine Cessna. The Wal-Mart planes would cost, if purchased new, about a million dollars each. But, in keeping with his frugal practices, Sam buys second-hand aircraft, at significant savings. (One dealer in Tulsa lamented that Wal-Mart is the hardest bargainer he's ever met.)

Over the years, Sam upgraded to more modern and faster personal airplanes. After the 1940-model Ercoupe and Tripacer, he owned the Beech Baron, a Comanche,

a Bonanza, and for many years his favorite twin-engine
Navajo. Sam usually has a plane that will carry up to
six. When he got his pressurized, twin-engine Cessna
414 in the summer of 1986, he bragged in the *Wal-
Mart World* that it was "a slightly used 1982 model,
but like new, and certainly the nicest airplane I've
ever flown." By happenstance it was painted in Wal-
Mart's blue and white and identified as N-5239-J. He
expanded on the importance of flying in his "Message
from Mr. Sam" in that *Wal-Mart World*:

> Our airplanes from the beginning have meant so
> much in helping develop our Wal-Mart Company.
> Doesn't seem possible that I've been flying in and
> out of Bentonville to our Wal-Mart stores since 1953—
> thirty-three years—lots of hours and situations. But
> I'm convinced that we could not have expanded as
> rapidly as we have through the years without the
> total utilization of our Wal-Mart air fleet (even if I
> have occasionally taken off bird hunting with my
> dogs). We never could have maintained the operat-
> ing controls or communications without having the
> ability to get into our stores on a consistent basis.

Sam's love of flying rubbed off in a direct way on
everyone in the immediate family, including Helen
and Alice. His three sons fly their own planes. The
daughter took lessons and learned to fly, but did not
take her examination for a private pilot's license. For
Helen a flying career was twice aborted. She once told
a friend:

"I learned to fly right after I got out of college. I got
in about four hours of solo and then had to quit when
civilians were cut off because the government needed
those little Cubs to train the young men going to war.

"In 1967 I took it up again and had about forty-five
hours solo in Sam's single-engine Bonanza. Then I left
on a trip to Europe. While I was gone he sold the
Bonanza and got a twin-engine plane."

Sam, present at the time, said: "Yeah, that Beech
Baron."

"And," Helen continued, "he sold the Bonanza. And the Beech Baron was always needed for business, and I never had an opportunity to learn to fly it. So I wasn't able to get checked out for a multiple-engine rating. I just gave up flying." She shrugged and laughed merrily.

Over the years, Sam has become rather notorious for putting his aircraft on autopilot and letting it fly itself. Sam will then turn his attention to the paperwork in his briefcase or read the newspaper. On one such occasion his passenger was Herbert Fisher, chairman of a New Jersey discount chain called Jamesway. They have been friendly competitors for years, are about the same age, and have battled each other on the tennis court. Fisher has admiringly called the Bentonville chairman "a living legend."

But when they were flying along two miles high and Sam put his plane on autopilot and began studying the computer printouts on the upcoming Wal-Mart store, Fisher became concerned for their safety, as he later told *Business Week* magazine, and upbraided Sam.

Pilot Walton was nonplussed and shrugged off the complaint. "Oh, it's a big sky!" Sam told Herbert Fisher.

Fisher was neither the first nor the last passenger to cringe or voice objections to Sam switching on the autopilot so he could be free to do something else. Perhaps the most bizarre such incident involved Burt Stacy, president of Sam's Bentonville bank, who was flying to Little Rock with Sam in the Cessna 414.

About fifteen minutes before they were due to land in the Arkansas capital, Sam set the autopilot and climbed out of his seat.

"What—what are you doing?" asked the startled banker.

"Oh, nothing," Sam responded in a casual way. He started to the back of the plane. "Just going to the bathroom."

Clarence Leis flew thousands of miles with Sam all over the country and vividly remembers one particular trip: "We came out of San Diego one time, just the two of us in the plane, and almost went head-on with a big jetliner. . . . Sam was one of those who turns his radio off when he gets out of the airfield and we didn't have the radio on. This was early one morning; we were coming back home. And, man, we saw that jet! And he was just doing everything to get out of our way! Frightening, man, it was frightening!"

Even brother Bud, the ex–torpedo bomber pilot, sometimes gets nervous with Sam at the controls. Years ago they were on a flight together in Missouri. "They were going to take off," recalled Tom Harrison. "It was a rural airfield, but the grass or wheat was up to the wings and it was wet. They took a couple of tries on the runway, but couldn't get up speed. Sam was going to take another run. Bud got out. 'Where are you going?' Sam asked. 'I'm not going in that plane,' said Bud. 'I'm gonna get a car or something.' I guess Sam took off solo."

Charles Gocio, a Bentonville lawyer and sometime quail-hunting companion, was flying home with Sam. Walton was in a hurry to get back to a meeting. Recalls Tom Harrison: "Instead of coming into the wind at our airport, they landed downwind. Charles said that they kept going and going toward that little old pond at the end of the runway. Charles said he practically jammed his feet through the floor.

"And when he finally quit rolling, right at the edge of the pond, Sam said, 'Whew! I didn't know whether I was going to get this thing stopped or not!' "

Several long time friends who also are pilots cautioned Sam to not take unnecessary risks in the air. One is W. H. (Bill) Conboy, an executive of Shelter Insurance Company of Columbia, who was a high school classmate.

"I have discussed flying with Sam many times," Conboy said. "I'm a flier myself. I'm a World War Two navy pilot, carrier, Korean war, and I'm still flying with my fifteen-year-old grandson now. I told Sam, 'Hey, here's the way you make the distinction. If you've got to work when you get there, don't work there and coming home. In other words, don't fly tired.' I could not convince him. Sam is a workaholic."

Said Bill Enfield: "Sam lives a charmed life to a certain extent. He can't be bothered with the usual sort of preflight checking of the plane that you're supposed to do. He goes to the airport and assumes that the plane is in proper condition because his people are supposed to keep it that way. He just jumps in and takes off. There have been times when we all have been really worried about him—because he wouldn't take time to check."

Safety concerns expressed by his family and business associates eventually prompted Sam to take some extra flying precautions. Doubtless he had already been "meditating"—one of his favorite words—himself on the need for the most modern equipment to avoid danger in the air. So he upgraded his airplane, as he disclosed in his column in the May 1989 *Wal-Mart World*:

> I'm getting my Cessna 414 modified and upgraded with one new engine, plus some additional horse-power to 325 per engine, and a wing modification as well. This means I'll have a slightly faster plane, but more important, in case of an engine failure, I'll have much better single-engine performance and safety. So it's probably worth the additional expense.
>
> I'm sure those Wal-Mart associates who are occasionally my passengers, as well as my bird dogs, will appreciate the investment. Until the plane is finished, I've been flying our Company's Navajo, which is a very fine airplane in which over the past six years I've probably logged some 2,000 hours visiting Wal-Marts all over our Wal-Mart Country.
>
> I truly enjoy flying, the challenges of contending with weather conditions, the planning required, as well as proving a quick access to our operations from Bentonville. . . . We could not have stayed in Bentonville and developed to our present size without the daily utilization of our Wal-Mart air fleet. That's just

one of our secrets. So, my hat's off to our very fine
aviation team, which does such a great job of providing safe, dependable transportation from here to
all our installations! It works for us—may not for
others— but, let's hold on to it!

Monday is the most frantic day of the week at the
Wal-Mart hangars at the Rogers airport. Company
executives are loaded aboard for flights to all parts of
the country. Each plane is fully loaded; a dispatcher
sees to that. Vice-presidents have priority for seats,
and then people in personnel and construction get
aboard. Sometimes a few passengers are bumped. Helen
has lamented she often has trouble hitchhiking on a
company flight. The planes fly 500 hours a month,
manned by a dozen pilots and serviced by a squad of
mechanics and fuel handlers.

Wal-Mart's aircraft fleet is made frequently to look
old-fashioned. Several corporate jets, costing $4 to $8
million apiece, fly in and out of Rogers and Fayetteville, bringing vendors who are making deals at the
Bentonville general offices.

Tony Lundquist, manager of the Wal-Mart aviation
department, says Sam does not favor buying jets, and
Wal-Mart really does not need them. He told me:
"Our turboprop craft get the job done. We can take
off from here and be in Fort Myers in about three
hours. Not bad." Lundquist, an ex-U.S. Navy pilot
and former operations director for an Arkansas com-
muter line, Skyways, volunteered that Sam is not too
old to fly: "Our check pilots have said that he is really
good. I have flown with him; I think he does a good
job when he's got his mind on it. A natural? Yes, I'd
say so. Just a good seat-of-the-pants flier."

Getting into the flying machine business brought to
the fore once again Sam's frugality and mania for
obtaining the very lowest prices. Walton learned that
Wal-Mart could qualify to buy aviation fuel, parts, and
supplies on wholesale terms if he was in the general
aviation business. In other words, if his aviation de-

partment was willing to serve the flying public with fuel, storage, and maintenance. He opened such a facility in his spare hangar at Rogers Municipal Airport and calls it Beaver Lake Aviation Company.

One of the Walton family planes, a twin-engine Piper Aerostar, was crash-landed by Jim Walton, but he escaped with minor injuries. He had taken off from Bentonville at 7:00 A.M. February 22, 1985, to fly to Little Rock. Barely ten minutes out, at 3,000 feet, one engine quit. Then hydraulic failure locked the landing gear still half down. Jim tried to land in a pasture near Springdale, clipped a fence, and skidded into a herd of cattle, killing two. The plane was badly damaged.

Jim Walton walked away but was put to bed for a week, fitted with a temporary neck brace, and on return to his office limped for a while.* The National Transportation Safety Board investigation attributed the accident to a broken oil line and imposed no penalty on Jim.

Only once since he got his private pilot's license in the mid-1950s has Sam Walton been caught violating FAA rules. In the summer of 1985, a few months after Jim's crash, Sam was grounded by the government for fifteen days.

Over a span of almost forty years he has logged several thousand hours in the air, flying more than a million miles. It fell to Kitty Acuff, an FAA inspector in Memphis, to suspend Sam's license, but she was charmed and impressed by his humble smile and mentioned to her colleagues that "he was a real gentleman."

The incident that grounded Walton occurred at the Memphis airport when Sam was attempting to depart in his twin-engine Navajo. Although Memphis is clearly indicated on aviation charts as a congested area and

---

*Because of the crash, Jim Walton still suffers occasional back pain. His mother lamented to a friend in 1990 it was a shame that a man so young couldn't even lift his two-year-old son. Rob Walton said the airplane manufacturer paid the Waltons for the loss of the Aerostar.

thus restricted for approach or departure under IFR (instrument) conditions, Sam apparently was then ignorant of that fact.

When he asked for clearance to take off, the control tower requested a flight plan. Sam, who was not qualified for instrument flying, filed a VFR (visual) flight plan—and took off.

The tower promptly reported him to the FAA. Handling the complaint, Kitty Acuff sent Sam a letter requesting an explanation and advising that he was subject to a thirty-day suspension.

"He didn't write," said Kitty Acuff. "He came to see me in Memphis. He explained it was a misunderstanding on his part, not intentional. His attitude was good. He had already started taking instruction to get his instrument ticket."

The Memphis FAA transferred the case to the Little Rock FAA office. An informal hearing was held, according to John Ciasca Jr., acting office manager, and Sam Walton accepted a fifteen-day suspension of his license. Sometime later he completed his instrument training and was checked out and licensed by the FAA examiner at the Rogers airport, Gwen Batie. (Later she told me she did not feel comfortable flying with him.)

Kitty Acuff said Sam's infraction had nothing to do with his age. She is aware of three or four corporate executives who are in the senior citizen category but still pilot their own planes in and out of Memphis. Across the country, there are a lot of private pilots who are even older than the Bentonville tycoon. If they can pass a physical, they can take up a plane.

In a curious way, Sam's two personal passions—flying and bird hunting—splendidly complement each other. In 1983 he flew to Falfurrias, Texas, to open a Wal-Mart store and discovered the Rio Grande Valley bobwhite. After one hunt, Sam was hooked on Texas quail. He took a winter lease on 20,000 acres—31 square miles—of the mammoth Dick Jones ranch, about 100 miles southwest of Corpus Christi. Such leases run

$5 to $8 an acre, so this tract costs Sam around $120,000 a year.

"I've never seen a more avid quail hunter," said Dick Jones. "He'll fly down in that plane of his, go to the ranch, load up his dogs in that old truck, and take off by himself. Couple of weekends a year he'll bring in a group of Wal-Mart managers.* But usually he hunts with just one or two guests."

The leased camp is not plush—three or four mobile homes clustered around water wells, windmills, a rick of mesquite wood for the sunken barbecue pit, a kennel for the dogs, and a barn for trucks and supplies.

"Sam won't buy a new truck." said Dick Jones. "He's got two old Chevys. As long as it's old, that's fine. He told me he likes one that rattles; that way his dogs can hear the truck and know where he's at, and he won't lose them."

The hunting camp has become a Walton family mecca. Nearly every Christmas his sons and their children gather there. Alice came for the first time in 1988. Brother Bud has a quail lease on the neighboring McBurns/McGill cattle ranch. Though known mainly as a world-traveling fisherman, Bud in the 1980s turned to quail, encouraged by a former rodeo cowboy, Walter Schiel of Waller, Texas who serves as guide and game manager on Dick Jones's spread. Walter Schiel also helps Sam train his dogs.

"They all enjoy coming down here and hunting,"

---

*Explaining to a friend how he utilizes the camp, Sam Walton said: "I get the officers and regional managers to come down here and hunt. About seventy-two in relays, maybe twenty or thirty at a time. They get a chance to talk to each other in an entirely different setting. It's the best thing of that kind I've ever done."

"No, it wasn't," said Helen Walton.

"Then what was it?"

"Bringing in the wives, the spouses, when you had the managers' meeting in Fort Smith. And that was my idea."

"I guess you're right, Helen," said Sam. "That was real good. Gave them a chance to understand our business, how it is all related, why everyone works so hard."

said Jones. "Helen came once or twice a year. Then she threatened not to come—the camp was too run-down for a lady. Those old trailers did need a lot of repair. Sam went right into town and ordered a new double-wide trailer. It'll be Helen's kitchen and entertainment center."

Out alone in his battered truck, Sam ran out of gas or got lost a few times on the desolate ranch. "His rattletrap truck is apt to break down," said Jones, "and that could be dangerous. We talked him into putting in two-way radios. That paid off pronto. He got stranded, called in, and we rescued him."

The first time he went out with Sam and his bird dogs, Jones was both startled and amused: "Sam just hollers at his dogs, and whistles at 'em. I mean he'll holler at 'em all morning. I don't see how his voice stands up—I'd get tired of hollering that long. He'll blow that whistle and stomp his foot and get mad at 'em—and then go at it again."

When the noon sun drives the temperature to 100 degrees, most south Texas hunters seek shade. Not Sam. Says Jones: "He'll get his gun and go right back out. . . . It's been a real pleasure having them as hunters on the ranch. They're wonderful people. They have a heck of a company. You've got to be impressed. Somebody asked me his secret of success. I don't know. I just think it's that he's on top of it so close, all the time. He knows Wal-Mart inside out. He knows everything that's going on."

Over the years, Sam gained almost as much stature as a quail hunter as he did as a merchant. Former President Jimmy Carter, who had a couple of hunts with Sam—one exceedingly memorable—praises him on both counts. Jimmy Carter refers to him not only as "probably the most successful retail merchant in the world" but also the most enthusiastic quail hunter he ever met and a true sportsman.

In December 1987, Jimmy Carter flew in to spend three days hunting Texas quail with Sam. The previous year Walton had been the former president's guest at a hunt in Georgia. Sam and Bud had met Jimmy Carter briefly in Washington when they were part of an Arkansas business delegation that visited the Oval Office.

It turned out to be a Texas quail hunt Jimmy Carter would never forget! Nor, for that matter, would Sam.

On the hunt with Sam and the former president would be Dick Jones and Walter Schiel, as guide, and several dogs, including Walter's superb young bitch named Streak. She was the daughter of Flash, Walter's best dog, but now too old to hunt.

At breakfast, talk turned to the danger of rattlesnakes. Jimmy Carter, wearing thick hunting pants but no snake leggings, was concerned. Walter tried to reassure him by saying he'd hunted the ranch eight years in regular clothes. "But if you see a rattler—jump! High, and away from him!"

They set out in Sam's rattling four-wheel drive pickup that had a high bench mounted behind the cab from which two hunters could observe the dogs as they ranged ahead and pound on the roof of the cab as a signal for the truck to stop when the dogs froze on point. The hunters would dismount, load, and flush the covey.

At midday it became unbearably hot. But Streak never slackened her pace. In front of a "mott"—in a thick clump of mesquite, prickly pear cactus, and prairie grass—she froze, her nose and eyes trained on the dense vegetation, her tail stiff as a poker. Dick Jones and Jimmy Carter went to the sides and Sam Walton moved straight in to flush the covey. Walter, not carrying a gun, stepped toward his dog. Everyone listened intently, awaiting the explosive whirring of wings as the quail covey erupted.

Instead came another sound—the chilling buzz of a rattlesnake. Walter looked down. His right foot was on the snake, just behind its head, pinning it down. The snake rattled wildly. Walter yelled, "Shoot him! Shoot him!" and leaped away, crashing into a mesquite tree. With his 28-gauge automatic shotgun, Sam

Walton shot from the hip, blasting off most of the
rattler's tail.

Streak dashed in thinking she was after a wounded
quail. The snake struck and sank its poisonous fangs
into her left jaw. Walter kicked the rattler loose. Sam
took aim and shot the snake dead. Walter picked up
Streak, grumbling that he'd jumped the wrong way
and left his bird dog in peril. Jimmy Carter said, "It's
not easy to do your best thinking when you're standing
on a rattlesnake."

Fortunately, the hunters found a veterinarian at an
adjoining quail camp. Streak's head was swelled twice
normal size, but she would live; a shot of serum and
ice packs would bring her around in a day or two.
Back at camp, Jimmy Carter slipped on a pair of
Levi's under his hunting pants before going out on the
afternoon hunt. They encountered no more snakes
and bagged their limit.

Most bird dogs that hunt in south Texas or out west
are "de-snaked." A special trainer will capture a rattler and surgically remove its poison sac (pulling the
fangs would be ineffective; they grow right back as do
an alligator's teeth). The dog, on a checkcord, will be
shown the snake and sharply yanked back if he tries to
rush it. The training is necessary; every year three or
four dogs around Falfurrias are killed by rattlers.
"Snakes are something we have to live with," said
Dick Jones. Wild pigs—*javelinas*—likewise are a menace in the region. One of Sam Walton's bird dogs was
cornered in 1988 by *javelinas* but escaped unscathed.

Sam, scheduled to fly to Alabama to visit some
stores, offered Jimmy Carter a ride home. On their
last night in camp, Sam suggested they get up at day-
break and have a quick hunt before boarding the
plane at midmorning. In his *An Outdoors Journal*,
Jimmy Carter writes:

> The next morning it was still dark when we had
> finished breakfast. After getting the dogs ready, we
> stood at the corner of the camp area and listened to

quail calling as first daylight brightened the eastern
sky. We began hunting a few minutes later, walking
through thicker grass than I had seen before on the
ranch, and found five coveys of quail before sunrise,
then several more before we had to quit hunting at
9:00 A.M. in time to pack. It was an unforgettable
experience.

One week later Sam was again taking off from
Bentonville in his Cessna for another hunt at the Texas
ranch with two new guests—Ferold Arend, the retired
president and one-time chief operating officer of Wal-
Mart, and his hunting pal from the sixties, lawyer
Charles Gocio.

On the outskirts of Dallas, the plane landed at Garland, site of the company's first Hypermart USA, a
giant one-stop superstore scheduled to open in a week
or two and offer everything from bananas to furniture
at bargain prices. Sam was anxious to see how his new
discount baby was doing.

"Sam and I were in our old hunting clothes," said
Gocio. "Ferold had on a shirt and pants. A big entourage took us through the Hypermart. How Sam was
dressed didn't bother anybody. He congratulated them,
told them what they needed to do, and then we went
back to the airport.

"We had seven dogs in the plane with us. Sam said,
'We'd better let these dogs do their business.' So we
got leashes and each took a couple of dogs and were
out there behind a hangar letting them relieve themselves. People at the airport were looking. Of course
they knew who Sam was; they must have wondered
what the hell we were doing. Anyway, we crawled
back in the plane and took off. It wasn't the most
pleasant trip with the smell of all those dogs."

On the Texas ranch, one of the dog handler's chores
is to keep track of Sam's guns. Says Walter Schiel:
"He'll bring a dog back to the truck for water and
prop his gun up by a bush, and drive off and leave it.
I've found one gun three times. Sometimes a gun will

bounce out of the truck, and we have to go look for it."

Sam Walton is regarded as a crack shot, usually able to get off two—sometimes three—shots at a flushed covey. "He doesn't miss too awfully much," said Charles Gocio. "Occasionally he'll miss. So will I. I've gone all day without missing. He has, too. You'll have your off days, just like a baseball pitcher; you're not getting it on—not getting that end of the gun barrel on target. If you don't, you ain't gonna shoot a bird down."

On the 1987 hunt Sam had his little gyp Queenie riding with him in the cab of his Chevy truck. Gocio and Ferold Arend were on foot trying to spot strays from a scattered covey. Sam suddenly let Queenie out, and the pup immediately pointed a quail. It was a tense moment; Queenie was a gyp, an untried pup. You mustn't let a gyp down on its first point. Gocio, closest to the bird, remembers:

"Sam said to me, 'Charlie, go over and flush that bird. Whatever you do, don't miss!' That old bird got up and just did a complete circle, and flew back over my head. I had to turn 180 degrees and shoot. That's hard. Those Texas quail fly fast! There was a lot of pressure on me, but I downed it. Queenie bounded over and immediately retrieved the bird. What a look on Sam's face! Was he ever proud!"

—27—

And the Race Goes On . . .

Flying his Cessna 414 across country or tramping quail fields behind his bird dogs in Missouri, Arkansas, or down in south Texas, Sam Walton can be momentarily free of the awesome day-to-day burden of corporate worry, but time is definitely becoming a factor for him. Seventy-two may not be old, but it's not young, either. Sam cannot forever keep his firm grasp of the Wal-Mart helm and weather the competitive storms raised by America's aggressive discount chains. Questions about the future of Wal-Mart, and that of its founder, arise as Sam grows older and remains secretive about his retirement plans.

Sam doesn't want to step aside. He tried that once, and it didn't work. He has backed away a bit, but at this writing he is still the boss, the chairman of the board. Nobody, in or out of the company, has the slightest doubt of that. The future of Wal-Mart seems equally assured.

After years of hovering close to the Sunbelt, Wal-Mart set off on daring invasions of new markets in New York, Pennsylvania, the Northeast, and even set targets in California, to cover virtually all of America. While these forays will be expensive, they hold enormous potential for broadly expanding the Walton profit base. Sam's plan is to keep scores of new stores springing up every year—until no appropriate locations remain.

Those close to him say he still has the same drive that has spurred him onward and upward all these years—to be number one. His ego is larger than his $9 billion fortune. He's out to topple K mart from the number two spot, and then go after the king of retailers, Sears. The most savvy Wall Street business analysts openly forecast that this will happen very soon, but it is still a very exciting race.

At the beginning of 1990, Sears and K mart distinctly led the field in number of stores in operation and total dollar volume in sales, and each had thousands more employees than Sam. But Wal-Mart was showing a higher percentage and faster rate of growth, and, more important, passed both rivals in profits earned in 1988 and 1989!

While Sam's outfit couldn't seem to do anything wrong, struggling Sears and K mart were unable to do much right. Here is how their race shapes up at a glance:

	1989		1988	
	Sales (billions)	Earnings (millions)	Sales (billions)	Earnings (millions)
Sears	$31.59	$ 646.9	$30.25	$524.4
K mart	29.1	322.9	27.3	802.9
Wal-Mart	25.81	1,080.0	20.65	837.22

Although Sam racked up the most profit for two straight years, he did it with fewer stores, having a total of only 1,525. Counting key subsidiaries, the K mart Corporation had 4,315, and Sears had 847 department stores and 884 specialty shops, a total of 1,731 merchandising locations. Wal-Mart more efficiently used its floor space, selling $227 worth of goods for each square foot of retail space. K mart, in contrast, sold only $139 per square foot.

The principal reason for K mart's terrible decline in 1989 earnings was the company's decision to take a

$640 million pretax charge for its program to upgrade stores and build new ones. Sears's poor showing was attributed by the industry to its internal struggle to find a new direction.

The swiftness with which Wal-Mart is overtaking K mart is shown in looking back only eight years. In 1982 K mart was called a cash cow with sales of $16.9 billion and earnings of $255 million while Wal-Mart was then just a cash calf with sales of only $3.4 billion and earnings of $124.14 million.

Sam definitely will pass K mart in both sales and profits, predicts retired Montgomery Ward president Sidney McKnight, a former Wal-Mart director. He told me in October 1989: "They'll overtake Sears, too, in another couple years. They'll be number one in the not-too-distant future."

But even to match the number two chain in stores, let alone surpass K mart in locations, would take Sam many years. At the start of 1990 there were, in 29 states, 1,402 Wal-Marts, 123 Sam's Wholesale Clubs, and 3 Hypermart-USAs, after the 14 dot Discount Drugs were sold off.

In comparison, his archrival, operating in all 50 states, had 2,215 K marts, 1,513 Waldenbook stores, 294 Payless Drug stores, 141 Builders Square hardware-lumber outlets, 47 Pace Wholesale Warehouses, 4 Office Square stationery stores, and one hypermart in Atlanta called American Fare. Sam boasted 250,000 associates, but the K mart stores alone had 350,000 employees, and Sears merchandising group 337,000.

The David and Goliath contest between puny Wal-Mart and the historic king of American retailers, Sears, Roebuck, is even more astounding. Ironically, all the while Sam's men have been creating market-share miracles from rustic Bentonville, the sophisticated leaders at Sears have been stumbling on Wall Street and shooting themselves in the foot with their customers and employees.

Looking back to just 1971, when Wal-Mart had but 38 stores and earnings of only $1.6 million on sales of $44 million, Sears had revenues of $10.1 billion and hogged

44 percent of the market share of the top 5 retailers. Sam then was not among the top 5, who were J. C. Penney, $4.8 billion and 21 percent; K mart, $3.1 billion and 13 percent; Woolworth, $2.8 billion and 12 percent; and Montgomery Ward, $2.3 billion and 10 percent.

By 1988, still leader Sears had upped revenues to $30.2 billion but saw its share of the top-5 market fall to 29 percent. K mart had bounded into second place on revenues of $27.3 billion, which gave it 26 percent. In third place was Wal-Mart with $20.6 billion revenues and 20 percent of the big-5 customers. J. C. Penney had fallen to fourth with $15.2 billion and 14 percent, followed by another newcomer, Dayton-Hudson with $12.2 billion and 11 percent.

Angered because Sears's merchandising earnings fell at an annual rate of 7.7 percent for five straight years, causing overall profit growth to remain flat and its stock performance to lag, powerful investors jumped down Chairman Edward A. Brennan's throat, demanding changes.

That triggered a company-wide shake-up blitz that *Business Week* (July 10, 1989) described as "hellish" on staffers, and strategic price-cutting that did little to brighten the cash flow. Sears paid Sam a high compliment by adopting his everyday low price policy, but analysts say it didn't cut much ice. On the other hand, while Sam prizes his "family" relationship with his workers, Sears fired thousands and destroyed the employee goodwill it once had. "Nobody trusts them," an ousted buyer told *Business Week*.

Whatever happens to Sears's bottom line, it would be a monumental feat for Sam Walton's outfit to supersede the Sears, Roebuck *physical* presence in the American marketplace.* It is just too big, with thou-

---

*In addition to its merchandising operations, Sears has 8,620 Allstate Insurance locations, at least 700 Coldwell Banker offices, and 365 Dean Witter brokerage offices. Also, Sears is hardly in danger of going to the poorhouse; its combined operations in 1989 had revenues of $53.79 billion and earnings of $1.508 billion.

sands of locations, given its diversification into Allstate Insurance, Coldwell Banker real estate, Dean Witter brokerage, and scores of other subsidiaries. In the merchandising group alone, before the ax began falling, Sears had close to 600,000 employees, about as many as K mart and Wal-Mart combined.

The crisis for Sears may continue for several years, Wall Street fears. New shake-ups and disruptions are on the horizon. Brennan decided to move headquarters out of the 110-story Sears Tower in Chicago, expecting he could sell the world's tallest building for $2 billion. He couldn't even find a buyer at $1 billion and finally mortgaged the building for $850 million.

The headquarters staff will be pared down and moved to new offices in a Chicago suburb, but—perhaps typical of the snakebite aspects of the company problems—Sears will have to continue to pay rent on the tower offices it leaves vacant. One would be flabbergasted to think Sam Walton would ever get caught in such wasteful corporate shennanigans.

Wall Street, which has great influence on American corporate strategies, also has been surprised, and disappointed, in K mart's recent decline. When Joseph Antonini became its chairman in October 1987, trade analysts rejoiced, expecting him to revive K mart momentum. Antonini had fresh ideas. "He's having a tough time getting them done," Oppenheimer & Company analyst Edward Comeau told *Business Week* (January 22, 1990). Antonini rushed in and tried to match Wal-Mart by cutting prices on 8,000 brand-name items. All that did, say Wall Street analysts, was to cause two problems. Some health and beauty aids became such popular bargains that all his stores ran out of stock and lost sales. Also the price-cutting savaged K mart's profit margin.

Antonini brought a $1 billion computer system, which when running in 1990 would monitor sales at stores and automatically reorder fast-moving products. Yet Sam had beat him to the punch on using such technology by linking all Wal-Marts to Bentonville headquarters via a satellite-computer network six years earlier. Despite all Antonini's efforts to upscale his chain's lackluster image, one marketing expert, Professor Louis Stern of Northwestern University, says bluntly: "K marts are depressing."

Sam Walton absolutely does not agree with Joe Antonini's decision, which eliminated one-fifth the items K mart stocks because they were slow sellers. Explains Sidney McKnight: "Sam and his people look for new items that customers are wanting. They add them, in quantity. Whereas Sears, Montgomery Wards, Penney, K mart—they try to eliminate slow items to improve their turnover. Sam is going in just the opposite direction, complete assortments. When you go into a Wal-Mart store you find what you want."

Wal-Mart does research casually and moves quicker to open stores. McKnight remembers Sam coming to visit him at McAllen, Texas, getting excited about the Rio Grande Valley, and saying he was going to put in some stores. "I thought that would take four or five years. But I was amazed at how quickly he was able to find locations, get the land and let contracts for buildings, and order the merchandise. In eighteen months he had stores popping up all over the Valley."

McKnight shares Walton's disdain for "number crunchers." He said: "A good retailer can drive around a town, take a look at the competition, development, street patterns, etc., and just instinctively know whether he can make a store go in that town."

The chairman of K mart has indicated he feels Wal-Mart breathing down his neck. Antonini has paid Sam the compliment of copying such Wal-Mart strategies as hiring greeters, applying the paintbrush, remodeling with wider aisles, and paying more attention to his shoppers. He echoed Sam when he told his people: "To keep our customers coming back, they must be serviced. They don't really have a lot of time to shop. They want things quickly. They don't want to have to wait in line or search around the store."

While keeping a sharp eye on the curious ups and

downs of his two great merchant rivals, Sam, to use the Bentonville vernacular, has his own fish to fry. And that means continuing to embark on bold new ventures. Sam was intrigued when a new kind of super supermarket came from across the Atlantic. Called a "hypermarket," it was a discount store occupying 200,000 square feet, selling food, apparel, and general merchandise. With the growth of these hypermarkets hemmed in by government restrictions in their native countries, European operators brought the concept to America. The first, Biggs, opened in Cincinnati in October 1984.

Sam and his lieutenants, intrigued by the possibilities of such a giant store and dazzled by the profitability prospects, leaped into action. They designed an American version of the hypermarket and dubbed it Hypermart USA. It also would require 200,000 square feet of space, which would mean a building large enough to contain a football field, a baseball field, a basketball court, an Olympic-sized swimming pool, three tennis courts, and a typical par 3-hole golf course. Characterized as "a mall without walls," it was designed to offer not only food, apparel, and general merchandise, but all sorts of extras such as a bank, dry cleaner, shoe repair, optical shop, hair salon, and a fast-food cluster and video rental. The floors were color coded to help guide customers. There were information telephones scattered around the mammoth store, as well as a number of play areas for children and parklike seating for tired shoppers. It was so large that someone decided the only way service representatives could get around fast enough was on roller skates. There were forty-eight checkouts!

Sam moved fast on this new idea. Wal-Mart teamed up with a Texas food wholesaler and opened its first Hypermart USA in a Dallas suburb called Garland in December 1987. Next they invaded Arlington, another Dallas suburb, and Topeka, Kansas, and Kansas City, Missouri, with similar hypermarts.

But they were not identical. Sam liked the salmon-pink color of ceiling in the Garland hypermart. In Topeka it was painted white because other executives thought that made the store look "brighter." Sam said try it; he was willing to tinker and experiment and find all the right combinations of elements. "We're not frozen," he said. "We'll try different things and see what is best. It may take a while. We're still learning. There's a lot we don't know.*"

The competition is already on Sam's coattails. K mart designed its own version of a hypermarket called American Fare. One requirement for a Wal-Mart hypermarket is a location in a metropolitan area adjacent to an interstate highway or a freeway intersection. Such locations are no longer easy to find. The Bentonville brass is still experimenting with the new stores to determine just what mix will best suit shoppers. They quickly determined that the customer's principal consideration is still lowest cost.

One alluring aspect of this new venture for Sam was the chance to get in on the food side of merchandising, something in which Wal-Mart could not claim much expertise. A decision was quickly made to buy out their Texas grocery wholesaler in the Garland hypermart and set up Wal-Mart's own grocery purchasing department in Bentonville.

It staggered Sam Walton to realize that Americans were spending $240 billion a year on groceries. He hoped that a large portion of that money would start to go through his cash registers.

His new interest in selling food led to the development of a fourth type of Wal-Mart store—the Supercenter, a 120,000-square-foot building that combined a standard discount store with an augmented warehouse

---

*Wal-Mart kept tinkering with the hypermart concept. In February 1990 when the fourth was opened in Kansas City, it had a new name and a new look. The new unit, which analysts thought possibly presaged changes at the three existing stores, was called Wal-Mart's Hypermart USA, discontinuing use of capital letters for HYPERMART. It stocked hundreds of additional items and had lower merchandise fixtures and wider aisles.

supermarket (or boxed food store) behind a 24-lane central checkout. The prototype, which opened in Washington, Missouri, in March 1988, also contained a pharmacy, an expanded garden center, snack bars, and an optical shop.

Other Supercenters, slightly different in size and content, were tested in Wagoner, Oklahoma, and Farmington, Missouri. All had wider aisles as well as a "bull pen" for consumer electronics. The idea was, according to David Glass, to "establish sales and operational parameters" before setting final goals for this probe of new marketing directions. The expected annual gross for a such a store was $30 million.

The Topeka hypermarket carried only 5,500 food items, about half as many as in the Garland Hypermarket USA. Wal-Mart is still trying to experiment and fine-tune the model store.

Sam Walton, remembering well his early years in the small traditional five-and-dime store on the Bentonville square, had to be astounded and overwhelmed at the variety of items his Topeka customers were piling in their shopping carts.

"It was a little shocking," Sam told David Glass, "to see one lady pick a dainty blouse off the rack and throw it in her cart on top of a package of hamburger."

Attending the opening of a new Supercenter, Sam immediately spotted one major problem—clogged checkout lines. And he observed shoppers getting frustrated as their frozen food purchases began thawing because of the delay. The boss promptly boosted the number of checkouts to twenty-four and moved the frozen food section closer to the front of the store to cut down on time out of the freezer.

Many national merchandise experts and market analysts think the Supercenter is the wave of the future for Wal-Mart. Some present stores may be retooled to take advantage of the new grocery add-on trend.

* * *

In the fascinating saga of Sam Walton and the amazing Wal-Mart phenomenon there are intriguing chapters yet to be written. Who knows what developments are coming? Will Wal-Mart become the biggest retailer in America? How many stores by 1995? What will be their pattern of development? Close observers believe the Supercenter seems the model most likely to be pushed to the fore.

As for who will rule as the chain's number one man, Sam Walton has not given any indication he plans to abdicate as chairman. Most of his contemporaries in the discount industry feel that staying active and on the job is what Walton lives for. If he ever steps down, his scepter as king of Wal-Mart most likely would be handed to David Glass, president and CEO and in 1990 only fifty-four years old.

Having built a fortune of $9 billion, Sam Walton is no longer in it for the money, which just keeps piling up. Wall Street calculated his net worth by early 1990 had leaped to around $13 billion. He disdains speculation about his wealth, but his generosity to his four children merits a little thought. It was back in 1954 that he and Helen did their estate planning and deeded each child 20 percent interest in the family fortune. In those one-store days, this "fortune" might have barely totalled $25,000. But how those one-fifth estate shares have grown! Now the Wal-Mart stock each child owns is worth $2 billion or more. It's nobody's business, of course; yet the public seems to find this kind of world-class legacy absolutely mind-boggling. Sam feels each child has fully earned his or her share of these riches by contributing administratively to the Wal-Mart success.

Of his children, Sam is most disturbed about his daughter—distressed and a little mystified by what he terms Alice's "stupid bad luck" in automobile accidents. He spent frantic days, friends recall, tracking down America's best surgeons to treat the broken leg she got in her accident in Mexico. Despite his best efforts, and twenty-two operations on her leg to cure a stubborn infection, Alice has a slight limp, which her friends fear is permanent.

The Walton family was again jolted in April 1989 when Alice, driving her 1987 silver Porsche coupe before dawn from her farm home to her office in Fayetteville, struck and killed a fifty-year-old woman factory worker crossing a wet and misty highway on the edge of Springdale.

The pedestrian, Oletha Hardin, was thrown onto the hood of the Porsche and her head smashed through the windshield, tearing her frightened face apart, showering Alice with broken glass and blood. The car went ninety feet before the corpse fell off, and slid another hundred feet to a stop.

Alice crawled out and ran back to where the victim lay in the road, and went into hysterics. Paramedics took Alice to the emergency room for minor cuts on her face and hands. Police said Alice was going fifty-four miles an hour in a forty-mile zone, and blamed poor visibility for the accident. State Police Sergeant Charles Westerman reported that although Alice was exceeding the posted speed limit, she attempted evasive action, but her brakes locked, and the Porsche went into a skid.

Alice told police she had been twice cited for speeding in the previous twelve months, but after a week of investigating, authorities decided not to file any charges in the fatal accident.

About eight o'clock the night of the accident, Alice showed up at the Hardin home, "about to cry," and told the victim's husband that she was sorry. "If she had been watching," Harold Hardin said when I interviewed him about his wife's death, "she could have stopped." The day following, Hardin said, a lawyer called offering to pay the $2,500 funeral expense. (Alice's lawyer, W.W. "Bill" Bassett of Fayetteville, says no such call was made by his firm.) Harold Hardin said; "That's not enough. A human life is worth more, but I'd rather have her back than have all the money

Sam Walton's got." He hired a lawyer, and the matter was settled out of court.

Sam Walton's own luck turned bad in November 1989 while he was down in his Texas quail-hunting camp. The scenario was commonplace, but troubling. Lady Luck was no lady that day. Sam came in from a day's bird hunting out on his enormous leased range to find himself a victim of carelessness. He was locked out of his house trailer. Somehow the keys had been left inside.

Determined to get inside, Sam climbed up on the shoulders of his dog handler, Walter Schiel, and attempted to crawl through a small window. It was a tight squeeze—too tight. Sam's dog whistle, dangling from his neck, got caught on the window and dug painfully into his sternum.

He felt sore the next day but went out with his dogs to hunt quail anyway. The pain persisted, and the bone in his arm began aching. Sam decided to fly to Houston and see his physicians. Perhaps, he thought, it had not been such a good idea to try to squeeze through a tiny window. He had no idea the freak episode would uncover a serious health problem.

Sam and the oncologist treating him for hairy cell leukemia, Dr. Jorge Quesada, had thought he was doing fine, with the blood cancer still in remission after more than seven years' treatment with interferon. Sam had undergone three complete evaluations during 1989 by Dr. Quesada and physicians at the Scott & White Clinic at Temple, Texas. These showed nothing adverse.

But on arrival in Houston with distressing pain and aches in his ribs and arm, Sam was given a bone scan. The test showed multiple lesions in the skeleton known medically as multiple myeloma, or cancer of the bone marrow.

"It is a malignant condition which presently has no immediate cure," Dr. Quesada told me. "That doesn't mean it cannot be controlled, but it certainly is a much more aggressive disease than what we were treating him for. The other disease is also fatal in long term, but because of the treatment we were able basically to put it in remission. If we are lucky, we might be able to do the same with this other one."

At M. D. Anderson Hospital immediate chemotherapy and radiation treatments began under Dr. Raymond Alexanian, a hematology specialist. Harvard educated, the physician has been on the cancer clinic staff for twenty-five years. Dr. Quesada also remains Sam's cancer consultant. This time Sam did not hesitate to follow doctors' orders, as he had in waffling over the decision to volunteer for the experimental interferon program.

In this newest untoward episode, Lady Luck was showing Sam Walton both her faces. Having the disease is terrible, but the lost trailer keys probably helped by indirectly leading to detection of his cancer.

"Had we found it three months ago," Dr. Quesada explained, "it would have been a little easier to treat him. But it didn't show at that time. . . . Cancer is a treacherous disease. Sometimes it takes a great deal of effort to find the disease in the early stages, and then when you turn your face it's already there—all over! That's the nature of cancer."

Dr. Quesada said that Sam Walton's prognosis depends on how well he responds to chemotherapy and radiation. "The response rate is high. . . . He has an excellent chance of getting into remission [for multiple myeloma]. But the problem is maintaining the remission for a long time."

It can be said for Sam Walton that he took the blow in stride.

His first thought was for his family—the 250,000 associates in his Wal-Mart stores. He wanted to give them the news before it became public.

At the M. D. Anderson Hospital on January 16, 1990, he wrote a two-page statement to go out over the Wal-Mart telecommunication network and to be read to all employees.

It was a characteristic Walton script. He began by asserting he was "excited about a couple of honors" just received by Wal-Mart and associates and felt "compelled to offer congratulations and thanks to all of you . . . that, plus a personal note that I'll also discuss briefly."

First he mentioned that the leading trade publication, *Discount Store News*, had designated Wal-Mart as the "Retailer of the Decade" and devoted 265 pages in its December 18, 1989, special issue extolling the company's history and success. He reiterated that $10,000 invested in Wal-Mart stock at the beginning would be worth $400,000 in 1990 if the market value remained as much as $44.

Next he expressed gratification that *Mass Market Retailers* had chosen for its gold medal for 1989 "not someone like our David Glass, Joe Antonini of K mart or Ken Macke of Target" but bestowed the honor collectively on the 250,000 Wal-Mart associates.

"This is an absolute first," said Walton's letter. "Never before has anyone given such recognition to any company's workers . . . associates . . . employees. You did it. You're the best."

The boss said he wished all 250,000 could go to New York to the award ceremony and that a large delegation would be sent.

"The personal matter I spoke of is really no big deal," said Sam's letter. "But I'd rather level with you and share the facts as to my current health than to have you hear many rumors, many that will likely be exaggerated or untrue."

He continued:

As most of you know, since 1982, or about seven and one-half years ago, I have been contending with a form of cancer called hairy cell leukemia. My treatment has generally been very successful here at M. D. Anderson Hospital in Houston along with the excellent doctors I have been using both in Bentonville and elsewhere. Currently I am continuing to take a drug called interferon, and my leukemia seems to be in remission at this time.

Last week I was informed that I have contracted another form of cancer called multiple myeloma, a bone disease, and that has apparently accounted for my aches and pains these past sixty or ninety days. And even so, I have been bird hunting, which probably accelerated this condition.

So, bottom line, this type of cancer as with my leukemia is a disorder of the cells in the bone marrow. They may be connected, but my doctors feel at this time there is no connection. They have also advised me that they have good success in treating this cancer if it is detected in time.

Over the past few days I have undergone two chemotherapy treatments and some radiation, and feel so much better already. I'll probably be here in the Houston area receiving treatment for two or three weeks, and hopefully in a month or two I'll begin my visitations over Wal-Mart country.

. . . We can continue to excel in the 1990s. With your dedication, prayers and concerns, your chairman will be back soon helping as I can in the years ahead as a most interested spectator, and stockholder. . . . Bless you all, and thanks again.

　　　　　　　　　　　　　　　Your friend, Sam

There's nobody like Sam Walton. As soon as he could break loose from M. D. Anderson Hospital for a few hours, he headed straight for a nearby Sam's Wholesale Club to check up on how his people were following Rule No. 1 and Rule No. 2.

Even more audacious, when physicians gave him a weekend off from treatment, Sam left Houston and flew back to Bentonville to spend forty-eight hours attending to routine Wal-Mart business. On Friday, January 26, 1990, he conferred with top management on strategy. The following morning, he strode into the headquarters auditorium—as he has done for so many

years—to listen and comment at the weekly Saturday
morning conference of frontline troops, store managers, buyers, department heads.

On home turf, Sam turned abruptly uncharacteristic
in another way—he talked, candidly, to the media.

When a reporter for television stations KHBS in
Fort Smith and KHOG in Fayetteville asked how he
felt, Walton said:

"I'm getting on a lot better, Kurt [Jefferson]. I've
been on this treatment for about a week now and
there seems to be a definite improvement in the way I
feel and the way I'm walking.

"I'm getting a lot of radiology on my back and my
bones. My bones have become soft and have developed holes in them. That's characteristic of this kind
of cancer. They're giving me chemotherapy along with
it.

"The two things seem to be improving and making
me feel better. That's the reason I was able to come
home this weekend. They don't treat me on weekends, so I have to go back for another couple of weeks
of this type of treatment.

"If this doesn't make the type of corrections that
need to be made in development of the blood through
the bone marrow, then I'll have to take heavier doses
of chemotherapy, with greater side effects and all the
rest. . . . I've got a good chance to recover, a sixty
percent chance, at least, with the type of medicine I'm
getting. So I think things are fine."

In Little Rock, one of the analysts closest to Wal-
Mart, J. D. Simpson, vice-president of Stephens, Inc.,
in January made the judgment that even though Wal-
Mart is fundamentally sound, Walton's absence would
hurt its performance in the stock market.

"I think the succession and the culture is there, the
execution is there," Simpson told the *Arkansas Gazette*. "But the king is the king. He's the patriarch
man, he started it, he changed retailing in the United
States. I think it will be perceived as a loss when
Walton is no longer working at Wal-Mart."

The report that Sam bounced out of the hospital to go visit one of his Houston stores brought a wry comment that probably would be echoed by hundreds of others familiar with Sam's workaholic habits.

Said Simpson: "Sam Walton's the type of guy that if he dies, he's probably going to die in a store."

The bone cancer struck the Wal-Mart chairman a harder and more crippling blow than any previous calamity he has experienced. He refused to give up. The pain was severe; radiation and chemotherapy gave him short-term relief. Then he had to resort to pain pills. His physicians were forced to experiment to try one thing and then another. Sam realized multiple myeloma is a disease not even the most experienced medical specialists can get a handle on easily.

In the spring of 1990 he had good days and bad days. But he dragged himself to the office, no longer getting there at five in the morning—now about seven o'clock. About noon he'd usually have to go home and lie down and rest. But he drove his own car. And he kept doing his usual things. An April visitor overheard him talking to a district manager.

"I've had complaints that people are having to stand in line at the checkouts," he said. He was talking about a store in a southwestern state. "I know Bill [the store manager] has done good in holding expenses down. But get him to hire more help up front. Spend the money. Our customers deserve to be treated right."

His friend Mike Smith dropped by Sam's home one afternoon last April and found him lying down, in great pain.

"I just wanted him to know everybody is pulling for him," Mike Smith says. "Helen was there and the phone was ringing all the time. Everybody is calling to wish him well. We talked about an hour. Sam made some remark about the Wal-Mart in Huntsville, Arkansas. I asked him if he'd been there. 'Yeah,' he said, 'I got in my Cessna and flew down there the other day.' 'By yourself?' 'Yeah, I came back before noon—because I knew I would not feel so hot in the afternoon.' ''

Sam told Smith that his mail brought a letter from a neurosurgeon at Mayo Clinic who wrote that he has had multiple myeloma for five years, and is still well enough to operate.

"Sam said he called and talked to the surgeon, and got really optimistic. 'If that Mayo doctor can whip it five years, and still keep going,' Sam told me, 'that means I've got a good point of reference. . . . That means, Mike, I think I can beat this thing!' ''

Epilogue

In the late spring of 1990, Sam Walton spent many a morning hour hunched over his cluttered desk doodling on a scratch pad. He scribbled down numbers, made calculations, and created projections. This was precisely the kind of homespun forecasting he had started doing in the pioneer fifties at his plywood-and-sawhorse desk in the loft of his lone five-and-dime on the Bentonville square. Even then he was setting goals and using his limited retailer skills mixed in with a lot of guesswork and optimism to chart the proper path for business growth in the unknown future. These amateur instincts had served him well for four decades.

Now, as he dabbled with self-made charts for the nineties and beyond, Sam perceived a remarkable fact of pure irony. It was the distinct and alarming contrast between his personal health and that of his mammoth discount empire: as an individual he was stooped and wracked by the deep pain of aggressive and chancy bone malignancies, yet his Wal-Mart operations had never been more vibrant, robust and promising. There was proof of this on every hand. Wal-Mart stock was steadily climbing on Wall Street, already beginning to top $60. And David Glass, Don Soderquist, and their cohorts, were planting more and bigger discount stores, while Al Johnson was rapidly opening a host of new Sam's Wholesale Clubs.

Just how big would his company be in the year

2000? That was the answer Sam was trying to come up with. Finally he thought he had it all figured out—the answer stunned him. It was so sensational he decided he must make his forecast public at the upcoming annual shareholders meeting.

When 9,000 employees, investors, Wall Street analysts and reporters crowded into the University of Arkansas' Barnhill Arena at Fayetteville, on June 1, Sam once again was typically down-home and upbeat, always the cheerleader. Getting down on one knee on the lighted stage, he announced a new two-for-one Wal-Mart stock split, the eighth, which would give the company more than 1.1 billion shares.

Wearing his trademark blue and white Wal-Mart baseball cap, but throwing off his suit coat, Walton stepped down to the floor of the vast arena to shake hands with many of the 1,300 store associates who had been bused in from across the country for the annual meeting. He pointed to his new shoes and said he bought them at Wal-Mart for $45. "I mean they feel good!" he said, with a big grin. Scores of the employees crowded around getting his autograph on their badges or fans. One man asked Sam to autograph his shirt. "I'll wear it to work every day!"

His every move was flashed on giant closed-circuit TV screens on the stage. Because of his serious illness, reporters, employees, and Wall Street experts alike scrutinized his every move. He was a little stooped (because multiple myeloma ravages the spine) but seemed, the business writers generally noted, reasonably spry and hale for a septuagenarian.

Moving around with his portable microphone, the boss finally got down to the message closest to his heart, saying in his folksy manner:

"I'm always putting down numbers, projections and goals, and I don't share them with anybody, ordinarily. But I don't mind sharing this with you folks, if you don't let it get out of this room." His face lighted up with a big smile and his eyes twinkled. "I believe it's possible for Wal-Mart to double its stores in the next ten years!"

His knowledgeable audience already knew that the discount chain would have 1,500 stores by the end of 1990, which meant the chairman was projecting 3,000 stores by the year 2000.

"This year we did $250 per square foot in sales," Walton said. "I wonder what we'll be doing by the year 2000. Let's just assume that the average store will be 80,000 square feet [by 2000]. I think it will be closer to 90,000.

"But if, in fact, we have an 80,000-square-foot store average, is $400 per square foot possible? Can we come from $250 to $400 in the average Wal-Mart in these United States?"

A shout rang from the floor of the field house: "Yes, we can!"

"If we do $400," Walton went on, "the average store would do $32 million a year. We've got a number of stores doing more than that now. And that's not even counting the Supercenters. If that thing grows and we flesh it out, we could blow past these numbers I'm talking about. And it very well could."

Multiplying out his figures, Sam Walton said the results indicated that by 2000 Wal-Mart sales would total $96 billion annually. "And that's not counting what we'll do in Sam's Wholesale Clubs!" he shouted.

"This year Sam's are going to do $6.5 billion," Sam said. "It's the largest wholesale club in the world and it started from scratch six years ago. Al Johnson [who heads the Sam's division] and his team are wild; they are on fire."

The wholesale clubs, he predicted, would grow from 135 outlets at the end of 1990 to 335 by 2000. "And Al, if you don't do $100 million average per store, we want you to lean over and we will administer a swift kick," Walton said, laughing.

The chairman's forecast startled many stock analysts present. What he had just said bluntly was that in a mere ten years Sam Walton's discount merchant empire could possibly turn the American retail industry upside-down by exploding from the present level of approximately 1,500 locations, doing $25.8 billion annual sales, to at least 3,335 discount stores and wholesale outlets with combined sales of $129 billion annually!

Nobody ever accused Sam Moore Walton of thinking small.

In 1991 Sam Walton achieved his dream of overtaking Sears as America's largest retailer. Wal-Mart reported annual sales of $32.60 billion while rival K Mart lagged behind with $32.07 billion in sales, and deeply troubled Sears Roebuck & Company trailed in unaccustomed third place with sales of $31.99 billion. The savvy investor who bought $3,000 worth of Wal-Mart stock in 1981 saw the value of this investment appreciate to $105,000 in 1991, according to figures in Wal-Mart's 1991 annual report.

Wal-Mart gained ground by invading the Northeast and California, increasing the number of Wal-Mart stores to 1,573 and Sam's Clubs to 148, upping the combined number of employees to 328,000, and racking up increases of 26 percent in sales and 20 percent in net income, enabling Wal-Mart to show a $1.291 billion profit.

The floundering chiefs at Sears had to be staggered; only one decade ago Sam Walton's sales of $2.4 billion a year were less than 12 percent of Sears' volume. One secret of Sam's success is that he continues to run a no-frills operation, holding sales cost to 16 percent, while Sears' overhead burns up 29 percent of sales, and K Mart's 23 percent.

What of Sam Walton's health? The reports from Bentonville are optimistic and Sam seems to be beating the odds on cancer. He was feeling well enough in the late spring of 1991 to fly alone in his Cessna 414 to visit stores in Florida, Wisconsin, New York and Arizona. Said a close associate: "He's just great. He's doing so good I tell you what, it's hard to keep up with him."

His Arkansas friends chuckle and say Sam Walton will never abandon trying to keep up his dawn-to-midnight work regimen as long as somewhere out there is one more merchandising record to break. And they're probably right.

Index

By the year 2000, 2 out of 3 Americans could be illiterate.

It's true.

Today, 75 million adults...about one American in three, can't read adequately. And by the year 2000, U.S. News & World Report envisions an America with a literacy rate of only 30%.

Before that America comes to be, you can stop it...by joining the fight against illiteracy today.

Call the Coalition for Literacy at toll-free **1-800-228-8813** and volunteer.

Volunteer Against Illiteracy.
The only degree you need is a degree of caring.

Vance H. Trimble is a Pulitzer Prize-winning reporter and the author of several books, among them *Plain Folks and Skunks: The Life and Times of Albert "Happy" Chandler* (with Chandler) and *The Uncertain Miracle*. He was born an Arkansawyer, barely an hour's drive from the headquarters of the Wal-Mart chain. He currently lives in Covington, Kentucky.